MW01201629

*Citizens or Papists?*

# Citizens or Papists?

## THE POLITICS OF ANTI-CATHOLICISM
## IN NEW YORK, 1685–1821

Jason K. Duncan

FORDHAM UNIVERSITY PRESS  NEW YORK 2005

Copyright © 2005 Fordham University Press

All rights reserved. No part of this publication may be
reproduced, stored in a retrieval system, or
transmitted in any form or by any means—electronic,
mechanical, photocopy, recording, or any
other—except for brief quotations in printed reviews,
without the prior permission of the publisher.

Hudson Valley Heritage Series, No. 3
ISSN 1534-1399

Library of Congress Cataloging-in-Publication Data

Duncan, Jason K.
    Citizens or Papists? : the politics of Anti-
Catholicism in New York, 1685–1821 / Jason K.
Duncan.—1st ed.
        p.   cm. — (Hudson Valley heritage series ; 3)
    Includes bibliographical references and index.
    ISBN 0-8232-2512-7 (hardcover)
    1. Anti-Catholicism—New York—History.   2.
Catholic Church—New York—History.   3.
Christianity and politics—New York.   4. New
York—Church history.   I. Title.   II. Series.
BR520.D86   2005
305.6'82747—dc22                          2005016811

Printed in the United States of America
07  06  05   5  4  3  2  1
First edition

To my parents, David and Kay Duncan

# Contents

# Acknowledgments

With so much thanks to give, I would like to express my deep appreciation and gratitude to my many outstanding teachers, beginning with those at St. Catherine of Siena School and Christian Brothers Academy in Albany. Special thanks go to Bernie Lammers and Ruth Kreuzer of St. Lawrence University and Richard Stites of Georgetown University. At the University of Iowa, where I began this project, I was fortunate enough to meet and work with the late Sydney V. James, who taught me much about the craft of history and of the pleasures of early American history. From my first semester in graduate school at Iowa, Allen Steinberg pushed me to do my best work and also took my scholarship on its own terms, for which I am very grateful. Linda Kerber's sharing of her deep understanding of the early republic and her important words of wisdom and encouragement have also shaped this work. Although Ellis Hawley was not involved in this project, I learned much from him, as I did from Shel Stromquist, Ken Cmiel, and Dwight Bozeman. Sarah Hanley and Mac Rohrbough were extraordinary in their generosity and hospitality. I would be remiss if I did not thank the staff at Iowa, especially Mary Strottman and Jean Aiken, for their friendship and assistance at many a key moment. Iowa City was also the scene of a lively graduate community during the 1990s; Dan Lewis, John Fry, Michael

Hau, Catherine Rymph, Phil Otterness, Greg Rohlf, and Gesine Gerard, among many others, including the folks in UE-COGS, all helped to make it that way. Friends and relatives whose generous hospitality on research and conference trips is much appreciated; they include the Cooneys, Jane Kennedy, Paul Marshall, Jeff Procak and Sara Winslow, J. B. Poersch, John Gadd, and Jay and Tricia Post. Jon Lauck, Dave McMahon, and Mark Milosch deserve not merely a mention, but a separate book.

No history can be written without the expert guidance and help from librarians and fellow scholars. The staffs at Iowa, Georgetown University, Catholic University, and the University of Notre Dame were especially helpful, as was James Folts of the New York State Archives in Albany, Lenora Gidlund of the New York City Municipal Archives, and Steve Bielinski and Father James Lefebvre of the Colonial Albany Social History Project. I am also in the debt of the Pew Program in Religion and American History at Yale University. I benefited greatly, too, from presenting my work to Alfred Young and the Early American History Seminar at the Newberry Library, to the American Catholic Historical Association, to the Society for Historians of the Early American Republic, and at the Cushwa Center for the Study of American Catholicism at the University of Notre Dame. Edward Countryman, Phil Gleason, Jay Dolan, Dan Cohen, John Fea, Patrick Carey, Dale Light, Emmet Larkin, Sam Thomas, David Waldstreicher, and David Hackett all made valuable suggestions in my research and writing, for which I am very grateful. My editor at Fordham, Bob Jones, has been a great help and a truly patient man; I would also like to thank Helen Tartar, Chris Mohney, Loomis Mayer, and Kate O'Brien for their efforts in the final stages of my manuscript becoming a book. The faculty and staff at Aquinas College, especially Chad Gunnoe and John Pinhiero of the History Department, Gary Eberle, Rosemary Schoenborn, and Ann Marie Schlichting of ITS, and Sally Reeves and Jeanine Weber have helped me to move things along at key moments. I also very much appreciate the faculty grant from Aquinas in the final year of work on the book, which helped me to complete it.

Finally, I would like to thank my family, especially my parents, David and Kay Duncan, who first noticed and encouraged my interest in history, and who have supported me on the long road to becoming an historian. Special thanks are also due to Sarah Dunn, who did not live to see this book, but whose generous support often proved to be essential. For their support, patience, and understanding over these many years, I also thank Mark and Pam, Ed and Mary Ann, little Heather, and Kae Lin and Sara and Dan; they witnessed, from back home in Albany, the often slow progress of this idea into what is now finally a book.

—Jason K. Duncan
Grand Rapids, Michigan

# Introduction

The relationship between Catholicism and republicanism in the
United States is long and complicated, and current historians are reconsidering it in light of their own experiences and with the questions they bring to the subject.[1] What follows is largely a political
history of Catholics in New York, especially in New York City, from
the colonial period through to about 1820. Its chief focus will be
on how Catholics (in particular, the men) developed, advanced, and
defended their own political interest in the decades after the American Revolution. Their struggle to achieve full equality in the republic
would have implications not only for the history of Catholics in
America, but also for the wider political development of the nation
as a whole, through the nineteenth century and even beyond.[2] Historians of the Jacksonian and antebellum periods agree that by some
point in the 1830s or 1840s, American Catholics had become a main-
stay of the Democratic Party.[3] One historian, Robert Kelly, went so
far as to assert that "it was the Catholic Irish who would give nineteenth-century American politics its fundamental structure."[4] At the
same time, many historians of the 1830–60 era have assumed, often
with little evidence, that the origins of the intense loyalty of American Catholics to the Democratic Party lie in the early republic, with

Catholics over time easily evolving from Jeffersonian Republicans to Jacksonian Democrats.[5]

By 1820, most Catholics in New York who had gained the right of suffrage were aligned with the Republicans, who were soon to become popularly known as Democrats. There has been little scholarship, however, that attempts to explain precisely how that partisan allegiance, which would have such important implications, developed during this formative era in the nation's political history. It is not widely known, for example, that both Federalists and Republicans competed for the support of Catholics in the early republic. In New York, there was no direct continuity from Anti-Federalists to Jeffersonian Republicans and then to early Jacksonians (who unequivocally supported political rights for Catholics) and various incarnations of Federalists opposing them with equal fervor. The actual history is much more winding and complicated. Republicans themselves, moreover, proved to be sharply divided on the question of whether Catholics could be genuine citizens of the republic.[6]

In recent years, historians of the early republic have done much to broaden our understanding of the politics and political culture that was current in the first decades after the ratification of the Constitution. The work of these historians has built on the studies of social and cultural historians of the past few decades. The best of this scholarship has enriched our understanding of what the Revolution changed, and did not change, in the political culture that the new nation inherited from colonial America. Consequently, it is now beyond dispute that the radicalism of the Revolution had distinct limits with regard to the aspirations of African-Americans, American Indians, and women to equality and full citizenship in the republic.[7]

Missing in this important new literature, however, is some recognition that Catholicism and American nationalism have frequently been in conflict since the founding of the United States. The roots of this antagonism date back to the founding of the colonies, and before that to the deep religious divisions that arose in Europe at the time

of the Reformation in the sixteenth century. The early republic is
fertile ground to study how Catholics sought to use the ideas and
rhetoric of republicanism to achieve equality with their fellow citizens. Religion and ethnicity in their own distinct ways were also
important political factors in the United States in the decades following the Revolution. New York's Irish and Catholic populations often
overlapped in the early republic, but there remained differences. Irish
immigrants of Catholic and Protestant heritage were received in different ways during the early republic. For example, it is hard to imag-
ine Andrew Jackson, if he had been born the son of Irish Catholic
immigrants rather than of Irish Presbyterians, emerging as a wildly
popular national figure in 1815, and then within a decade becoming
a serious contender for the presidency. New York is an ideal location
for a political study of Catholics in the early republic, partly because
of the singularly traumatic experience that Catholics endured in the
colonial period. During the 1680s, Catholics were disproportionately
represented among the authorities of the provincial government in
New York. As a result of what historians have called Leisler's Rebellion, an aftershock in New York of England's Glorious Revolution of
1689, Catholics in the province were systematically denied all religious and civil liberties. These prohibitions remained in place
throughout the remainder of the colonial period; there would be oc-
casional outbursts of anti-Catholic agitation, including bizarre episodes such as the slave conspiracy of 1741. The Catholics who
remained in the province were very much on the margins of public
life. Only until the course of the American Revolution shifted the
site of ultimate sovereignty away from the Protestant monarch in
London did Catholics gain religious freedom. After this, the main
goal of Catholics in the early republic was to achieve equal citizenship
with New Yorkers of other religious denominations. During the early
republic, American Catholics generally faced the problem of reconcil-
ing their religious and national identities at a time when their fellow
citizens were defining American nationalism as something that was

free from European control. Catholics in New York sought to de-
politicize their religion and make loyalty to the state and republic a
matter independent of religious affiliation. In New York, this task
was not an easy one. Catholic men demanded that political parties
treat them as civic equals by nominating them for office, a measure
of genuine citizenship since the time of ancient Greece.

This story is also part of the broader history of American Catholicism. In most general histories of the United States (except for cur-
sory references to the Catholic origins of colonial Maryland),
Catholics are not introduced until the narrative reaches the 1840s, or
perhaps at the earliest the 1830s. Yet the history of Catholics in the
United States has not received all that much attention from historians. One scholar, Tim Walch, called in the 1980s for more scholarship
to help close the gap between Catholic history and the "mainstream
of American historiography." A decade later, however, Leslie Tentler
lamented that American Catholic history is in some important ways
still essentially "ghettoized." She attributes this to the mistaken as-
sumptions of many of her colleagues that the history of American
Catholics is not particularly interesting, and that Catholics have had
a minimal impact on the nation's development.[8]

If there is some truth to Robert Kelley's assertion, Catholics did
have an important effect on the character of American politics in the
nineteenth century. In the most recent significant studies of the politics and political culture of the early republic, however, Catholics are
ignored. The inherent tension between Catholicism and American
republican nationalism has all the elements needed for a compelling
ideological conflict. Catholics, by definition, accept the ecclesiastical,
teaching, and moral authority of the hierarchy of their church. The
assumption that Catholicism was not a political issue in the United
States until the middle of the nineteenth century has proven difficult
to dislodge.[9]

Historians of American Catholicism have also tended to neglect
the early republic. These historians, looking backward to colonial per-

secution of their church and forward to the nativism of 1830–60, have portrayed the early republic as a period in which Catholics were almost effortlessly woven into the fabric of the new nation. One major survey claims that the late eighteenth and early nineteenth century was a "Republican Interlude" marked by "a prolonged period of cordial relations between Catholics and Protestants."[10]

The difficult history of Catholicism in New York accords with the most radical members of the state's political society in the early republic becoming advocates of Catholic political equality in the early nineteenth century. At the same time, the most conservative elements tried to deny Catholics that equality. For the former, the cause of Catholics was crucial to the development of a genuinely American republicanism in New York. Historians generally did not consider religion, much less Catholicism, when looking for episodes of radicalism in the American past. Those historians who have found an intersection between religion and a democratic ethos usually locate it among those of unorthodox beliefs, such as deists and freethinkers. Their republicanism was often infused with a conscious rejection of traditional Christianity and clerical authority. One leading historian has also uncovered a source of economic radicalism among low church Protestants who believed that an "evangelical Christian equalitarianism" was the foundation of a just social order. Yet, given the history of Catholicism in New York, the struggle for Catholics to gain full citizenship was radical in its own right.[11]

While this study is mainly concerned with how Catholics acted in the wider political arena, it also presents an opportunity to examine how the Catholic Church adjusted to minority status in a predominantly Protestant state with no established church. There was a contest between clergy and laity for control of the Catholic Church in New York, and the laity itself split into competing factions within the church. These divisions, and how they were ultimately resolved, often mirrored the way Catholics found themselves in different parties and factions in the wider political arena of the early republic.

This battle is a further reminder that Catholics in New York were not monolithic in the first decades after they had gained religious freedom in the 1780s. They were divided in several ways, including at times along lines of economic condition and ethnicity. These two factors were ultimately the most significant in determining the partisan loyalties of Catholics, as a whole, by 1820.

Race is a secondary factor in this story. The roots of anti-Catholicism in New York were religious and political, not racial. Irish Catholics in New York faced discrimination based on their religion and national and ethnic heritage. However, the origin of some of the tension and hostility between Irish Catholics and African-Americans in New York, which reached a nadir during the Civil War draft riots, may be found in the early republic. There is little evidence to suggest that conflict between the two groups during this time was violent. In fact, a leading scholar on this topic acknowledges that Irish and African-Americans lived in proximity to one another without undue incident until at least the 1830s. When Irish Catholic immigrants in New York engaged in violence on a large scale in the early nineteenth century, it was with white Protestants. Irish Catholics and African-Americans generally found themselves in different political camps during the early republic, however. This partisan rivalry may have contributed to the later social tensions between them.[12]

In early New York, which has been too easily credited by historians for its tolerance and pluralism, Catholics faced a particularly daunting task in seeking to be both loyal citizens of the state and dutiful members of their church. Although they achieved some notable successes in this regard in the early nineteenth century, nativism and anti-Catholicism would return to American public life with a renewed vigor not long after 1820. By the time that had happened, however, Catholics had secured religious and political liberty, rights that were guaranteed by law, as well as powerful allies to help them to defend their hard-earned freedoms.

# Prologue

## "Disorder to None But Papists": Leisler's Rebellion and the Making of Anti-Catholicism in Colonial New York

In the spring of 1691, English authorities in New York City executed Jacob Leisler and Jacob Milbourne for the crime of treason. Leisler, born in Frankfurt, had come in about 1660 to what was then New Amsterdam, the capital city of the Dutch colony in North America. He was the leader of a party that had claimed power in the province of New York in the wake of England's Glorious Revolution of 1688–89. At that time, the Catholic King James II was forced to flee England; he was replaced by Protestant monarchs William and Mary, who had been living in Holland. Jacob Leisler and his faction believed that their main duty was to put into place the Glorious Revolution in New York, a conviction that Leisler maintained until the end of his life. As acting lieutenant governor of the province, Leisler had pursued a vigorous policy designed not only to eliminate Catholic influence from New York, but also to deny individual Catholics all religious and political liberties. A bitter and tragic irony thus surrounded the execution of Leisler and his son-in-law, Jacob Milbourne, a radical Protestant who had immigrated to North America from England. Defiant to the end, Leisler declared on the gallows that he had acted only "to maintaine against popery or any Schism or heresy whatever the interest of our Sovereign Lord & Lady that now is & the reformed Protestant Churches." He also urged his fellow New Yorkers with his final words not to hesitate in "uniting . . . against a Common enemy" to advance "the Glory of the protestant interest." Proclaiming their devotion to the Protestant cause, Leisler and Milbourne were put to death on May 16, 1691. A martyr's fate at the hands of the hated "papists" would surely have made more sense to Leisler and Milbourne, given their worldview, than being dispatched by those acting in the name of King William and Queen Mary.[1]

Even as official New York prepared to execute Jacob Leisler, it was locking into place the core of his agenda, which did in fact deny Catholics all political and religious rights. Although the years from 1689 to 1691 have generally been thought of as "Leisler's Rebellion," those who took part referred to it as a "Revolution," or "Reformation" (which has religious overtones), and it illustrates how the Leislerians believed themselves to be acting on behalf of Protestantism and in firm opposition to Catholicism. Just three days before New York authorities carried out the death sentences of Leisler and Milbourne, the provincial government enacted laws guaranteeing the right to religious freedom. Under these statutes, Catholics, who had the legal right to worship publicly under laws passed in the 1680s, were now expressly denied the right to practice their faith openly. The new law stipulated that "always provided that nothing herein mentioned or contained shall extend to give liberty for any persons of the Romish religion." This measure was in keeping with English policy; New York's new governor, Sir Henry Sloughter, in his official instructions from London, was ordered to "permit a liberty of conscience to all Persons (except Papists)." In England itself, Catholics were denied political and religious equality in the aftermath of William and Mary coming to power. This directive to Governor Sloughter, however, required no change from the spirit or policies regarding Catholics that Leisler had championed. As he prepared to die, Jacob

Leisler may have felt a measure of vindication as the central principles of his program were written into law in New York.[2]

The ramifications of the Glorious Revolution were especially important for the history of colonial New York. The province had been originally established under Dutch auspices earlier in the seventeenth century and was called New Netherlands. It had been subsequently conquered by English forces and was briefly retaken by the Dutch before the English reestablished their rule in the 1670s. Unlike that which prevailed in less diverse New England and the southern colonies, the people of early New York were marked by an impressive array of ethnicities and religions. New York was also home to the only two Catholics to serve as governors in the thirteen English colonies in North America between Spanish Florida and French Canada. Thomas Dongan and his predecessor, Anthony Brockholls, had been appointed governors of New York during the 1680s by the Duke of York, who became James II in 1685.[3] They and other Catholic officials governed in New York at a time when the Protestant–Catholic rivalry still shaped much of the character of European, and by extension, North American politics. The Thirty Years War, the longest and bloodiest conflict between Catholics and Protestants in Europe, had been over for only thirty-five years when Dongan became governor in 1683. The throne in England, a full century and a half after Henry VIII had taken his kingdom out of communion with Rome, was itself the scene of competition between Catholics and Protestants in the 1680s. Charles II had been officially a member of the Church of England, but was widely believed to harbor Catholic sympathies. His brother, James, who succeeded him, was an avowed Catholic. James II had decreed that New York be part of the Dominion of New England. This expanded polity included the five New England colonies, along with New York, New Jersey, and Pennsylvania. Its governor was the haughty and unpopular Sir Edmund Andros, an Anglican and an ally of the Stuarts. At the time of the consolidation, Dongan had ceased to be a provincial governor, although he remained in New

York as its most prominent Catholic. In London, English Protestants were reluctantly prepared to accept the new king's religion, as long as James, who ascended the throne without a son, eventually passed on the monarchy to one of his two Protestant daughters. But when James's wife, Queen Mary, gave birth to a son in 1688, the future suddenly looked much different. Both Whigs and Tories in England called for James II's eldest daughter, Mary, and her husband, William, Prince of Orange, to come to London from Holland to assume the English throne. They did so; James fled the country, and England had its "Glorious Revolution," as its adherents famously called it.

Other British colonies in North America were also uncertain as to who possessed legitimate authority after James II's fall from power. For nearly three years, for example, Massachusetts had no generally recognized government in the aftermath of the Glorious Revolution. When the new governor finally arrived there in 1692, he found the jails full of "witches." In New York, something similar was happening. Jacob Leisler's preoccupation with Catholics was so consuming that it caused him to suspect those Protestants who did not share his fixation on Catholics of being in league with "the papists." The persecution of Catholics in New York between 1689 and 1692 never equaled the scope of the terror that engulfed Salem, but there are parallels. Witchcraft in Massachusetts was feared as the greatest threat to Puritan Christianity. In religiously and ethnically diverse New York, Roman Catholics, who had just prior to 1688 been disproportionately represented among the province's authorities, became a prime target. The Leislerians focused on Catholics as the root cause of instability and unhappiness and a menace to both Protestantism and English authority. They consequently declared Catholics unfit for civil society, and wrote that inclusion into the province's laws.[4]

Back on the gallows in New York, Jacob Leisler could hardly have imagined his end, given the circumstances in which he came to power. On May 31, 1689, a contingent of the New York militia took possession of Fort James, doing so in the name of the new Protestant monarchs in London, William and Mary. They also justified their action in part as a response to the oppression that the people had allegedly suffered under Governor Dongan. The members of the militia also mentioned the disturbing presence in the fort of Irish "papist" soldiers. Declaring themselves "to be Entirely and Openly opposed to papists and their religion," the militia insisted that they would maintain control of the fort until they received orders from legitimate Protestant authorities in England. A few days after occupying the fort (the name of which they promptly changed from James to William), the soldiers announced that they were under the command of Jacob Leisler, who assumed the title of Lieutenant Governor of New York. Leisler, a prosperous merchant and one of the wealthiest men in the province, was from a family that had distinguished itself on behalf of Protestantism in its rivalry with the Catholic Church. His father, a French Huguenot, had been banished from his home by Catholic authorities at the end of the Thirty Years War. Jacob Leisler's Calvinist brand of Protestantism was international in its scope; he had been instrumental in aiding the Huguenots in their efforts to settle in New York. Hundreds of them had come to New York after King Louis XIV of France in 1685 revoked the Edict of Nantes, which had guaranteed a measure of religious liberty to French Protestants for a century. This stunning action provoked great fear among many Protestants in the North Atlantic world, including Calvinists in New York. Leisler and his allies were also convinced that the influx of Catholic officials into New York in the 1680s had been part of a conspiracy by the Catholic Duke of York (who became King James II in 1685) and his minions to establish Catholicism in the province. In defending their seizure of power to the newly crowned king of England, the party led by Jacob Leisler gave thanks that God had provided William as an "instrument in our deliverance from Tyranny, popery and slavery." They also pointed out that overthrowing the previous authority in New York was made necessary because "most in command over us being bitter papists." Leisler strongly supported William as the leader of the Dutch House of Orange, which since the sixteenth century had been a leader among Calvinist Protestants and was adamantly opposed to reconciliation or cooperation with the Catholic Church.[5]

A large part of the problem in New York was that the province's small population of Catholics were disproportionately represented among officials and soldiers, and this fostered a conspiratorial view among some Protestants. Governor Dongan and the Duke of York had appointed several Catholics to prominent posts in New York during the 1680s. They included Jarvis Baxter as commander of the fort at Albany, Bartholomew Russell as ensign at the fort in New York City, and Matthew Plowman as collector of fees for the port of New York. Despite the presence of these men in positions of authority, Catholics as a whole made up only a small fraction of New York's population. As late as 1682, a minister of the Dutch Church noted that "As to Papists, there are none; or if there are any, they attend our services or that of the Lutherans." Dongan himself reported to London in 1687 that there were "few Roman Catholics" in the midst of a community that included members of a dozen different religions and dominations, with members of the Dutch Reformed Church the most numerous. The most liberal estimates of the number of Catholics in New York in the 1680s have them comprising at most five percent of the population.[6]

Jacob Leisler's main priority after gaining power became the elimination of all Catholic influence in New York. It is not clear that he had any political or constitutional goals much beyond the boundaries of the Protestant–Catholic rivalry. One observer commented after Leisler's death that he "was especially anxious to allow no Papist to remain in any office." King William had issued a proclamation limiting all offices within his realm to Protestants, a directive with which the Leislerians swiftly complied. A week after Leisler's regime eagerly proclaimed that William and Mary were now the rightful monarchs in London, Matthew Plowman, one of Dongan's appointees, was ordered to appear before the provincial council. When he did so, he was summarily informed that "he was no protestant, that therefore he was not qualified to continue as Collector of the Revenue." Other Catholic officeholders were quickly relieved of their positions and most fled the province. The new regime made sure to disenfranchise Catholics as well. In October of 1689, elections held in New York City were expressly limited to "Protestant Freemen."[7]

The Leislerians did seek to forge a new political-religious consensus in New York, one based on a common Protestantism that transcended ethnic, national, and denominational differences. In reconstituting the provincial militia, Leisler asked every town on Long Island to "send us two known Protestant, trusty soldiers, armed." In July of 1689, a month after he had assumed power, Leisler sent out his troops to "disarm the papists." He noted with pride that the soldiers charged with this mission hailed from many parts of the North Atlantic world, but were bound together by religious ties: "all known Protestants, born in N.Y., England, France, Holland, Germany and Switzerland." The new militia that Leisler put together was a reflection of New York's ethnic diversity; it demonstrated that his movement was not strictly national, that is, Dutch, in its ethnic makeup. Supporters of Leisler, in fact, took pains to deny that their movement was in any way a "Dutch plott." His party further justified its campaign against Catholics by claiming that on the day in June of 1689 in New York that William and Mary were proclaimed the sovereigns of England, a massive bomb planted by Catholics in Fort William "was discovered by one Neger, and fort, city and the people were trew Gods mercy miracouslusly saved of that hellish designe." This was a distinct, perhaps even a deliberate, echoing of a celebrated episode in the history of Protestant–Catholic conflict, namely the foiled attempt in 1605 of Catholic conspirators, led by Guy Fawkes, to blow up the Houses of Parliament in London while James I was in attendance. The Leislerians thus placed themselves squarely in the English tradition of Protestant heroes who thwarted

Catholic intrigues at the last possible moment. Coincidentally, many of the Leislerians were of Dutch ancestry, and so they were especially anxious to build solidarity with the English in New York. Associating themselves with the traditions of English Protestantism, Leisler's government celebrated Guy Fawkes Day, which originated in England, and in America had been commemorated in New England as "Pope's Day." New York officially marked the day in November of 1689 as it "solemnise[d] with bonefires and burning the pope."[8]

As there were few Catholics in New York to resist the "Revolution" and "Reformation" against their religion, the Catholic institutional presence collapsed quickly. Leisler's supporters closed the Catholic chapel in the fort and a Jesuit school that had been opened while Dongan was governor; the Jesuits themselves fled the province. The government issued warrants for the arrest of Dongan and Anthony Brockholls, the other former Catholic governor of New York. Leisler claimed popular support for his actions in that "the people being much against papists beinge in office." Commenting on the presence of half a dozen families of "rank French papists" at Saratoga, on the northern frontier of New York, he concluded that they must have been "there for a bad designe." He believed that no Catholic in the province could be trusted, whether living within sight of the king's fort on Manhattan Island or lurking on its frontiers. Leisler conceded his obsession with Catholics, admitting that "the bad creatures among us give me great occupation." He also took the initiative among leaders of the other British colonies in North America. Leisler alerted the governor of Barbados to the dangers that that colony faced from Catholics and communicated to the Maryland Assembly that Dongan, whom he believed had "ranged all the country" meeting with other "papist grandees," was organizing Catholic resistance to the king. He assured the Marylanders that he would take all necessary action against the Catholics: "I shall omitt nothing if I learne of them to secure them."[9]

The Leislerians' apprehension of imminent danger from Catholics stemmed in part from New York's proximity to French Canada. In

February of 1690, during the first winter after the overthrow of James's government in New York, the French and their Indian allies attacked Schenectady, a small trading post just west of Albany. The raiding party, which killed many of the inhabitants of the settlement, consisted of French soldiers and at least 150 "Indians, the most of them French converts from the Mohawks, commonly called the praying Indians." French soldiers were ordered to take oaths of allegiance from "any Catholics on whose fidelity he considers he can rely"; conversely, French expatriates of the "pretended Reformed religion," that is, the Huguenots who had found sanctuary in New York just a few years earlier, were to be captured and returned to France. After the attack on Schenectady, Jacob Leisler, "fearing too great a Correspondency hath bean maintained between ye sd French & disaffected P'sons amongst us," ordered the arrest of all Catholics and those who had commissions from Dongan. Leisler took the advice of a delegation from New England, whom he had invited to New York, and whom had urged him to decree "that no papist be suffered to come into ye fort" and that Catholics not be allowed to possess arms.[10]

One of the ironies of Jacob Leisler's eventual downfall is that it can be traced in large part to the character of its leader's fervent opposition to Catholicism. Leisler tried to organize an invasion of French Canada in response to the raid on Schenectady, but when he failed to generate enough interest in the other colonies for the venture, his credibility suffered. Ultimately, Leisler proved unable to limit his accusations of "popery" to Catholics only. Despite the constant affirmations of Protestant unity and solidarity, Leisler and his party, in the words of their opponents, did not blanch at "terming all Papists or popishly affected who did not favour his designes." The Leislerians insisted that true Protestants had nothing to fear from them; they meant to cause "disorder to none but Papists and Jacobites." The Leislerians were especially critical of Lieutenant Governor Francis Nicholson, who was Governor Edmund Andros's representative in New York. Nicholson's authority stemmed from his commission from the deposed King James, and thus in the eyes of the Leislerians, his claim to authority was illegitimate. They accused Nicholson, an Anglican, of being a "pretended protestant" who was guilty of "countenancing the Popish party," and given to "entertaining secretly at the same time severall souldiers wholly strangers to the Towne being some Irish." One witness testified that in 1686 he had seen Nicholson "Several times in Ye Masse" and "upon his knees before the Alter in the papist Chappel." Nicholson, in the eyes of the Leislerians, had been too sympathetic toward Catholicism while in office. Although he appeared to comply with popular demands that "images erected by Coll. Dongan in the Fort" be taken down after the Catholic governor left office, Nicholson had actually moved the religious statues and icons to a secure room in the fort. The Leislerians would brook no such halfway measures. After the government of the Dominion of New England fell, the Leislerians advanced their "reformation" (as they referred to it) by acting in the tradition of Protestant iconoclasts and smashing the physical remnants of Catholicism in the fort.[11]

The Leislerians drew a firm line between Protestantism and Catholicism in the province, forcing New Yorkers to choose between the two. Officials who enjoyed their offices by the grace of King James and who seemed slow to acknowledge the legitimacy of William and Mary became suspect. Leisler himself accosted several "English gentlemen," calling them "Popish Doggs" and accusing Captain Nicholas Bayard of the militia of hosting illicit cabals with the "popish." Bayard, who was thrown into prison, later maintained that this climate of fear caused some New Yorkers of means to leave the province lest they be caught up in the web of accusations. Others, too, who had done nothing more than to maintain amiable personal relations with Catholics came under suspicion. Leisler accused a Captain McKenzie of the militia of being "popishly affected" because he had heard him refer to Father John Smith, a Catholic priest at the fort under Dongan, as a "very good man." McKenzie did not deny the charge, saying "I do still say he is a very good humoured man, but I never called him so because he was a Papist." Noting that Leisler "put on a more angry look" before accusing him of Catholic sympathies, the embattled McKenzie defied Leisler by insisting that "I am as much a Protestant as you or any man in the country."[12]

Even the Protestant clergy was not exempt from the hail of accusations. Alexander Enis, a minister of the Church of England, was denounced by one of Leisler's supporters for speaking well of the Jesuits and Roman Catholicism. Several ministers of the Dutch Reformed Church, known as dominies, were also accused of secretly cooperating with Catholics. Godridus Dellius of Albany was denounced for corresponding with a Jesuit priest, "according to what we have long had reason to suspect"; the pressure on him became so intense that he fled to Puritan New England, known neither for its religious tolerance nor its Dutch population. Jacob Leisler unleashed a harangue on a Reverend Selyns during services at the Dutch Church in New York; Selyns later said of the Leislerians that "Neither could the Protestant Ministers in the province Escape their Malice & cruelty's." Another member of the Dutch clergy, Rudolphus Varick of Long Island, was summarily dragged out of his house and imprisoned for "Treasonable words against Capt. Leysler and the Fort." This testimony supports the Leislerians' claim that devotion to Protestantism, and not ethnic identity, was their standard for loyalty to the new power in the province.[13]

However, by not limiting the object of his crusade to Catholics alone, Leisler and his party eventually crossed an important line. They ran afoul of persons of wealth and influence in New York. Three dozen merchants and Dutch Reformed clergy sent a communiqué to the English government in London complaining that supporters of Leisler were nothing but "rabble," a "drunken crue," "ignorant Mobile," and—in an apt historical comparison to the English Revolution of the 1640s—"Olliverians," as in adherents of Cromwell. An affluent New Yorker characterized Leisler's supporters as "the meanest and most abject common people"; a contemporary observer commented that "almost every man of Sence, Reputation or Estate" opposed Leisler. Those who had the most to lose in New York had good reason to fear that the mercurial Leisler and his inflammatory rhetoric of "Reformation" and "Revolution" threatened their own economic and social interests.[14]

Authorities in London subsequently made the decision to remove the crusading Leisler from office. Although Jacob Leisler himself was clearly committed to keeping New York within the English Empire, some of his Dutch supporters harbored dreams of making the province once again a colony of Holland despite Leisler's efforts to build a pan-Protestant movement. He and his allies were brought down by representatives of the Protestant monarchs in whose names they had originally taken power. Major Richard Ingoldsby arrived in New York City in January of 1691 with a military party in advance of Henry Sloughter, whom King William had appointed governor of the province. Ingoldsby demanded that Leisler turn over possession of the fort, which Leisler refused to do because he believed that Ingoldsby did not possess a royal commission. A brief skirmish followed, during which a few of Ingoldsby's soldiers were killed. The Leislerians charged that Ingoldsby's force had recruited "several Papists and Negroes" in New York City to aid them in their attack on the fort. The Leislerians sought to discredit Ingoldsby's claim to rightful authority by accusing him of committing the egregious crime of arming those, that is, Catholics and African slaves, who were most opposed to stability, order, and the Protestant regime in a reformed New York. The allegation was also in the tradition of Protestant fear of Catholic violence, a cultural inheritance from Europe on which Leisler had drawn upon throughout his time in power.[15]

Henry Sloughter finally arrived in New York in March of 1691 to take up his duties as governor. Jacob Leisler surrendered Fort William to the duly constituted English Protestant authorities, just as he had promised to do when he took possession of the fort two years earlier.

Sloughter's party, however, promptly arrested Leisler and seven of his closest supporters, including his son-in-law, Jacob Milbourne, and charged them with treason. In a clear signal that London considered Leisler to have crossed an important line, authorities also charged Leisler with illegally imprisoning and exiling some of the king's "Protestant subjects." There was no mention in any of the official proceedings of Leisler's campaign against Catholics, which implies approval by London of all that Leisler had done in the name of re-moving "popery" from New York. And so while Leisler had done much to inflame both ethnic and class tensions in New York, his campaign against Catholics seems to have raised no serious com-plaints among those in authority. Having succeeded in achieving his main goal, one carried out explicitly in the service of England's new Protestant monarchs, Leisler now faced the maximum punishment from those who came to do the bidding of those same monarchs.[16]

New York officials also drew on Leisler's legacy as they sought to bring greater stability and coherence to the province. After a dizzying thirty-year period in which New York twice went from being a Dutch colony to an English one and then experienced the chaos of Leisler's Rebellion, sources of unity were at a premium. The govern-ment of New York tried to heal some of the divisions by encouraging a sense of shared Protestantism among the province's many ethnici-ties and Christian denominations. New York, especially New York City, in the last quarter of the seventeenth century, was becoming more English and less Dutch in population and character. Anti-Ca-tholicism was a cause around which English, Dutch, French Hugue-nots, Congregationalists of New England birth and ancestry, and other Protestants could rally. Provincial authorities issued a procla-mation of thanksgiving in September of 1692 calling for celebrations marking the end of the "late confusions and debaucheries." The proclamation affirmed the "preservation and security of the Holy Protestant Religion" as an official policy of New York. Moreover, New York continued to hold, with official approval, the Guy Fawkes celebrations that Leisler had initiated in 1689. Official decrees from London also helped to complete a comprehensive, Leislerian policy toward Catholics. King William ordered in 1691 that all officials in New York swear oaths under the Test Act. These oaths consisted chiefly of a series of declarations against the spiritual and temporal authority of the Catholic Church, as well as its religious practices. All who took the oath were required to deny the Roman Catholic doctrine of the transubstantiation and affirm their belief that the adoration of the Virgin Mary and the saints, as well as the Catholic Mass, were "superstitious and idolatrous." Potential officeholders also had to swear that they had not received a special dispensation from the pope that absolved them from taking the oath in good conscience.[17]

By the middle of the 1690s, the Catholic presence in New York had been reduced dramatically. Some of the Catholics who had been living there at the outset of Leisler's Rebellion in 1689 fled to Pennsylvania, where the Quaker leadership was more tolerant than their counterparts in New York. Among those Jesuits who fled New York, some eventually made their way to Maryland, where they continued their ministry. Thomas Dongan avoided capture by Leisler's forces and went to England, which proved to be a safer locale for him than was New York under Leisler's rule. The former governor was allowed to live in England as a free man and eventually was granted noble status. Those Catholics who did remain in New York were predominantly the "humbler adherents of the ancient faith" who endured official and popular hostility. Two Catholics from Albany (New York's second-largest city), Frans Pruyn, a tailor, and Peter Villeroy, a laborer of French birth, "who by reason of their Perswasion" refused to take the Test Oath or sign an association denouncing "Papist" treachery, although they did agree to take a simple oath of loyalty to the king. For Pruyn, Villeroy, and other Catholics of modest means who did not have the resources to leave New York for opportunities elsewhere, their religion prevented them from becom-

ing fully trusted subjects of the king and politically engaged inhabitants of the province.[18]

During the war between England and France that lasted until the
middle of the 1690s, Catholics in New York continued to be suspected
of divided loyalties. Two soldiers who came to New York in 1696 as
part of an English force were found to be Catholic. Their superiors
promptly took Charles Moreill and James Wood out of the ranks
and shipped them back to England. That same year, the New York
government disarmed all Catholics in the province and held them in
prison until the authorities could be satisfied that they posed no
threat to public safety. There was also an official investigation to
identify all Catholics in New York City. Following an investigation
in 1696 by the mayor of New York City, only ten men (including
Anthony Brockholls) could be clearly identified by military authorities in New York as being "reputed Papists." They were of English,
French, and Irish ethnicity. Five years later, an observer noted that
there were "not 20 papists or Jacobins in the whole province." When
the suffrage for Assembly elections was broadened in 1698, Catholics
were again specifically excluded from the franchise. Even so, it seems
that a few Catholic men may have tried to vote in provincial elections,
because in 1701 New York felt it necessary to deny the suffrage to
any "Papist or Popish recusant." The province of New York not only
denied Catholics the rights and privileges of subjects, but also made
civic life itself and the practice of Catholicism mutually exclusive and
incompatible.[19]

One of Jacob Leisler's immediate successors as governor of New
York, Richard Coote, the Earl of Bellomont, championed legislation
banning Catholic priests from the province. He argued that Jesuit
missionaries on the province's frontier were inciting the Iroquois to
attack. The provincial Assembly in 1701 enacted that bill into law.
Under its provisions, Catholic clergy were strictly forbidden from
living in or entering New York under pain of life imprisonment (or
death in the event of escape and recapture), and Catholics in New

York who gave refuge to their priests were to be punished with heavy fines and time in the stocks. The law also gave New Yorkers broad permission to "apprehend without a warrant" any person they suspected of being a Jesuit and promised a reward if those they turned in to the authorities turned out to be members of the Catholic clergy. This law effectively deputized the entire people of New York in the battle against Catholicism.[20]

■ ■ ■

Within a decade of Thomas Dongan becoming governor, the place of Catholics in the overall polity and society of New York had fallen dramatically. The results of this transformation had a major impact on the whole province. Jacob Leisler succeeded because his brief regime essentially Protestantized New York's political life by its vigorous insistence that those who held power be suitably anti-Catholic. It implemented England's Glorious Revolution in an especially aggressive manner in New York, an outcome that had unfortunate consequences for the province's remaining Catholic population for more than three-quarters of a century. The settlement of the Glorious Revolution in New York helped to shape the province's political and religious culture, which was unique among the British colonies in North America. Unlike in New England, where one variant of Christianity held itself above all other churches, Protestantism itself became the end point in New York. Theological disputes among the various denominations, in political and social terms, mattered for little. Although the Church of England was officially established in four of New York's southern counties, it never gained the preeminence that that denomination did in Virginia or that the Congregational Church enjoyed in much of New England. Loyalty to the English crown, its interest in North America, and to the Protestant cause in general was what counted. Catholicism in Leisler's "reformed" polity became an outlawed and thoroughly politicized religion. All political activity by any avowed Catholics who remained in New York was strictly prohibited. That meant, among other things, that the chance that any leader or faction in the province would be able to portray their opponents as "Romish" or "popishly affected" was greatly reduced. New York's politics for the remainder of the colonial period would remain exceptionally competitive and contentious, but never again would there be such chaos and uncertainty as when Leisler ruled. Thus, the excesses of Leisler's regime would be prevented in the future by maintaining in practice Leisler's core ideas—the forced and systematic exclusion of Catholics from all religious and, especially, political liberty.

Leisler's Rebellion and the shattering impact it had on Catholicism in the province notwithstanding, historians have written approvingly of early New York's ethnic and religious diversity and its pluralistic character.[21] This portrayal is part of a larger interpretation of the middle colonies (generally understood to include New York, New Jersey, Pennsylvania, Delaware, and sometimes Maryland) as harbingers of the future republic because of these same traits. The middle colonies have been held up as more representative of the type of society that the United States eventually became than were the more homogenous societies of colonial New England and Virginia.[22] New York *was* diverse in religious and ethnic terms, and even after 1700 it was relatively tolerant compared, for example, to Massachusetts. A flaw in the portrait that historians have drawn of colonial New York, however, is that it fails to recognize the extent to which religious pluralism was secured in New York concurrently with the forced exclusion of Catholics.[23] Colonial New York appears less pluralistic and tolerant when the perspective shifts to the historical experience of Catholics.[24]

The banishment of Catholics from New York's religious and civil life has its history. Catholicism in New York was linked in the minds of Protestants not just to distant Rome, but to the French colony in Canada that posed a genuine military threat to English interests in North America. But anti-Catholicism in New York was more than a foreign, external threat; it sprang from internal sources as well. The king's decrees and statutes that became law in New York after 1689 were not merely imposed on the province from without. Protestant New Yorkers embraced the mandates that excluded Catholics from the province's religious and political life and easily integrated these mandates into the fabric of the province. The events of the late seventeenth century gave Protestants in New York their own history of triumph over, and deliverance from, Catholic oppression. This ascendancy extended well into the eighteenth century, long after Leisler himself had been deposed and executed. For New York Catholics, then, the province's own Glorious Revolution, that is, Leisler's Rebellion, proved to be a complete disaster, one from which their fortunes would not recover for generations.

# CHAPTER 1

# "The Hand of Popery in this Hellish Conspiracy"

## *The Legacy of Anti-Catholicism in Colonial New York*

After the departure of Catholic officials in the wake of Leisler's Rebellion, the small Catholic population that lived in the province was
scattered and unorganized. Fear of Catholicism, in the context of England's rivalry with France and Spain, remained part of New York's
political culture. During a span of twenty years in the middle of the
eighteenth century, Catholicism once again became directly linked
to England's rivals for empire in ways that posed a direct threat to
New York. Catholicism as a religion continued to be outlawed in the
province through the first three quarters of the eighteenth century.
Although Catholics who entered New York could not become naturalized subjects, some did live in the province as laborers and slaves.
Early in the eighteenth century, Catholic freeborn subjects of Spain
were captured by privateers along the Atlantic seaboard and sold into
slavery in New York. Authorities believed some of them to be the
leaders of a 1712 slave uprising in New York City that left several
whites dead. A group of slaves deliberately set a fire, waited in hiding,
and then killed some of the residents of the city who came to extin-
guish the flames. In response, the New York government enacted a
law in 1713 that naturalized all foreign-born Protestants living in

the province. Under its provisions, all those who became naturalized subjects of New York were required to take the Test Act, in which they abjured any allegiance to the Roman Catholic Church. There is scattered evidence suggesting that at least a few enslaved New Yorkers continued to identify with Catholicism despite the prevailing circumstances. When Alexander Saxton ran away in 1733, his owner described him as one who "professeth himself to be a Roman Catholic" who wore clothes marked by a "cross on the left breast."[1]

## THE 1741 SLAVE CONSPIRACY

As they had during the turmoil surrounding the Glorious Revolution, New Yorkers in the middle of the eighteenth century associated violence and threats to the public order with Catholicism. In 1741, the threat became perhaps even more terrifying because Catholics, both lay and clergy, had appeared to have inspired slaves to rebel. The Protestant reaction in the 1680s against Catholics stemmed from their positions of prominence in the colony. After half a century of officially suppressing Catholicism, New York officials now saw a very different type of Catholic threat, one that emanated not from the governor's chair and the fort, but rather from New York's murky world of dank basements and grogshops, where poor whites, Irish soldiers, and enslaved Africans could meet away from the watchful eyes of the authorities. As Jacob Leisler himself had said as his regime was collapsing, there had been fears in New York of a possible alliance between African-Americans and Catholics, two groups on the margins of society with little apparent reason to uphold the established order. An even stronger parallel between 1689 and 1741 was that New York Protestants continued to link Catholicism with a foreign enemy; in this case, it was Spain.

Colonial New York City was, in many ways, an unstable place in the 1740s. Between a fifth and a sixth of its population were enslaved people of African and other ancestries. Irish Catholics, whose loyalty to the crown New York authorities had good reason to doubt, served as soldiers in the city's garrison. Catholic missionaries were believed to be hiding on the province's frontiers, encouraging the Iroquois to make war on New York. New Yorkers were particularly uneasy in the winter of 1740–41. The weather that season was unusually harsh, there were fears of a slave revolt such as that which shook South Carolina in 1739, and rumors of an invasion by the Spanish were circulating as well. New York authorities received word from Governor James Oglethorpe of Georgia that the Spanish had secretly deployed priests to the principal cities of British North America to direct plots aimed at burning those places to the ground. The province's officials were acutely conscious of their location as a "frontier province," one that made them particularly vulnerable to attack from England's enemies, as they would periodically remind London. Toward the end of the long winter of 1741, rumors were abroad in New York "that there had of late been Popish priests lurking about the town." A search failed to turn up evidence of any Catholic priests, but the speculation must have contributed to New Yorkers' sense that they were under siege. An outbreak of fires of unknown origin, the most serious of which damaged Fort George on March 18, 1741, convinced New York authorities that the province had indeed become the target of an international conspiracy. Officials' reaction to the fires became so extreme that one New Englander, relishing the irony after New Yorkers had long pointed to the Salem trials of 1691 as a prime example of Puritan intolerance and fanaticism, characterized the proceedings in New York as a witch hunt. New York officials initially suspected African-American slaves; they later came to believe that the fire in Fort George was the result of "a horrid conspiracy" entered into by slaves and John Hughson, a poor white resident of the city.[2]

For Judge Daniel Horsmanden, who presided over the trials of those charged in the alleged conspiracy, the affair was at bottom a plot conceived and executed by Irish Catholics. He was convinced that it was not coincidental that the most dangerous fire had been set "on St. Patrick's night," that is, March 17. The very timing of the fire helped to persuade the judge that Irish Catholics had led their African partners in this conspiracy. "For on this night, according to custom, their commemoration of their saint might be most likely to incite those of the infernal league with boldness and resolution, for the execution of this terrible enterprize." Several British soldiers of Irish birth were brought to trial for their involvement in the conspiracy. Will, a slave, just before he was burnt at the stake, accused William Kane of being "always reputed a Papist" and of plotting with John Ury, a priest, to burn the Anglican church in New York City. Kane denied the charge, maintaining that he was a Protestant and that "he never was at any Roman Catholic congregation in his life." Irish soldiers Andrew Ryan, Peter Connolly, Edward Kelly, and Edward Murphy were also accused of being involved, but the case against them was dropped when no one appeared to testify against them. Even so, Judge Horsmanden was convinced of their treason and duplicity. "Many of the Irish Catholics, . . . being confederated with the conspirators; they could not have pitched upon a fitter season for perpetrating their bloody purposes."[3]

Another intimation as to "Whether or how far the hand of popery has been in this hellish conspiracy" came from the confessions of two African-American slaves. They testified that they were offered absolution from their sins by Father John Ury, whom authorities arrested for "being a Roman Catholic priest, exercising his religion, and seducing the people." One of the chief witnesses for the province at the trial, Mary Burton, placed Ury, who arrived in New York in late 1740, at the center of the entire conspiracy. She alleged that he had mixed among New York's slaves and poor whites, baptizing them and assuring potential rebels that he had the power to forgive all their sins, including those committed in the course of overthrowing New York's government. At his trial, John Ury denied that he was a Roman Catholic priest. In his private journal, he had rejected the

Catholic sacrament of penance, insisting that "it is not in the power of man to forgive Sins, that it is the prerogative only of the Great God." It is most likely that Ury was a member of the Church of England who did not recognize the legitimacy of William and Mary's accession in 1689. That view in itself would have put him at odds with New York's authorities, but the charges against Ury were his alleged Catholicism and supposed inciting of slaves to rebellion.[4]

New York authorities were especially fearful of a lethal mixture of illicit religion and the wrath of those who were enslaved. They believed of Catholics that the "juggling tricks" that they possessed in their "hocus pocus bloody religion" made it easy for them to "pick the pockets of credulous people," presumably uneducated African slaves. This dangerous combination of presumed Catholic superstition and African gullibility was illustrated for the all-white, Protestant jury by Attorney General Richard Bradley, who described a scene at the house of John Hughson, one of those whom Ury had allegedly baptized for Rome. Ury had stood in front of a group of slaves and proceeded to "make a round ring on the floor with chalk, and stand in the middle of it with a cross in his hand, and swear the negroes into the plot." The prosecution also argued that Ury encouraged the slaves to rebel by telling them that the Spanish and French would arrive to aid in their insurrection. Although John Ury denied all charges made against him, he was convicted and sentenced to death. Caught in a web of fear and persecution, his vow, "I lift up my hand and solemnly protest that I am innocent" was almost certainly true. He was executed by hanging both for encouraging slave revolts and for violating the 1701 law barring Catholic priests from New York under pain of death.[5]

As the prosecutions continued into June of 1741, officials became even more convinced that Catholicism lurked behind the frightful specter of slave rebellion. Margaret (Peggy) Kerry, who along with the Hughsons was targeted as one of the principal white conspirators, was alleged "to be a papist," and "it is suspected that Huson [Hughson] and his wife were brought over to it." All three, along with the Hughsons' daughter, Sarah, were hung for their roles in the plot. John Hughson's father and three brothers were among those imprisoned and suspected of being Catholics. Lieutenant Governor George Clarke reported to London in August of 1741 that "it is now apparent that the hand of popery is in it . . . we have besides several other white men in prison and most of them [it is thought] I wist Papists." Most troubling of all, from the standpoint of Protestant New Yorkers, was their suspicion that guileful Catholic priests had infiltrated their city, seeking to use the raw strength and anger of the slave population to undermine the community. What is more, they could not be convinced, despite all their investigations and prosecutions, that they had completely eradicated the menace. Therefore, Daniel Horsmanden took little satisfaction in seeing that Juan de Sylva, an enslaved Catholic convicted of conspiracy, just before his execution, "behaved decently, prayed in Spanish, kissed a crucifix, insisting on his innocence to the last."[6]

## Anti-Catholicism and the Political Culture of Mid-Eighteenth-Century New York

In the middle of the eighteenth century, Guy Fawkes, or Pope Day festivities, first held during the days of Jacob Leisler, were a regular part of New York's political culture, both official and popular. In 1737, the "Assembly and Corporation and the other principaled Gentlemen and Merchants" of New York City called on the governor, made several toasts, and ordered the fort's cannon and fireworks to be set off. Royal officials used Pope's Day in New York during the 1730s to buttress support for the monarchy and to remind any potential rebels that the perpetrators of "that horrid and Treasonable Popish Gun-Powder Plot to blow up and destroy King, Lords and Commons" were executed for their efforts. Ordinary New Yorkers celebrated November 5 in their own ways. On Pope's Day in 1748, a substantial number of them led a march, "the first of its kind in these Parts," through New York City, breaking the windows of homes that were not lighted in support of the procession. A critic derided the celebration as that *"filthy practice"* and expressed the hope that "as it was the first, so may it be the last of the Kind." What made this Pope's Day celebration novel was the popular disorder that surrounded it. As in Boston's November 5 observances, Pope's Day in New York City had become a vehicle for the "lower sorts" to assemble and exhibit their own politics. "A large body of the Mobility in town assembled as usual" on November 5, 1755, parading effigies of the devil, the pope, and the pretender around the city on a bier. "The Mob," as a newspaper described it, stopped at the home of a captured French general (this was during the Seven Years War), but authorities ordered a guard to the scene, which prevented any violence from breaking out.[7]

These anti-Catholic rituals took place in the absence of any organized Catholic community. The lack of any outward signs of Catholicism led one observer to note approvingly in 1748 that New York was free of "the least face of popery." Thomas Jones, who lived in New York in the middle of the eighteenth century, believed that one of New York's defining characteristics was the broad religious tolerance that so many enjoyed. He noted that in addition to his own Anglican churches and the many congregations professing the Dutch Reformed faith, New York was home to "Presbyterians, Moravians, Seceders, Lutherans, German Calvinists, those of the French Reformed Church, the people called Quakers, and even the very Jews." Jones found in the 1750s that all of these disparate religions and ethnicities "lived in perfect peace and harmony. This, if I may be allowed the expression, was the *Golden Age* of New York." He left unmentioned the systematic denial to Catholics of religious liberty, an exclusion that was also part of colonial New York's character and political culture.[8]

## THE SEVEN YEARS WAR AND PROTESTANT UNITY

Britain's last imperial war with France was a force for unity in a province that was known for its intense factional politics. The Seven Years War buttressed the Protestant identity of New Yorkers, which expanded to include even more denominations and churches. As inhabitants of a province that shared a border with Canada, many in New York believed that the war with France represented a serious threat to their liberties. One Protestant minister, in encouraging members of his congregation to volunteer for the militia, asked: "Ye that love your religion, enlist, for your religion is in danger. Can Protestant Christianity expect quarter from heathen savages and French Papists?" The war was yet another trial for Catholics in New York because the conflict led to heightened scrutiny for French Catholics who lived in the province. All French people were liable to be detained until they could give a good account of themselves, that is, prove that they were Huguenots. Far to the northeast of New York, in Nova Scotia, French Catholics known as the Acadians were driven from their homes and dispersed around the thirteen colonies, in part because they refused to renounce their Catholic faith. In 1756, about 150 of them were forcibly sent to New York, where authorities "distributed them in the most remote & secure parts of this colony," and made sure that the children were placed in Protestant homes. The Acadians were neutrals in the war; even so, New York went to great lengths to prevent the establishment of any Catholic enclaves in their midst.[9]

The circumstances of the Seven Years War, ironically, led to an increase of Catholics in New York. Catholics were legally barred from serving in the British military. In order to fill their ranks, however, British officials recruited Catholics in Ireland and Scotland to serve overseas, a practice that began in earnest during the Seven Years War. Consequently, Irish Catholics came to New York in the 1750s and 1760s as members of the British army and navy. Once there, they had incentives to desert, including to escape fighting for Britain or to avoid returning to meager prospects in Ireland. One such Irishman who did so was Patrick Dunn of Galway, Ireland, who was a Catholic priest. He was captured in New York escorting Edward Jefferys, an English soldier who was fleeing to Canada. Jefferys was executed for desertion. On September 23, 1756, Dunn was also executed; he died "a strict papist," although it is not entirely clear if Dunn was found guilty of breaking the 1701 law banning Catholic priests in New York or for aiding a deserter. Others were more successful. In January of 1758, Thomas Gland, John McEvey, and John Burn, all natives of Ireland, fled from a British warship in New York harbor. Some of the Catholic soldiers on the loose in New York were Americans from other colonies. "A great number of Irish Papists and Transports who were enlisted from the back parts of Pennsylvania and Mary Land" deserted in New York, and some of them hid out among the Iroquois.[10]

The ideology of the conflict, with its emphasis on a shared Protestantism and corresponding anti-Catholicism, buttressed, if anything, the prohibitions against the Catholic faith that had been in place in New York since the late seventeenth century. Lieutenant Governor Cadwallader Colden proclaimed at the conclusion of the war that August 11, 1763 would be a general day of thanksgiving to celebrate the Anglo-American victory over France. New York's religious pluralism and diversity was on full display at that moment. Clergymen at New York City's various houses of worship, including the Anglican, Presbyterian, Dutch Reformed, Baptist, and Jewish congregations, preached sermons based on biblical texts. A Moravian preacher, representing the latest Protestant denomination to gain acceptance in New York and one that had been persecuted in the 1740s, was given the honor of delivering the primary sermon at an ecumenical service. Centering his remarks on the 29th Psalm, he sought to strike a unifying tone as he proclaimed that "The Lord will bless his People with Peace."[11]

## CATHOLIC RELIGIOUS IDENTITY IN LATE
## COLONIAL NEW YORK

By the third quarter of the eighteenth century, the logic of empire
and economics had help to generate a shadowy population of Catholics. It included immigrants from Ireland and New France, Irish and
Irish-American soldiers who were assigned to defend New York, the
descendants of Spanish-speaking slaves captured in imperial wars,
and indentured servants from Ireland. Despite the probable increase
in the number of Catholics living in New York by the 1770s, the
strict prohibitions on Catholicism continued to discourage any Catholic religious community from emerging fully. When William Tryon
became New York's royal governor in 1771, his official orders from
London required him to "permit a liberty of Conscience to all persons
except Papists," the same language that had been given to every provincial governor, upon taking office, since 1691. At the same time,
New York's rich diversity of churches and denominations was becoming even more striking. Members of various Protestant denominations opened approximately seventy-five Protestant churches in
the province between 1750 and 1775, with Dutch Reformed, Presbyterians, Congregationalists, and Quakers the most numerous. Without a church of their own, Catholics had to find other ways to meet
their spiritual needs. Individuals who had the means to do so, such
as John Leary, an affluent merchant and horse importer, traveled to
Philadelphia to hear Mass at one of the Catholic churches in that city.
Others who had been baptized as Catholic either gave up religion
altogether or joined one of New York's various Protestant congregations. Most of the latter turned to the Anglican churches. The congregation of St. Peter's (Anglican) Church in Albany included some
Irish Catholics. Among them was Cornelius Mullone, who at his Anglican baptism in 1771, promised "to conform to the rules of the
Church of England," a pledge that other new members of the church
were not required to make. John Jenkins and Thomas Barry, who
many years later became active members of Albany's first Catholic

parish, were also members of St. Peter's in the 1770s. The situation for Catholics in New York City was similar. It was in the graveyard of the Anglican Trinity Church in Manhattan "that the oldest Catholic gravestones now standing in New York are to be found."[12]

Despite the official ban on their faith, Catholics in New York City by the early 1770s were apparently meeting in secret to hear Mass at the home of a German immigrant on Wall Street. They were ministered to by Father Ferdinand Farmer, a German-born Jesuit. Father Farmer was remembered as having "visited N.Y. before the revolutionary war, when the legal punishment was death for priests or Jesuits presuming to set foot on that Province." He had come to Maryland in the 1750s, and from there he ventured outward "in search of little flocks scattered in the wilderness." Father Farmer would enter New York by stealth, dressed in disguise, his visits so clandestine that he made no official record of them. Even so, the priest's sojourns to New York City were evidence that there was now a group of Catholics there who had taken an important step toward claiming religious freedom for themselves.[13]

# CHAPTER 2

# "The Encouragement Popery Had Met With"

## Catholics and Religious Liberty in Revolutionary New York

The legacy of anti-Catholicism in New York became evident in an early republican political club that became prominent late in the colonial period. One of the leading factions in the province was comprised in part of Anglicans, and their opponents included many dissenting Protestants. The latter had historically prided themselves on their religious and political distance from the Catholic Church and its center in Rome. In the 1750s, members of that faction, including William Livingston, William Smith, and John Morin Scott, formed a Whig club. The goals of the three, in the view of one of their political opponents, included "pulling down the Church, ruining the Constitution, or heaving the whole province into confusion." A member of the Anglican DeLancey family derided them as "presbyterian and republican fanatics" who "had in the proceeding century brought their Sovereign to the block," a reference to the execution of Charles I in 1649. The leaders of the Whig Club, although viewed by some as a threat to the established order of colonial New York, saw themselves as heirs to a political tradition that would have offered the province's scattered and unorganized Catholics little encouragement that a change in New York's political culture and structure might be of some benefit to them. At the weekly meetings of the Whig Club, members would proudly and defiantly toast "the immortal memory of Oliver Cromwell."[1]

It is not surprising that at the start of the imperial crisis between Britain and its American colonies in the 1760s, members of the province's dissenting Protestant denominations led the opposition to the crown in New York. Whigs, or Patriots, couched some of their initial opposition to British rule in religious terms; promising the greatest change to the status quo in New York, they raised the cry of "popery" to discredit those who continued to support the crown. Anti-Catholic rhetoric and imagery retained its ideological currency at the outbreak of the crisis that led to revolution. Celebrations of Pope's Day, for example, served as a disguise for ideas and actions that were subversive and potentially revolutionary. During the uproar over the Stamp Act in November of 1765, the Sons of Liberty posted signs throughout New York City warning of "the storming of the Fort this Night under cover of burning the Pope and pretender unless the Stamps were delivered." The phrase "under the cover of burning the Pope" had a double meaning. The Sons were proclaiming their dissatisfaction with particular imperial policies. At the same time, however, they affirmed the Protestant heritage they shared with Great Britain by celebrating the anniversary of the defeat of the Catholic plot to kill the English king in 1605.[2]

Patriots in New York used a religious controversy to distance themselves further from British rule in the province. Thomas B. Chandler, an Anglican priest from Elizabeth, New Jersey, published a pamphlet in the late 1760s calling for an Anglican bishop to be assigned to America. To circumvent potential charges that he was encouraging the introduction of "popery" into Protestant America, Reverend Chandler insisted that America's Anglican prelate would be a "primitive Bishop" in the tradition of the ancient Christian church. William Livingston led the protest against Chandler's proposal. Writing under the pseudonym, "The American Whig," he denounced the suggestion as incompatible with the history and culture of a Protestant people. Livingston said of the possibility of a bishop coming to the colonies, "America is a Virgin as yet, undebauch'd by proud tyrannical Ecclesiasticks . . . [and] the Man of Sin who always steals a Rape under a Priest's Garment." In seeking to link Chandler's plan to Catholicism, "The American Whig" contended that the papacy itself was rooted in the development of a strong and vigorous episcopacy, arguing that "the *Man of Sin* is to this day a monument of the supreme height to which this ambition has mounted." Even more bluntly, he accused Chandler of justifying the "horrid rites of idolatry and the solemn fooleries of popery." Also, in protesting the involvement of some New York merchants in the British tea trade, Patriots held a rally outside the coffeehouse in lower Manhattan on Guy Fawkes Day, November 5, 1773.[3]

Livingston also connected the religious controversy to politics. He compared the Anglican desire for a bishop with the widely hated Stamp Act, claiming that "the high-flying Tory party are resolutely bent upon establishing the episcopal government in the colonies." Furthermore, Livingston claimed that there was a direct correlation between British policy and Anglican plans for a bishop. "The late Stamp-Act was intended to squeeze out of the colonists a fund which they probably had hopes of applying to prelatical purposes." Chandler had said that opposition to an Anglican bishop came from Whigs in America. Livingston, oblivious to the possibility that Catholics might be living in New York, eagerly pointed out that Chandler "could not find any other type except some of his own party, and the papists in Maryland." Livingston's point was that New Yorkers (and by extension, all Americans), were not merely subjects of King George III, but also Protestants who would jealousy guard not only their political liberties, but their religious freedoms as well. Livingston and other Whigs further tried to isolate the Church of England in New York by suggesting that it was beginning to lose some of its Protestant character. In calling for a bishop, "The American Whig" argued that Chandler was forgetting that the Anglican Church, which had a prominent place in the history of New York, was distinguished by its "reformation of their doctrines in opposition to the Church of Rome."[4]

A division between some Anglicans and other Protestants was one mark of the growing political crisis in New York. Thomas Chandler was not the only member of the Church of England to feel the sting of the Patriots' zeal in 1774 and early 1775. The Reverend William Mansfield, an Anglican priest in Queens County, New York, was denounced as a "Tory, a Papist, and an enemy of my country, by the adherents of the present unnatural rebellion." A Patriot newspaper published a satire called "The Tories' Creed," in which adherents declared their belief in "all arguments and positions that the Jesuits (those enlightened advocates for passive obedience) have ever maintained or published." The Sons of Liberty, mocked as a "Presbyterian Junto," by one of their opponents, distributed broadsides in New York City that read "No Placemen, Pensioners, Ministerial Hirelings, Popery, nor Arbitrary Power!"[5]

New Yorkers had their belief in Britain's commitment to Protestantism shaken further in 1774. After taking possession of Canada from France after the Seven Years War, Britain faced the problem of establishing its dominance over the predominantly Catholic population in its new colonies. Part of its solution to this problem was issuing what became known as the Quebec Act. The act stated that Catholics in Quebec "may have, hold, and enjoy, the free Exercise of the Religion of the Church of Rome, subject to the King's Supremacy." The measure also specifically provided for the "Encouragement of the Protestant Religion, and for the Maintenance and Support of a Protestant Clergy within the Province." For their efforts to guarantee religious liberty to both Protestants and Catholics in Canada, the British provoked an intense outcry from the thirteen colonies. The opposition was such that the Patriots came to regard the Quebec Act as one of the Intolerable Acts. General Thomas Gage, the commander of the British military in the colonies, thought that rural Americans in their outrage over a perceived threat to their religious liberties became further united with their urban counterparts who were resisting British economic policies.[6]

The Quebec Act generated dissent because it threatened the colonists' sense of themselves as a free, British, Protestant people. The protests were particularly intense in New York; only in New England was the response arguably more impassioned. New Yorkers were the first colonists to denounce the Quebec Act in print. Even while the bill was still only a proposal in England, the New York Assembly listed it as a grievance; New York and Massachusetts were the first colonies to register their official disapproval. In communicating their grievances to British authorities in early 1775, the New York Assembly declared that the "indulgences" granted to Roman Catholics in Quebec had "given great uneasiness to the minds of many of your Majesty's American subjects." As one New Yorker put it, if America were also to be subjected to Catholicism, "which country will exist for the liberties of Protestants and Englishmen?" The campaign against the Quebec Act in New York was led by members of New York's dissenting denominations. In the provincial Assembly, George Clinton, a son of Irish Presbyterian immigrants from rural Ulster County, New York, proposed that a resolution denouncing the Quebec Act should also condemn Catholicism as a "sanguinary religion equally repugnant to the genuine simplicity of Christianity, and the maxims of sound philosophy." Combining Protestant fervor with the rationalism of the Enlightenment, Clinton's measure reflected two major elements of the mindset of the revolutionary movement in America. Adherents of both defined themselves in part by their rejection of Catholicism.[7]

From the fall of 1774 through the spring of 1775, in the streets and in the taverns of New York, Patriots used anger at the Quebec Act and fear of Catholicism to build popular support for resistance to British authority in America. The wide denunciation of Britain's toleration of Catholicism in Canada gave Protestants in New York the opportunity to unite once again across denominational lines. For Anglicans who favored united action by the colonies against Britain, opposing the Quebec Act was a way to identify themselves as Protestants and Patriots. Alexander Hamilton, an ambitious young émigré from the West Indies, quickly grasped how unpopular the Quebec Act was in New York. He said of the British, "If they had been friends to the Protestant cause they never would have provided such a nursery for its greatest enemy." The General Committee of Association, a Patriot group in New York City, in May of 1775 denounced the "establishment of Popery" in Quebec because it defended the "those invaluable rights which are the common inheritance of Britons and Americans."[8]

Through the early months of 1775, even those most adamant in their resistance to British authority in the American colonies were careful to treat the unifying force of the monarchy with respect. One New York crowd in March of 1775 assembled under a banner that proclaimed, "GEORGE III REX. AND THE LIBERTIES OF AMERICA. NO POPERY." It was not until after the battles at Lexington and Concord that Patriots set out to break the remaining political link between the colonies and Britain—allegiance toward His Majesty, George III. At that point, they began using the specter of Catholic tyranny to portray King George as having become implacably hostile to the colonists' liberties. At an outdoor meeting on April 29, 1775, Patriot leader Isaac Low charged that "the King was a Roman Catholic, nay, a Roman Catholic tyrant; that he had broken his coronation oath, had established the popish religion in Canada." King George was still very much the head of the Church of England and Defender of the Faith. But Low, appealing to both emotion and logic, sought to drive a wedge between the king and his subjects. His goal was to dispel any guilt or that fear New Yorkers might have had about rejecting the authority of the king, which was a treasonable act. If George III, in countenancing Roman Catholicism in Quebec, had in fact *broken his coronation oath,* then it was he who had severed the ties between country and colony; New Yorkers, by "rebelling," were only recognizing that reality. Low's speech had the desired effect, as his remarks were "approved of in loud huzzas by the rabble."[9]

In his 1776 pamphlet *Common Sense,* Thomas Paine also employed anti-Catholic themes as he tried to shatter whatever was left of the bond between the English king and his American subjects. He made reference to Catholicism not to enter into a religious debate, but rather because he knew that his audience would readily approve of, and understand, that rhetoric. Paine insisted that "monarchy in every instance is the Popery of government." Responding to the argument that America ought not to separate from the "Mother Country," Paine said that that phrase "hath been jesuitically adopted by the king and his parasites, with a low papistical design of gaining an unfair bias on the credulous weakness of our minds." Paine appealed to the Protestant ethos of the colonists as he encouraged them to think of themselves as American rather than English. In tapping into a distinctly Protestant vision of America, Paine, although he himself was a deist who belonged to no church, declared that the discovery of the New World itself was directly related to the birth, survival, and growth of Protestantism. He reminded his audience that "The reformation was preceded by the discovery of America, as if the Almighty graciously meant to open a sanctuary to the persecuted in future years."[10]

EARLY CATHOLIC LOYALISM

The potential for any alliance between members of the dissenting congregations who led the agitation against Britain and members of the Catholic Church would have been dimly perceived, if at all, at the outset of the Revolutionary War. Patriots had shown little concern in the early stages of the conflict that their insulting references to Catholicism might discourage actual Catholics from joining their movement. At the beginning of the war in New York, it looked as if Catholics might align with those resisting a break with Britain. A group of immigrants, most of whom were from the Scottish Highlands, but also including some from Ireland, migrated to New York's Mohawk Valley in the early 1770s. These immigrants, some of whom were Catholic, became tenants on land owned by Sir William Johnson, who was an agent of the crown in New York. Among the group was John McKenna, a Catholic priest from Meath, Ireland. Although McKenna's presence in New York was illegal, it was countenanced by Johnson, who himself had been born Catholic in Ireland. Like other ambitious Irish Catholics in the first British Empire, Johnson converted to Protestantism, joined the Church of England, and became a staunch supporter of it in America. His own attitudes toward Catholicism were complicated; one observer in New York maintained that Johnson had prevented his Catholic tenants from practicing their faith.[11]

By the early 1770s, however, the pressures of the Patriot challenge to British authority in America had begun to erode the primacy of defending the Protestant interest above all others in New York. Before leaving for America, Johnson's tenants had proclaimed their loyalty to the British throne. The loyalty of the Johnson family to the king made the Highlanders a suspect group to the Patriots once the war started. In January of 1776, several thousand Patriot troops, under the command of General Philip Schuyler of Albany, marched into the Mohawk Valley and disarmed and plundered the immigrant Loyalists. Even so, Schuyler's army sought to persuade the immigrants to join the rebellion. They refused, in part because Father McKenna had warned them that the Patriots in New York were hostile to Catholicism. Johnson's immigrants and their priest eventually made their way out of New York and into Canada. British authorities there organized them into two companies, the Royal Highlanders and the Royal Yorkers, with Father McKenna serving as chaplain to both. The Loyalists returned to the Mohawk Valley as invaders, taking part in Lieutenant Colonel Barry St. Leger's siege of Fort Stanwix in 1777. Some retained their Catholic faith, as evidenced by Father Mc-Kenna's account of his experience in the war: "It is extremely diffi-cult for me to say Mass everyday, but nothing is more important." The one place in New York where royal authorities permitted Catho-lics to practice their faith had led, in part, to Catholic support for the king's cause. The Patriots had yet to adopt similarly pragmatic poli-cies regarding Catholics; the demands of war and international diplo-macy, however, would give them an opportunity to do so.[12]

### BEGINNINGS OF A CATHOLIC–PATRIOT ALLIANCE

Despite the natural ease with which Patriots used anti-Catholic rhet-oric in the first decade of the resistance movement against British power in the American colonies, especially in New York, the demands of forging a national army caused the Patriots to reconsider their relationship to Catholics. General George Washington, the com-mander in chief, ordered a halt to Pope's Day celebrations in the ranks of the Continental Army. He understood that such blatant dis-plays of anti-Catholicism would offend Catholic troops from Mary-land and Pennsylvania, as well as needlessly complicate efforts to persuade the Canadians to join the Revolution. This new national attitude was made evident in New York as well. In the spring of 1776, John Carroll, a Catholic priest from Maryland, entered a grim New York City that was preparing for an invasion by the king's forces. Despite the unlawful nature of his stay in the embattled city, Carroll was in no danger, at least not from the Continental Army. He was on his way to Montreal with a diplomatic commission that the Conti-nental Congress had appointed. The commission included his cousin Charles Carroll (also a Catholic from Maryland), Benjamin Franklin, and Samuel Chase; the four were charged with enticing Canada to join the thirteen colonies in their struggle against Britain. Carroll made no mention of meeting any local Catholics during his "disagreeable days" in New York. The mission was later welcomed upriver at Albany by General Philip Schuyler, who was just months removed from his punitive expedition in the Mohawk Valley. Schuyler entertained the unlikely diplomats "with great politeness and very genteely." Although the delegation ultimately failed to woo the Canadian, (a major reason being that Jean-Olivier Briand, the Catholic Bishop of Quebec, was a firm Loyalist), the mission did signify that the American Revolution itself was beginning to change. It was now generating its own internal logic that was making traditional loyalties, especially ones based on religion, less important. The interests of Patriots and Catholics in America were beginning, slowly, to converge.[13]

Patriots in New York directly confronted the question of what place, if any, Catholics had in their revolution when delegates elected to draft a constitution for the new state gathered in Poughkeepsie. The Convention of the State of New York, as it was formally known, met up the Hudson River because the British had indeed invaded and captured New York City since Father John Carroll's visit. No doubt influenced by New York's long tradition of relative religious pluralism, delegates quickly agreed that the state constitution should include a broad guarantee of religious liberty. The decision was also in keeping with New York's history and culture, however, that the only contentious aspect of the deliberations on protecting freedom of religion centered on whether the prohibitions against Catholicism should be retained. The delegate most determined to deny Catholics religious freedom was John Jay, a wealthy Anglican and one of the more conservative New York Patriots. His reluctance to abolish such a long-standing pillar of the old order—the prohibitions against Catholicism—befits one who saw the Revolution as primarily a political dispute with London. Jay, as one of the leaders of American society, did not think that the war should threaten the place of men of property and distinction. After failing to win approval of a broadly conceived amendment that would have given the state wide authority to investigate any church or denomination it deemed a threat to public safety, Jay offered a narrowly crafted measure aimed specifically and exclusively at Catholics. He urged that religious liberty in New York be denied to "the professors of the Church of Rome, who ought not to hold lands in, or be admitted to a participation of the civil rights enjoyed by the members of this State," unless they first swore oaths before the state Supreme Court denouncing the idea that the Pope could absolve them from allegiance to the state. Under the terms of Jay's amendment, Catholics would also be required to deny the doctrine that the pope and other clerics had the power to forgive sins, which was "prohibited by the Holy Gospel of Jesus Christ," and to renounce that the pope could absolve them from the terms of the oath itself. He borrowed this language almost verbatim from seventeenth-century English laws denying religious freedom to Roman Catholics. The Catholic sacrament of penance was objectionable politically as well as theologically in New York because it implied that Catholics recognized an authority outside of the state.[14]

John Jay's efforts to continue the prohibitions against Catholics in part stemmed from his family's history. He carried with him the inherited memories of the persecution that his Huguenot ancestors suffered in France during the reign of Louis XIV. Jay may also have wanted to remind his colleagues of their common Protestant heritage and of their once (and future?) common adversary, the present conflict notwithstanding. Doing so would provide political room for his fellow Anglicans who did join the revolt against England. However, John Jay was not well positioned to lead the fight against religious freedom for Catholics. Some of his New York co-religionists in the Church of England remained loyal to the crown. Jay's appeals to Protestant solidarity fell short; his amendment was defeated by a vote of 19 to 10, on March 20, 1777. Although the constitution would not go into effect for another month, and the British occupation of New York City would make it impossible for Catholics to practice their faith openly, the eighty-six-year prohibition against Catholicism in New York legally came to an end at that moment.[15]

Jay's effort had failed, in large part, because the Revolution was changing the way that New Yorkers made sense of the connections between religion and politics. A long-standing common Protestant ethos had unexpectedly become creaky with members of various denominations now fighting on both sides of the war. The rationale for denying Catholics religious freedom in 1777 was much less clear than it had been just a few years earlier. Catholics had long been suspect in New York of not being sufficiently loyal to the Protestant monarchy in London and its representatives in North America. That imperative had now suddenly disappeared. It was now to Catholics' advantage that they would have been regarded as having little stake in upholding the old order. This was particularly true in New York, which was fiercely contested, harbored many Loyalists, and whose largest city was occupied by British troops.

As soon as Catholics had won the right, in the abstract, to practice their religion, their rights as citizens were challenged. The draft version of the New York Constitution stipulated that any male immigrant could become a citizen by making a simple pledge of allegiance to the state. John Jay, once again taking the lead, moved that all those applying for citizenship be required to declare that they "abjure and renounce all allegiance and subjection to all and every foreign king, prince, potentate and state, in all matters ecclesiastical as well as civil." The convention adopted the proposal, which would effectively deny Catholic immigrants to New York the rights and benefits of citizenship unless they first renounced allegiance to the pope. Although unlike the debate over granting Catholics religious freedom, a majority of delegates shared Jay's doubts about whether Catholics would possess undivided loyalty to the new republican state. The naturalization law, however, did not apply to Catholics already living in the state (and would presumably not discourage them from supporting the Revolution).[16]

Delegates to the convention who wrote the New York Constitution singled out Catholics for other potential civil disabilities. They gave election inspectors the authority to request potential voters to take an oath of allegiance to the state, one identical to that required of those seeking citizenship. If election officials decided to require the oath of them, future Catholic voters would have been forced to choose between their religion and their state. Distrust of Catholics now involved the question of independence versus dependence, a key element in republicanism. Foreign-born Catholics, delegates agreed, could not yet be granted without reservation the full benefits of citizenship in republican New York. As there was little visible Catholic presence in New York in the 1770s, and no Catholic delegates at the convention to object, it was convenient for the convention to grant religious liberty to Catholics in the abstract and then to erect legal barriers to discourage them from entering the state and deny full citizenship to those already living there.

Patriot ambivalence toward Catholics in New York gave the British hope that they might reap some military advantage from it. The British ability to recruit Catholics in New York as late as 1778 indicates that Catholics were not necessarily united in support of the Revolution. In 1777, a group of Catholics in Pennsylvania (where there was genuine religious liberty for all faiths before the Revolution) formed the Roman Catholic Volunteers to fight for the king. The following summer, they moved to New York City and sought recruits there. The Volunteers enlisted 150 men, bringing the total in their ranks to about 330. These gains were temporary, however, as two captains of the Volunteers were court-martialed, and the discipline of the unit collapsed. British authorities transferred the 80 men who remained in the ranks to another regiment, the Volunteers of Ireland. The fact that only 80 men remained in the Roman Catholic Volunteers suggests that either the recruitment totals in New York were inflated from the outset, or that many of those who initially enlisted never reported for duty were found to be unfit, or deserted soon after.[17]

What progress the British and their supporters were able to make in recruiting Catholics to their cause ended with the announcement of the American–French alliance in May of 1778. This arrangement, all but unthinkable a decade or so earlier, worked to change the attitudes of both Patriots and Loyalists toward Catholics. The decision to enter an alliance with Catholic France was a national one. It caused Patriots in Congregationalist New England to re-examine their beliefs toward Catholicism; in New York, where Protestantism had been a unifying political force, the earlier break with Britain made the Catholic alliance perhaps easier to accept. One indication of this shift is that Patriots in New York during the Revolution did not identify Catholics as potential subversives, as had provincial authorities in colonial wars. The Commission for Detecting and Defeating Conspiracies, a remarkably thorough investigative arm of the Revolution, compiled a long list of those thought to be potentially hostile to the Patriot cause. Those whom the commission had determined bore close watching included slaves, Shakers, Tories, deserters, Hessians, neutrals, robbers, spies, and Quakers. Notably absent from among the officially suspect were Catholics.[18]

The British became much less interested in cultivating Catholic support after the Patriots had sealed their alliance with France. The Reverend Henry de la Motte, a French priest of the Augustinian order and a chaplain to his country's forces, was captured in the Chesapeake and brought to New York City in 1779 as a prisoner of war. Father de la Motte was allowed to leave the ship and walk around the city. During one of his strolls, a group of Catholics in Manhattan asked him "to say Mass," adding the caveat that "a law of this Province prohibited the exercise of the popish religion." Although this was after the New York Constitution, which granted Catholics religious liberty, had gone into effect, that document had no standing behind British lines. Father de la Motte took the step of getting the permission from the British commander in New York before he would agree to the Catholics' request to say Mass. The commander turned down the priest, who either misunderstood due to language differences or decided to ignore the ban. In any event, de la Motte then proceeded to say the Mass, "for which he was taken up and put into confinement." Under different circumstances, a more flexible approach by the British might have been to dispense with a law that seemed archaic during the Revolution and continue to work toward an alliance with New York's long-oppressed Catholic population. The British, by this point in the war, however, most likely saw Catholics as now part of the Patriot coalition, as both the alliance with France and the New York Constitution had become operational. There would be no bold, creative stroke designed to reach out to a group that might have been persuaded to join the British cause, as was the case in Virginia. It was there that Lord Dunmore's tactic of granting freedom to slaves who ran away from their Patriot masters was at least a partial success. The British, however, saw no reason in New York to accommodate the religious needs of Catholics, and they chose to follow the law of the old regime to the letter. Their arrest of Father de la Motte showed that they had now consigned New York Catholics to the ranks of their enemies.[19]

NEW YORK LOYALISTS AND ANTI-CATHOLICISM

Loyalists enthusiastically approved of the British refusal to compromise with Catholicism. They eagerly pointed out that Patriots had recognized the aspirations of Catholics for religious liberty, comparing "the encouragement popery had met with in consequence of the French alliance" to their own policies toward Catholicism, and invited all to see "how differently it is treated within the King's lines." After the Patriots and French sealed their alliance, New York Loyalists appropriated anti-Catholic rhetoric and imagery and featured it in their critique of the Revolution. In the fight to preserve New York's old order, they vigorously championed one cornerstone of it, hostility to Catholicism. Loyalists were more numerous, and were a greater percentage of the population in New York than in any other state; the middle colonies as a whole produced more adherents to the crown than did any other region. The relationship between Loyalism and anti-Catholicism was not a simple one. New England, with its own long tradition of antipathy to Catholicism, was home to few Loyalists. Many Loyalists in New York were members of the Church of England; yet in Virginia, where Anglicanism was the dominant religion, there were only a small number of Loyalists. The very diversity and competition among New York's ethnicities and churches had long contributed to its sharp divisions; colonial New Yorkers had indeed been "A Factious People." In part due to the alliance with France, the old Whig agrarian party, religious dissenters who fiercely opposed ecclesiastical hierarchies, had shed much of their initial anti-Catholicism in pursuit of independence from the Protestant mother country. It was ironic that Anglicans, who had periodically been accused of "popery" in colonial New York, were in the end left to carry the banner of Protestantism that the Leislerians had raised at the end of the seventeenth century. Loyalists cast the Patriots' rejection of Protestant England and embrace of Catholic France as hypocritical. One of them contended that the many Patriot Presbyterians continued to "hate popery, and would eradicate its principles, if they could, from the face of the earth." Loyalists attacked the Franco-American alliance on religious grounds. "But behold now the *cloven foot* discovered! These same men, have made a solemn league and covenant with the *Popish French King*." They denounced Patriots for taking up arms "against our gracious sovereign King George the Third, under whose strong protection *Protestant* refugees find asylum."[20]

Loyalists argued that the Patriots' alliance with France had dangerous implications besides religious ones. After all, it was a powerful European nation that was bringing Catholicism to America. "All the bigotry, all the superstition of a religion abounding in both beyond any which the world has beheld, all in his Royal hand to be used at his Royal will and pleasure." Loyalists did acknowledge that there was some merit in the Patriots' initial dispute with Britain, conceding that "one main reason and motive for taking up arms against our gracious King, and mother country, was to oppose and prevent the introduction of popery." That understandable concern about the establishment of Catholicism in Canada, however, did not, in the Loyalists' view, justify a full-fledged rebellion against Britain. They clung to the belief (or at least professed to publicly) that anti-Catholicism was too deeply rooted in New York's political culture to have disappeared so quickly; their hope was that a general antipathy to Catholicism would somehow regain its vibrancy and would ultimately outweigh any military benefit that the French might provide the Patriots. Loyalists claimed that "the people daily grow more and more disaffected to the Congress' Alliance with a popish King." The defenders of the king tried to revive a sense of Protestant solidarity that cut across denominational lines. One of their number, Richard McGinnis, contended that the French alliance should "be held in everlasting detestation and abhorance by every true and sincere Protestant of the Church of England." McGinnis claimed that other Protestants had similar reason to be outraged at Patriots who "are likewise to be held in abhorance by them who profess to be Presbyterians if they adhere to the Confession of Faith as professed in the Church of Scotland, etc." Loyalists encouraged New Yorkers to face squarely the possible consequences of the Patriot–French alliance. To Jacob Duche, an Anglican priest who had initially supported the revolution but who later became a Loyalist, the Patriots' alliance with France made clear the larger meaning behind the conflict. "Whatever may be the opinion of some to the contrary, it is absolutely certain that on the part of many, the present is a *religious war.*" One Loyalist pleaded that New York not "lend France a helping hand, to overturn and pull down the *Protestant Church* on purpose to build the *Popish Church* on its ruins." Another Loyalist noted that Americans had traditionally been "peculiarly attached to the Protestant faith. Is America unacquainted with the tenets of popery? What then has America to expect from a popish alliance, but shoals of priests under every possible disguise?" They cast their religious appeals in the broadest terms, in keeping with New York's history of diversity and Protestant pluralism. "Act like Englishmen, like Protestants, like Christians" was one such exhortation.[21]

New York Loyalists described how immersed in Catholic practice and ritual Patriot leaders had become. One of their newspapers gave an account of a reception in Philadelphia held in honor of a foreign representative to the United States that was marked by the "great signs of the cross." Jacob Duche, the Anglican priest, lambasted the Continental Congress for attending a Catholic Mass in Philadelphia, ridiculing "American rulers who not only permit their wives to attend Mass, but attend it themselves in person and offer up their *devotion* in the language, service and worship of Rome." The implication was that the Patriots had abdicated their responsibilities as Protestant men to protect their impressionable wives from the seductions of Catholicism. Loyalist writers argued that Patriot leaders had in effect "sold their souls" for temporal gain. A prime example was an occurrance during a funeral Mass that Congress attended for a Spanish official in Philadelphia. During the service, Samuel Huntington, the president of the Congress, was presented with holy water. At that moment, he encountered the sort of Catholic rite that his Protestant sensibility had previously taught him to scorn. "The Calvinist paused a considerable time, near a minute, but at length his affection for the great and good ally conquered all scruples of conscience, and he too sprinkled and sanctified himself with all the adroitness of a veteran Catholic." Politics, or more to the point, political expediency, had in his case triumphed over religious truth. Adherents of the British cause in New York also presented a strange incident at the same funeral as emblematic of how Patriots had been duped by their Catholic allies, and how hollow that confederation really was. A few curious members of Congress peeked under the bier, only to find it empty, as the body had been buried earlier. Although the members of Congress who realized that the ceremony was a façade were temporarily angered, the mysticism of the moment won out. "The bier was surrounded with wax candles. And every member of this egregious Congress, now reconciled to the popish communion, carried a taper in his hand." Whether this was a genuine representation of an actual event or a partially fictional account, its significance resides in the Loyalists' attempt to discredit their enemies by portraying them as not only willing participants in Catholic rituals, but also as having in some real sense become Catholics:

> Protestant Americans! Did you imagine that in so short a space as seven years, a Congress of your own creating, would *on your own ground* have exhibited that profligate apostasy from the reformed faith, of publicly attending at a Roman Catholic Church, to countenance that impious religion?[22]

A society governed by Catholic principles would be grim indeed, Loyalists warned. One of them sardonically remarked that one "advantage" of the alliance with France and Spain would be that "we would then be *certain* of being admitted within the pale of the Holy Catholic Church, of receiving papal absolution, and being freed from the terrors of purgatory." Although it was seemingly much too late for such a politics of nostalgia, Loyalists hearkened back to an earlier time, when New York Protestants, although differing in doctrinal specifics and denominational traditions, united around a shared aversion to Catholicism. The vibrant Protestant pluralism of the colonial period, New York's "Golden Age," as Loyalist Thomas Jones characterized it, would now be supplanted by a dreary epoch of enforced Catholic uniformity. Fearing a New York that would be both Catholic and republican, one Loyalist remarked that "the names and jarring opinions of Calvinists, Lutherans, and Arminians, of Churchmen, Presbyterians, Congregationalists and Seceders, of Baptists, Anabaptists, Methodists and Quakers" would be gone. Instead, "all their controversies will be buried in oblivion, and we shall peaceably unite in the venerable title of *true Roman Catholics.*" In this ironic and disturbing vision of a Patriot future, America would after all be subject to the dictates of an arbitrary European power, which was what the revolutionaries had feared all along, except that now they would be oppressed not by London, but by Rome.[23]

There were unintended consequences of the Loyalists' sustained effort to link the Patriots with Catholicism. These consequences inadvertently worked to erode the legitimacy of the anti-Catholicism that had long held sway in New York. It was not, however, only the alliance with France that was beginning to make overt hostility to Catholicism less acceptable in New York; the Loyalists' anti-Catholicism also contributed to its becoming an increasingly inconvenient feature of American political culture. A case in point is that of Benedict Arnold, the most prominent Loyalist to cite fear and distrust of Catholicism as influencing his decision to side with the British. To those who supported the revolution, Arnold was much more than a Loyalist; he was the most notorious traitor in America. At that time and ever since, Americans have usually attributed his betrayal to greed or to resentment at being passed over for promotion. Arnold himself, however, claimed more principled reasons for his decision; prominent among them was his disgust with the Patriots' supposed embrace of Catholicism. *Rivington's Royal Gazette* featured for weeks the proclamation that he had made to the officers and soldiers of the Continental Army upon his defection. In it, he made clear that at least this one New England native (Arnold was from Norwich, Connecticut) retained his region's traditional antipathy toward the religion of the Patriots' European ally:

> Do you know that the eye which guides this pen lately saw your mean and profligate congress at Mass for the soul of a Roman Catholic in purgatory and participating in the rites of a church, against whose anti-Christian corruptions your pious ancestors would have witnessed with their blood?[24]

It could not have but helped the cause of Catholics in New York that as the revolution reached its final years, the most prominent voice seeking to make a political issue of their religion now belonged to none other than Benedict Arnold.

Catholic Responses to the Revolution

The international dimension of the Revolutionary War also benefited American Catholics. Along with the impact of the alliance with France were the contributions of prominent European Catholics such as Pulaski, Kosciusko, and Lafayette. Thousands of Catholics, many of them from Maryland and Pennsylvania, joined the Continental Army and the state militias. A small but influential group of prominent American Catholics from those two states, which were home to most Catholics in colonial America, also demonstrated that religious affiliation need not disqualify one from occupying a position of trust and authority in the Patriot movement. Stephen Moylan, John Barry, and Thomas Fitzsimons of Pennsylvania and John, Charles, and Daniel Carroll of Maryland were all in the ranks of military and political leaders of the revolution. No Patriot of comparable stature emerged from among New York's subterranean Catholic population. However, many Irish and Irish Americans, some of whom were Catholic, filled the ranks of the New York militia and the New York Line of the Continental Army. The New York legislature decreed in 1778 that all able-bodied men (American Indians and slaves excluded) between sixteen and fifty years of age were required to enlist in the militia if they were not already in the Continental Army; the only exemption granted for religious reasons were those given to pacifist Quakers. The New York Line of the Continental Army did not bother to inquire into the religious affiliations of its enlistees.[25]

Catholics who remained behind British lines in New York City adapted to wartime circumstances in a variety of ways. There were Irish Catholics who supported the British cause and sought to profit from it. Patrick McDavitt, a merchant immigrant who after the war became a member of the state's first Catholic parish, sold "new muskets and bayonets" and other military gear to the British army. Martin Doyle was proprietor of a public house called "The Faithful Irishman and Jolly Sailors." Elizabeth Power ran a tavern in New York City, but feared that she had failed her customers in "not accommodating them heretofore equal to her wishes, as being a lone woman." She then entered into a partnership with Patrick Doyle; the two opened "Cornwallis's Arms," serving "the army, navy and public in general." Other Irish women were not on as friendly terms with the occupiers. Catherine Barry, a native of Capoquin, Ireland, along with Margaret Smith of Waterford, Ireland and several other women were imprisoned on charges that they had attacked and maimed a British soldier. Not firmly aligned with either side was a Mrs. Carroll; she boarded in her home several captured rebel officers with whom she socialized. Her political allegiance could shift easily between "Tory or Whig, as best suited the company she happened to be in." Then there were Catholics such as John Kelly, who left New York when it fell to the British, but returned after the war and helped to establish the city's first Catholic church.[26]

Catholics in New York had begun to practice their faith more openly as the long war drew to a close; the prevailing circumstances gave them opportunities to receive the sacraments. Father Ferdinand Farmer returned to New York in 1781, ministering to Catholics living in Westchester County, which was behind Patriot lines. He apparently did so with the permission of local revolutionary authorities, who in contrast to the British who arrested Father de la Motte in New York City when he tried to say Mass, allowed the priest to perform his religious duties. Paradoxically, it was during the upheaval of war that Father Farmer felt secure enough to make an official record of his ministry in New York. Some of those he baptized were the Acadians whom the British had exiled during the Seven Years War.[27]

■ ■ ■

From the perspective of Catholics in New York, the American Revolution's unpromising beginning, with its impassioned anti-Catholic rhetoric, had slowly given way to a new toleration of their religion. Catholics of different political views found opportunity and danger as members of a church that had been outlawed in New York for eighty years. This story within the larger narrative of the revolution also reveals how three of the main groups in the conflict—Patriots, Loyalists, and British—dealt with the legacy of anti-Catholicism in New York. The experiences of four Catholic priests who were in New York during the war illustrates how the relation of Catholics to the American Revolution changed significantly over its course.

The first priest, Father John McKenna, served Loyalists in the Mohawk Valley who had retained their allegiance to the British crown due, in part, to the anti-Catholicism that the Patriots had initially displayed. John Carroll's diplomatic mission to Canada took him through New York under the protection of the Continental Army. This demonstrated how the Patriots' desire to defeat Britain and win independence early on took precedence over traditional American Protestant antipathy to Catholicism. Augustine de la Motte's tragicomic ventures in New York City were testament to how the American–French alliance eradicated much of the remaining rationale of religious discrimination against Catholics. The French priest's travails in New York City also illustrated how rigid the British were about maintaining the colonial penal codes against Catholics. The experiences of the fourth priest, Ferdinand Farmer, were probably the least political. However, Father Farmer's trip to New York at war's end anticipated the religious liberty that the American Revolution generated for New York Catholics.

The defeated British and thousands of Loyalists finally sailed away from New York City in late 1783 as the most recent standard-bearers of New York's long tradition of hostility to Catholicism. Not long after their departure, the New York legislature, having moved out from under the shadow of war and occupation, unanimously repealed the 1701 law banning Catholic priests. This represented the fall of the last of the long-standing colonial legal barriers to Catholics practicing their faith openly. The logic of the American Revolution had done away with the old imperial demand that made fealty to the crown a matter of both politics and religion. British nationhood had been inextricably connected to Protestantism for two centuries; as Americans disengaged from the empire, they explicitly renounced not just their political allegiance, but in effect their ecclesiastical fealty to the throne in London as well. Therefore, it no longer made sense for the Patriots to discriminate against Catholics on the grounds that they were not loyal to George III, the Protestant Monarch and Defender of the Faith.

In rebelling against Britain, Patriots had implicitly rejected *all* European authority, the alliance with France notwithstanding. Whether the new republican state of New York would allow Catholics, with their ecclesiastical connections to Rome, to be full citizens was yet to be determined. However, it must have occurred to Catholics in the state, as they began to work toward opening New York's first Catholic Church since the days of Dongan and Leisler, that they had indeed lived through a revolution.

# CHAPTER 3

# "No Foreign Ecclesiastical Authority"
## Catholics and Republican
## Citizenship

Despite their sudden gain of religious liberty, New York Catholics remained concerned about their status as citizens of the new republic. Soon after the Americans reclaimed Manhattan from the departed British forces after their long occupation in late 1783, the "Roman Catholic Inhabitants of the City of New York" sent a petition to Congress. They were apparently troubled that the clause in the New York Constitution of 1777 might well discourage Catholics from migrating to the state by requiring that anyone seeking naturalization take an oath of allegiance, thereby renouncing all foreign religious authority. Congress responded that it had no jurisdiction over the matter and referred the petitioners back to the New York government. The Catholics who sent that petition to their national government were a small and obscure religious minority in New York during the 1780s. The first Catholic priest to arrive in New York City following the war, Father Charles Whelan, identified about two hundred people as comprising the congregation, although Father John Carroll of Maryland, the de facto leader of the Catholic Church in the United States, estimated the number of Catholics in New York to be "at least fifteen hundred" in 1785.[1]

ST. PETER'S IN THE 1780S: EUROPEAN
BENEVOLENCE, FEDERALIST LEADERSHIP

New York Catholics did have at least one important asset as they
began their efforts to establish a church of their own in the nation's
capital. They were able to draw on the legacy of the United States's
alliance with Catholic France and Spain in recruiting Father Charles
Whelan to New York. He had served as a chaplain to the French navy
during the Revolutionary War, ministering to thousands of Spanish
and French prisoners, as well as to a few American Catholics. In the
years immediately following the revolution, Catholics worshiped at
the residences of Don Diego de Gardoqui, the Spanish ambassador to
the United States, and Hector St. Jean de Crevecoeur, a French diplomatic consul. They also gathered for Mass in the home of Jose Ruiz
Silva, a wealthy merchant who had immigrated from Portugal.[2]

New York Catholics sought aid from secular authorities as they
began to build their church. They negotiated with the city government through an intermediary, Crevecoeur, who was not a Catholic.
Father Whelan described the French diplomat, however, as "a very
staunch friend of the Church" who "helps our cause as much as
possible." Crevecoeur introduced Father Whelan to the revolutionary hero Marquis de Lafayette, who himself previously had inter-
ceded on behalf of Catholics with Governor Clinton and the mayor
of New York City. A group of twenty-two Catholic men, acting "in
the name of all our brothers of this city," told Crevecoeur that they
"were encouraged by the happy tolerance accorded by the new constitution of this State and the privilege of professing publicly our
religion here." They asked the French diplomat to obtain on their
behalf from the city government a "suitable site on which we can
construct a church." Crevecoeur brought their request to the New
York City Common Council. In the tone of a supplicant, he pleaded
on behalf of a minority, painfully aware that its religious liberty had
only recently been granted, expressed the hope that this freedom

would be permanent, and looked for tangible aid from the government in order to exercise that right. Crevecouer sought to bolster the Catholics' case by claiming that the "Christian and tolerant spirit" of the New York Constitution "has inspired them [Catholics] with the most lively gratitude," and expressed the hope that the constitution "has become a new tie which shall attach them for ever, as well as their descendants, to the prosperity of this State, of which they have the happiness to be citizens." Despite these entreaties, Catholics did not receive much cooperation from their municipal government. They asked permission of the New York City Common Council, once again through Crevecouer, to use the Exchange, a large public meeting place, for Mass. This request was denied, as the council claimed that the Exchange, which had been damaged during the war, was unsafe. The rejection, however, spurred Catholics toward completing their own church. They finally secured some critical aid from New York's Trinity Church (formerly Anglican and now Episcopalian, and whose congregation included many of the city's commercial and political leaders), which leased property to the Catholics at a nominal fee. Trinity had also been home to many Loyalists during the revolution, and some of the popular Whigs had sought to punish the church after the war by seizing its property.[3]

The legal founding of St. Peter's parish dates to June of 1785, when a small group of Catholics, including affluent merchants and diplomats such as Crevecoeur, Jose Ruiz Silva, James Steward, and Henry Duffin, declared themselves to be "The Trustees of the Roman Catholic Church in the City of New York." New York law required each religious body to have a board of trustees consisting of representatives of its laity. These trustees, who were defined by the statute as men, would "take the charge of the estate and property belong[ing] to the respective churches . . . and to transact all affairs relative to the temporalities of their respective churches." This law was based on a Protestant model of church governance and became New York's contribution to a major struggle within the Catholic Church in the

United States in the decades after independence, that being between the clergy and laity over control of the parish church. Crevecoeur's election as a trustee highlights the importance, at the outset, that the parishioners of St. Peter's placed on their connections to the Catholic allies of the U.S. The fledgling parish also drew on their European co-religionists for funds to build the church. The trustees appealed directly for financial support to King Charles III of Spain and King Louis XVI of France. Despite Crevecoeur's efforts, the French government offered little monetary assistance, although the French embassy was of more help. The French minister to the United States, Barbe Marbois, said in 1785 that "the establishment of the legation chapel at New York will give Catholics of that city all the spiritual aid they can desire." Eventually, however, it was the king of Spain, Charles III, and his government, who emerged as the primary sponsor of St. Peter's in the crucial years 1785–86. The Spanish King became St. Peter's chief benefactor when he donated 1000 *pesos fuertes* to the parish. Catholics thanked Charles for the "attention and friendship" that he had shown them. In acknowledging the king's gift, New York Catholics emphasized their appreciation for all that the Spanish monarch had done in extending to them his "Royal protection." They promised that in honor of his generosity, they would "take the liberty of erecting a tribune in the most distinguished place and of reserving it for His Majesty's use" in the event that Charles ever visited New York City and St. Peter's.[4]

New York Catholics recognized that their receipt of the Bourbon monarch's generosity could put them in an awkward position in republican America. They portrayed their reliance on the generosity of European governments as necessary, given the uncertain state of their religion in New York: "The infancy of our congregation is indispensably the reason why its funds are so reduced, and the meagreness of our means the cause of our being obliged to have recourse to the liberality of the powerful and well-disposed servants of His Majesty." In acknowledging the paradox of an American church receiving such assistance from a European benefactor, the lay leaders of St. Peter's declared, somewhat defensively, that "we judge it to be the only means of enabling us to continue our enterprise of promoting and adding respect and credit to our faith and Republic." Thus Catholics turned toward Europe to enable them to participate fully in the experiment of America's now genuinely universal religious liberty.[5]

European benevolence was literally much in evidence at St. Peter's from the very foundations of the church. The ground breaking for Manhattan's first Catholic church since the days of Dongan and Leisler in the late seventeenth century took place on November 4, 1785. That date was chosen to begin work on the church because it was the feast day of St. Charles Borromeo, for whom King Charles of Spain had been named. The *Packet,* a Spanish ship in New York Harbor, was decorated brightly for the occasion and it fired many salutes in honor of the king. New York Catholics gave Don Diego de Gardoqui, the Spanish ambassador to the United States, the honor of laying the cornerstone of the church. Afterwards, a public Mass was celebrated at his residence, following which the Catholic diplomat "gave a very elegant entertainment to the first personages of this City." This auspicious and quite public Catholic celebration was a striking departure from the history of eighteenth-century New York. As Father Whelan himself noted, "In the past a priest would have been sentenced to death, if he had there said Mass or administered the sacraments." The removal of those prohibitions against Catholicism also made New York a much more appealing locale for ambitious Catholic European merchants than it would have been before the revolution. Dominick Lynch, born into a wealthy and long-established Catholic family in Galway, Ireland, was among those who helped to establish St. Peter's. He entered into a business partnership with Thomas Stoughton of Flanders, another scion of an affluent European Catholic family. Stoughton opened the mercantile house of Lynch and Stoughton in the spring of 1783 in New York City;

Dominick Lynch and his wife Joana followed him to New York two years later. The Lynches moved into a stylish town house at 36 Broadway, next to Don Diego de Gardoqui. The row of houses were described by a contemporary as "by far the finest buildings my eyes ever beheld, and I believe they excel any on the continent." Lynch assumed a leadership role at St. Peter's soon after his arrival; the firm of Lynch and Stoughton was involved in the plans for building the church.[6]

In addition to the opportunity for religious freedom in New York, Lynch also saw the economic potential of the new state: "New York seems to be well calculated by nature for commerce and must in time vie with the first state," he concluded. In his politics, the Irish merchant did not favor a state-centered government with agrarian leanings that would interfere with the imperatives of international commerce. He strongly disapproved of the punitive measures taken by the state legislature against British interests in America; this was from the initiative of the popular Whigs, whose influence reached its peak in the 1780s. The legislature passed a bill in 1784 that doubled duties on British shipping; Lynch believed this to be one of a series of destructive policies that would continue to hamper trade unless "Congress are empowered by the different states to regulate commercial treaties." If Congress were not given such authority, Lynch feared, "we shall drive from this state the little navigation left, and throw the same into the channel of other states." Lynch became acquainted in the 1780s with an important kindred spirit on these matters of political economy. He joined in a partnership with Alexander Hamilton that also included Henry Knox; they subsequently hired a teacher for their children (among them was George Washington Custis, step-grandson of General Washington) in New York City. Lynch and Hamilton also shared an opposition to the representatives of the overwhelmingly Protestant yeomanry and their vision of New York as an insular polity dominated by small producers. Hamilton, a leading critic of the agrarians, characterized them as men of *"the levelling*

*kind''* who threatened ''the security of property'' and who should be
challenged by ''all men of respectability, in the city.'' The respectable
men of the city now included Catholic merchants such as Lynch and
Staughton.[7]

Although prosperous merchants and diplomats were the most
prominent members of St. Peter's, the parish included many others
who did not live in the fashionable row houses of lower Manhattan.
Father Whelan, soon after arriving in New York, found his parishioners to be ''very poor, but very zealous.'' During preparations for
the opening of the church building in 1786, a New York newspaper
praised the wealthier people of St. Peter's, who ''forgetting the dig-
nity of rank and fortune, have for these several days united with their
brethren of less affluent circumstances, in removing the rubbish, and
getting the house in order for the approaching solemnity.'' The
''brethren of less affluent circumstances'' included Irish Catholics
who had lived in New York City as servants, laborers, and soldiers
before the revolution. In the 1780s and after, about one quarter of
the parishioners who lived in New York City were unskilled workers
employed as cartmen and day laborers. Approximately a third were
artisans, and a much smaller percentage were highly skilled crafts-
men. A significant number of Catholics owned and operated small
enterprises such as taverns (the owners of which included women),
groceries, shops, and liveries.[8]

The parish was also diverse in terms of the national origins of its
members. The number of ethnicities within St. Peter's required,
Father Whelan noted, that a ''priest know at least the Irish, English,
French and Dutch languages, because our congregation is composed
of these nationalities, as well as also of Portuguese and Spaniards.''
There was also a small number of Catholics who claimed African
ancestry. The parish's French Catholics included Acadian refugees
and their descendants, and another group of French Catholics who
had fled Quebec for New York during or after the American Revolution. People of French ancestry were well represented among the

wealthiest Catholics of New York City. A French priest, Father Huet De La Valiniere, ministered to them. That Catholics migrated *to* New York as a safe haven from Canada, and found refuge there in the 1780s, also demonstrates the realignment in religious and cultural geography that the revolution had produced in North America. Although there was clearly ethnic and racial diversity within the parish, Irish immigrants and people of Irish ancestry were, from its beginning, the dominant national group at St. Peter's. Soon after taking up his duties at St. Peter's, Father Whelan reported to Rome of his parishioners that "for the greater part they are Irish." John Carroll later that same year went so far as to describe St. Peter's as an "Irish congregation." The first census of the United States supports Father Whelan's assertion; of the Catholic heads of families that have been identified as residing in Manhattan in 1790, thirty-nine were Irish, seven were French, and three were German.[9]

The first major dispute that broke out at St. Peter's arose not out of ethnic conflict, however, but rather from the question of who had the proper authority to appoint and dismiss priests at the church. Father Charles Whelan was well regarded personally for his piousness and humility, but some harbored doubts about whether he possessed the energy and rhetorical skills needed to rouse and organize a faithful emerging from such difficult circumstances. His mild nature did not necessarily serve him well at St. Peter's; Father Ferdinand Farmer thought that Whelan "does not for want of eloquence seem able to establish a congregation out of a people that had almost lost or forgot their religion." The lay trustees of the parish thought likewise, and so they recruited Father Andrew Nugent to come to St. Peter's. Like Whelan, he was an Irish priest of the Capuchin order, but he possessed the flamboyant speaking style that Father Whelan lacked. He was something of a loose cannon, however, having been suspended from his duties in Ireland by the Archbishop of Ireland, although it is not clear if the St. Peter's trustees were aware of this.[10]

A split in the congregation developed soon after Nugent's arrival in 1785. Most of the trustees, including Lynch, Stoughton, and the

"respectable part of the congregation" favored Nugent over the mild-
mannered Whelan. The division became public on December 18,
1785. At Mass on that Sunday (probably held in the chapel of either
the French or Spanish embassy), two supporters of Father Nugent
seized the collection basket, causing an uproar.[11] There was a problem
in church governance with all of this. Father Nugent had come to St.
Peter's without official sanction from a Catholic bishop. Father John
Carroll of Maryland, whose position as Superior of the Mission in
the United States allowed him to function much as would a bishop,
was troubled that the trustees had taken it upon themselves to recruit
Nugent with the intent of having him replace Father Whelan. Carroll
feared that if the laity assumed the right to hire and dismiss priests,
"the unity and Catholicity of our Church would be at an end; & it
would be formed into distinct & independent Societies, nearly in the
same manner, as the Congregational Presbyterians of your neigh-
bouring New England States." Now that Catholicism as a religion
was on equal legal footing with other faiths in diverse New York,
Carroll was fearful that the laity would adopt practices more in keeping with Protestantism and eventually come to reject the Catholic
tradition of obedience to ecclesiastical superiors. He warned Lynch
and Stoughton that he was alarmed that they were prepared to use
the legal authority of the state (under the provisions of the trustee
law) to remove Father Whelan from his station. "You can take no
step more fatal to that respectability, in which, as a Religious Society,
you wish to stand, or more prejudicial to the Catholic cause." The
Maryland priest was also worried that the disruptions and disagreements within the congregation would bring shame and dishonor on
the Catholic Church in New York just as it was emerging publicly.
Turmoil and discord, he believed, "in the presence of other Religion-
ists, would breed disunion amongst yourselves, and make a very dis-
advantagious impression to the prejudice of the Catholic cause, so
soon after the first introduction of public worship into your city."
Father Whelan averted a showdown by leaving New York City in

February of 1786. Carroll then exerted his clerical authority and appointed Nugent as priest of the parish. Whelan's forced departure from St. Peter's was a victory for the lay trustees.[12]

Although the construction of the church building was not yet complete, the parish went forward with its plans to consecrate St. Peter's on November 4, 1786. That date was traditionally the eve of the Pope's Day, or Guy Fawkes's, celebrations in the Anglo-American world, including New York. The new acceptance of Catholicism in New York was on display for all to see, with the festivities surrounding the first Mass at St. Peter's. Pope's Day, it seemed, would now be celebrated only in England. The opening Mass at St. Peter's did illustrate, despite the promise of the day, some tension between Catholicism and a main current of American nationalism. Most citizens of the United States were forging their national identity, in no small part, through a conscious rejection of European authority and influence. Catholics in New York, conversely, chose November 4 to open their church because it was the Saints Day of King Charles of Spain. The diplomatic representatives of the kings of Spain and France were present at the opening Mass, which Father Nugent said, assisted by the chaplains to the French and Spanish embassies.

A primary theme of the day was the gratitude that parishioners of St. Peter's owed the Spanish monarch for the benevolence that he had shown toward them and their church. Father John Carroll had been invited to attend, but was not able to make the trip from Baltimore to New York; however, he did prepare some remarks for the occasion. In them, Carroll urged the congregation to remember King Charles's "noble generous benefaction and encouragement for the erecting of this house of prayer, afforded you by that illustrious prince." Charles's devotion to the Catholic faith, Carroll said, was marked by a genuine universalism. His "zeal for the service of God . . . refuses to be circumscribed by his own dominions." Carroll also praised the efforts of the representatives of the Spanish and French governments, "whose active benevolence, whose sincere zeal for the honorable establishment of Religion have opened on you the sources of royal munificence." The influence of the Spanish was on vivid display as Catholics consecrated St. Peter's; Don Diego de Gardoqui and his family sat at a place of honor at the Mass. John Carroll asked parishioners to give thanks for the startling impact of the American Revolution, brought about by "that infinite goodness, which by a series of wonderful events, has opened to the professors of our Holy Faith, access, protection, favour in this State and city!" Father Nugent dismissed the congregation at the end of Mass with a "very Christian exhortation, reminding them of their obligation of giving thanks to the Almighty and of praying for the health and happiness of the Catholic King and the Royal Family." At a banquet that Diego de Gardoqui hosted afterwards at his home, the guests included Governor George Clinton (who as a young member of the New York Assembly had harshly criticized the Catholic Church in the wake of the Quebec Act), the President of Congress, and the Cabinet of the United States government. At the celebration, the guests first toasted the royal families of Spain and France, then the United States of America, George Washington and Count Rocheambeau, and finally to "a lasting and close friendship between His Catholic Majesty and the United States of America."[13]

Despite the wishes of Father John Carroll that Catholics in New York remain unified and respectful of church tradition, more trouble soon arose at St. Peter's. Father Nugent, who had initially been supported by the trustees of the parish, soon fell into their disfavor. Not only did Nugent and the trustees disagree over the former's salary, but also the priest's erratic behavior offended some of his more affluent, original supporters. As a result, "the principal Gentlemen" of the congregation, including Dominick Lynch, called in Father John Carroll to mediate. Carroll and Lynch dined together during the priest's stay in New York in 1787, leading Nugent to accuse Carroll of being in league with his enemies. Carroll then attempted to suspend Nugent from his duties, but the renegade priest refuse to give up his position. Nugent later prevented a visiting Carroll from saying Mass from the altar at St. Peter's one Sunday that same year. The following week, when Carroll again sought to say Mass at St. Peter's, a raucous group of Nugent's supporters shouted him down; Carroll and most of the congregation retreated to the Spanish embassy for services. Presumably, this group would have included the diplomats and merchants who were opposed to Nugent and his supporters among New York's less genteel Catholics. Carroll, with the support of the trustees, then turned to secular authorities as they took Nugent to court. A New York City magistrate ruled in favor of Carroll and the trustees, finding Nugent "guilty of a riot." Carroll subsequently appointed Father William O'Brien of Ireland to succeed Nugent, telling O'Brien that he considered his "arrival in America, at so critical a period, as a providential designation of you to repair so dreadful scandals."[14]

O'Brien began his duties, but although he had been deposed, Nugent retained some of his following among the poorer members of the parish. He celebrated Mass with his supporters in a private home in New York City for a few years after his dismissal from St. Peter's. Nugent eventually left New York, but only after the trustees agreed to finance his passage to Europe, as the priest's own, less affluent supporters were unable to pay his way out of New York. In approving the request of Nugent's supporters for the priest's travel fund, the trustees of St. Peter's made the point that they were "actuated by pure motives of Benevolence towards the Revd. Mr. Andrew Nugent." But the trustees' desire to strengthen their position as lay leaders of St. Peter's also lay behind their largesse toward the departing Nugent.[15]

During the protracted dispute involving Father Nugent, merchants and other men of property and influence had consolidated their positions as lay leaders of St. Peter's. On April 13, 1789, the day after Easter Sunday, Dominick Lynch, Thomas Stoughton, Andrew Morris, George Barnewell, John Sullivan, Charles Ncylon, William Mooney, Patrick Farrell, and Jose Ruiz Silva were elected as trustees of St. Peter's. Although the list of those voting in St. Peter's trustee elections have not survived, the state law that established the office of trustee stated that "every male person of full age who has statedly worshiped with the said church . . . shall be entitled to a voice at such first election." The law, which effectively gave the Catholic laity a legitimate voice in church affairs, pointedly excluded women. There was little within the Catholic tradition or American republicanism that would have encouraged the women of St. Peter's to argue that they deserved to participate in the governing of the parish on an equal basis with men. The trustees, who came from a variety of ethnicities, united around the idea that as the wealthiest and "most respectable" members of the parish, they were entitled to speak for the entire Catholic laity. These men of property had made some important social connections with each other. Among those elected in 1789, John Sullivan was a grocer, and George Barnewell was an import merchant who owned a store on Water Street, near the Merchant's Coffee House in the first ward of the city. Andrew Morris was a wealthy chandler and soap maker; he was also a friend of John Carroll. Don Diego Gardoqui was the sponsor, or godfather, of Alexander Lynch, son of Dominick and Joana, at his baptism in 1788. The Spanish consul, Thomas Stoughton, was married to Margaret Lynch, sister of Dominick; Stoughton was also the godfather of Eleanor Morris, daughter of Andrew and Eleanor Morris. These trustees had forced two priests of whom they disapproved to leave New York; in the first of these instances, they had successfully challenged the authority of the higher clergy, Father John Carroll, in doing so. In the late 1780s, this group of lay leaders at St. Peter's proved to be supporters of a strengthened national government; they had little reason to put their hopes in a New York governed by locally and state-oriented popular Whigs who would soon unveil their opposition to the political aspirations of Catholics to be full citizens.[16]

## FEDERALISTS, ANTI-FEDERALISTS, AND CATHOLIC POLITICAL RIGHTS

The rather sudden introduction of Catholicism into New York may have alarmed rural Protestants who were determined to build a republican state free of the influence and trappings of European monarchies. The concentration of Catholics in New York City and their conspicuous ties to foreign powers was what most likely triggered the agrarians' suspicions and led them to revive anti-Catholicism as a political issue in early 1787. In their political culture and ethos, New York's popular Whigs had little in common with Catholics in the 1780s. Few Catholics lived in rural New York, and the representatives of the yeomanry may well have feared in the 1780s that urban Catholics might soon be governing them. Wary of hierarchies and centralized authority, both political and religious, they and their constituents favored a polity that was egalitarian and locally oriented. The Whig political tradition in Anglo-American politics, to which they were heirs, included a sharp distrust of episcopal churches; many of the yeomanry in New York belonged to "low church" or dissenting Protestant sects. Several popular Whigs in the New York Assembly in the 1780s had tried to claim the land of Trinity Church in New York City, which had been part of the Church of England and spiritual home to many Loyalists during the Revolution, for the state of New York. This was the same Trinity Church that aided Catholics in the building of St. Peter's Church. The popular Whigs had also persecuted former Loyalists in New York, even after the war was over, for lacking devotion to the cause of American republicanism. Their worldview, not surprisingly, also included suspicion of the Catholic Church.[17]

In New York politics, however, the popular Whigs suffered a setback in 1786, as Alexander Hamilton rallied the merchants and landed gentry, and supported by some urban artisans, scored an impressive victory in elections that year. The popular Whigs now comprised a minority in the state legislature, the institution that they asserted best reflected the will of the yeomanry most directly. Their leader, Governor George Clinton, had served the revolution entirely within New York. As a young assemblyman in 1775, Clinton, a Presbyterian, had been an especially sharp critic of Catholicism in the controversy over the Quebec Act. Those popular Whigs who remained in the legislature in 1787 then sought to reclaim some influence over the state's politics. The state legislature met in New York City between 1784 and 1788, where assemblymen and senators (and Governor Clinton) would have observed firsthand that Catholicism had indeed established itself in their state. Although the legislature was not in session when ground was broken for St. Peter's Church in November 1785 or when the church was dedicated a year later, members of that body could have learned of the strong presence of the European Catholic powers at these events. In any event, they reintroduced, and suddenly so, the question of whether Catholics could be admitted as full members of the republican polity in New York.[18]

Samuel Jones, a supporter of Governor Clinton from Queens County, submitted legislation in the Assembly that would have mandated that election inspectors require potential voters to take an oath renouncing allegiances to all foreign powers, both civil and ecclesiastical. The language of this proposed oath was identical to the naturalization oath in the 1777 state constitution, which had also permitted, but did not require, election inspectors to demand that same oath of all who sought to exercise the suffrage. Supporters of the bill that Jones put forward contended that as the state constitution required immigrants to renounce all foreign allegiances, nothing less should be expected from voters. The question of whether the oath would discriminate against Catholics quickly became the center of debate. Jones avoided any open mention of religion in putting forth his measure, maintaining that he championed it "on the ground of the Constitution, and no other." Likewise, William Harper of Montgomery County, a popular Whig stalwart throughout the 1780s, specifically denied that there would be "any difficulty that Roman Catholics or any other denomination of people could make in taking such an oath." Even so, the clear implication of the legislation was that Catholics could not be fully admitted to republican citizenship until they formally declared their allegiance to the state took precedence over and above their religious loyalty and identity.[19]

The popular Whig party was less than forthright in denying the impact that their proposed oath would have on Catholics; they could hardly have believed that Catholics would willingly take an oath that demanded that they renounce formal ties to their church. They were compelled, however, by the changes in New York's political culture that resulted from the revolution to be circumspect in this matter. No political party in New York before 1775 would have hesitated to name Catholics as the target of punitive legislation. As late as 1777, John Jay had explicitly tried to deny Catholics religious freedom. The experience of the revolution itself, however, including the Loyalists' fervent use of anti-Catholic rhetoric, had made overt discrimination against Catholics, in its own way, contrary to the cause of American republicanism.

The arguments in the New York Assembly against Jones's legislation came from opponents of the popular Whigs, especially those from New York City, where most of the state's Catholics lived. William Malcom of Manhattan pointedly addressed the implications of the legislation, claiming that it would "exclude all the Roman Catholics in the state from their right of representation." Conceding that the language of the bill was taken directly from the New York Constitution, Malcom insisted that "it was now applied to a purpose for which it was never intended." William Denning, also from New York City, agreed with Malcom that the oath would infringe on the voting rights of Catholics.[20]

It was Alexander Hamilton, also representing New York City, who was most vociferous in his opposition to the legislation. Hamilton asserted that native-born Catholics were "unincumbered with that dangerous fanaticism, which terrified the world some centuries back; but which is now dissipated by the light of philosophy." Hamilton also turned to the New York Constitution to rebut the Clintonians' arguments, as he "insisted strongly on the distinction drawn by the Constitution," meaning the one between "Roman Catholics already citizens and those coming from abroad." To Hamilton, Catholics who were already living in New York were without question citizens of the state; to restrict their voting rights would amount to nothing less than religious bigotry. He also admitted that the principle of oaths of allegiance that demanded abjuration of all foreign loyalties was written into the New York Constitution, but like his ally William Malcom, he questioned the propriety of extending it to matters of voting. Hamilton believed it gratuitous to require a Catholic born in New York to take such an oath, for "he knows no fealty to any power upon earth; nor is it likely that his mind should be led astray by bigotry or the influence of foreign powers." If the state enacted this measure into law, Hamilton contended, it would unnecessarily and foolishly weaken the allegiance of Catholics, who were "born amongst us, educated with us, possessing our manners, with an equally ardent love of his native country." He asked of the native-born Catholic, "what has he to abjure?"[21]

As he became invested in creating a more powerful central state, Hamilton grew impatient with those who sought to keep alive old rivalries and suspicions at the expense of a genuinely national polity. The contemporary role of the Catholic Church in Europe was much less central than it had been previously, he argued. And those who feared Catholic power in America were mistaken, "for the dangers are now only imaginary and are void of existence, at least with respect to us." Hamilton had not moved to New York until just prior to the outbreak of the revolution; he had little direct experience with the anti-Catholicism that pervaded colonial New York. He served in the Continental Army, with its soldiers and officers of many ethnicities and religions, including Catholics. In the early 1780s, Hamilton had been one of New York's delegates to Congress, and it was there that he formed alliances with those committed to strengthening the powers of the national government. Among them were Thomas Fitzsimons of Pennsylvania and Daniel Carroll of Maryland, both Catholics and citizens of states where they could enjoy full civil rights. Hamilton's understanding of the meaning of the revolution was forged in a national arena. Although he has long had a historical reputation as being more concerned with centralizing power than with protecting civil and political liberties, Hamilton in this instance was conspicuously aggressive in defending the rights of a religious minority. He was motivated by more than altruism, however; economics was also a factor. Dominick Lynch and other Catholic merchants brought with them to New York both capital and an interest in international commerce that impressed Hamilton, who was preparing to represent New York at the national convention, and was charged with revising the Articles of Confederation in 1787. For the purposes of the franchise, Hamilton argued in the New York Assembly, the more equitable approach would be to limit such oaths to civil matters only, as in requiring voters to renounce their loyalty to the king of Great Britain. William Malcom made a motion in the Assembly to that effect, which carried easily and thus defeated the popular Whig effort to disenfranchise Catholics.[22]

The following year, the New York legislature considered a bill similar in spirit to that which Hamilton and his allies had defeated. The 1788 measure required that anyone who was elected governor, elected to the state legislature and Congress, or appointed to a civil or military office take an oath of allegiance to the state renouncing "all allegiance and subjection to all and every foreign king, prince, potentate and state, in all matters ecclesiastical as well as civil." The bill was first introduced in the Senate, where it was shepherded to passage by John Haring of Orange County, in the Hudson Valley, and John Williams of Washington County, northeast of Albany. Both Haring and Williams were confirmed popular Whigs who later that year voted against ratification of the U.S. Constitution at the New York Convention. Supporters of the proposed constitution were still in control of the legislature. This time, however, they did not contest their opponents' (whom they now called Anti-Federalists) implicit claim was that Catholics could not be trusted with political power; by this inaction, Federalists essentially allowed Anti-Federalists to limit the political rights of Catholics. Politics in New York in 1788 was dominated by debate over the proposed federal constitution. While the legislature was considering the oath bill, the campaign to elect the delegates to the state convention that would decide if New York would ratify the proposed federal constitution was reaching its peak. Newspapers across the state were full of essays extolling the virtues and vices of the constitution. Federalists may have been reluctant to defend political rights for Catholics at an extraordinarily sensitive moment in the political history of New York and the nation. Their overriding goal was to achieve ratification of that document by the states, and there was considerable doubt in early 1788 as to whether they would be able to do so in New York. Without much debate, the legislature passed the oath measure. Governor Clinton, now the leader of the Anti-Federalists in New York, signed the bill into law in February of 1788.[23]

The Anti-Federalist animus toward Catholics differed from John Jay's efforts at the New York Convention in 1777. Although a leading scholar of church–state relations in New York has described the 1788 oath of office act as one "long desired by men like John Jay," clearly the impetus for it had come from Anti-Federalist legislators. On the whole, Anti-Federalists favored relatively small, homogenous polities. Although New York was quite diverse, forbidding Catholics to hold state office was one way to simplify its politics and build a state that was closer to their republican ideal. New York's Anti-Federalists, at the same time, were not necessarily opposed to religious liberty for Catholics. It had been the popular Whigs who had controlled the state legislature in 1784 when it swiftly removed the colonial law

banning Catholics priests from New York. However, the Anti-Federalists were not ready to concede the right of full political participation
to a group that seemed to embody many of the characteristics of a
new national order—the imperatives of distant, arbitrary authority
and the influence of urban merchants—that they feared the federal
constitution was ushering in. The 1788 law may also have been motivated in part by the Anti-Federalists' dismay that no religious test
was established for U.S. offices under the proposed Federal Constitution. Opponents of the constitution around the country pointed out
that in the absence of such a standard, Jews, pagans, infidels, Mos-
lems, and Catholics would be permitted to serve in public offices; it
was even conceivable, as one Anti-Federalist put it, that the "pope of
Rome might be elected President." Be that as it may, Anti-Federalists
in New York took steps to insure that neither the successor of St.
Peter nor any who recognized his authority would be eligible for
election to their state legislature.[24]

The struggle in New York in 1787–88 between Federalists and
Anti-Federalists over the political rights of Catholics was part of a
larger battle between two emerging political orientations, one that
had an important cultural aspect to it. The most dramatic example of
this conflict in the 1780s broke out in Massachusetts, where yeoman
farmers took up arms in protest of mounting debt and a state government that they believed was dominated by mercantile interests in the
port and capital city of Boston. The Shayite rebels of central and
western Massachusetts, however, were also troubled by the cosmo-
politan nature of life in Boston, and the seemingly easy acceptance of
the gentry and merchants there of cultural differences. It seems that
many of those same fears were also at work in New York, and the
political fortunes of Catholics in the state suffered as a result.[25]

During the subsequent ratification campaign in New York, the
question of Catholicism in American politics was not raised directly
by either side. This was true of the essays that Alexander Hamilton,
John Jay, and James Madison wrote in New York newspapers in sup-

port of the constitution in the state. In the pages of the *Federalist*, the two New York writers, Jay and Hamilton, had starkly different public records on the question of religious and political rights for Catholics. However, it was the spirit of tolerance and equal political rights for members of all faiths that was featured, albeit briefly, in the *Federalist*. Hamilton and Madison, in one of their essays, portrayed the Swiss Cantons as an example of a republic flawed in part by the divisions between primarily Catholic and Protestant jurisdictions, a disability that they promised would not hamper a federal union among the United States. The animosity toward Catholicism that John Jay had harbored a decade earlier when New York was drafting its own constitution was missing here. The Federalist political philosophy was developing a vision of a United States that would shed old European animosities in favor of a secular republic in which religion would be a publicly protected private right, and not a matter for politics. This attitude was also evident when New York adopted male suffrage, without property or religious qualifications, at the urging of the Federalists, for the election that would elect delegates to New York's convention to ratify the proposed constitution. The Federalists, though, had to tread lightly. Although conspicuous anti-Catholic rhetoric had fallen out of New York's political discourse since the revolution, open defense of Catholics at that moment carried with it risks. Federalists could not discount the threat that anti-Federalists would try to link them with Catholicism. The memories of how Patriots had accused Loyalists of "popery" at the outset of the revolution were still fresh. Anti-Federalists, moreover, had just demonstrated their willingness to make a political issue of Catholicism earlier that year.[26]

The Anti-Federalists, for their part, were not too concerned with how their advocacy of the oath of office bill would affect their standing among Catholic voters. An important part of their argument was that the proposed constitution was dangerous due to its centralization of power and disregard for local authority. Anti-Federalists were worried that the federal constitution would bring to power an aristocracy that would eventually abolish their liberties. One Federalist, mocking those fears, posed as "Squire Artifice," a fictional, Anti-Federalist politician. The Squire warned his supporters that the new constitution would lead to the loss of freedom of the press and trial by jury, as well as to higher taxes, which would be used to "provide a place for the great men's sons, who would be appointed officers in the navy and army, and tax masters over honest farmers." The "Squire Artifice," in this satire, tried to alarm Anti-Federalists by claiming that the supporters of the new constitution would use that document to crush religious freedom, and "popery, or no religion at all, would be established in its stead." In other words, Protestantism in New York would be endangered by a new federal constitution. This parody signaled, in subtle fashion, that the Federalists, aware that Anti-Federalists were now the primary inheritors of anti-Catholic politics in New York, used this knowledge to portray their opponents as narrow-minded and foolish. This notwithstanding, Anti-Federalists won a large majority of votes cast in April of 1788 and more important, forty-six of the sixty-five delegates elected to the New York State ratification convention. Their strength was in the rural counties upstate; Federalists had their strongest showing in New York City, home to most of the state's Catholics. Although religion had not been a focal point of the debate over the constitution in New York, the "Spirit and Independency of the Yeomanry," to which one observer attributed the anti-Federalist victory, was clearly more Protestant in tone than Catholic.[27]

The interests of Catholics in New York, as a whole, were best served by the establishment of a national government under a federal constitution. Ambitious Catholic merchants such as Dominick Lynch wanted to preserve the economic opportunities that they saw waiting for them in the United States. The Spanish ambassador to the United States, Don Diego de Gardoqui, favored the proposed constitution. De Gardoqui had criticized Robert Yates and John Lansing, Jr., two

of New York's delegates to the Constitutional Convention in Philadelphia, for leaving the proceedings early and not signing the document. Antoine de la Forest, a French diplomat assigned to New York,
claimed that Lansing and Yates had abstained from signing the proposed constitution "under various pretexts"; he praised the document as "a plan of general Government that seems contrived with
Great Wisdom." Immigrant Catholics of modest means would have
seen benefits in the naturalization clause in the federal constitution,
which could allow them to become citizens without having to renounce their religious beliefs by supplanting the New York Constitution on that important point of law. Father John Carroll, too, declared
that American Catholics had overwhelmingly supported ratification
of the federal constitution:

> They concurred with perhaps greater unanimity than any other
> body of men, in recommending and promoting that govern-
> ment from whose influence America anticipates blessings of
> justice, peace, plenty, good order and civil and religious liberty.

If Carroll's claim was largely true, there is little reason to assume
that any significant number of Catholics in New York would have
been in the minority among their co-religionists across the country
on the question of the constitution.[28]

The Catholic clergy had similar reasons for favoring ratification of
the constitution. They certainly did not want the laity to take any
oaths in which they renounced allegiance to Rome. John Carroll was
in general quite hopeful about the opportunities that the revolution
had presented to American Catholics. Even in regard to the New York
naturalization law, initially he was "willing to suppose liberality in
the framers of your Constitution, I endeavoured to reconcile it with
Catholicity." It was only reluctantly that Carroll concluded that as
the Pope was clearly an ecclesiastical authority, "the obvious, & I
from private information, fear the intended meaning of the words is
incompatible with our profession." Carroll and Father Andrew Nu-

gent had clashed on ecclesiastical matters, but both had serious misgivings about the potential impact of the New York Constitution on the future of Catholicism in the state. Carroll had written to Nugent in 1786: "With you, I am of the opinion, that the oath of office (meaning the oath of naturalization for the office of citizen) required in your state is inconsistent with our tenets." More than any other religious denomination in New York, Catholics clearly stood to benefit from the adoption of a federal constitution that protected religious liberty and did not make religious tests a qualification for citizenship or officeholding.[29]

The vigorous debate surrounding the question of the constitution in 1787 and 1788 gave Catholics some idea of their place in the competitive politics of New York State. At the New York ratification convention at Poughkeepsie, Anti-Federalists raised the question of what kind of people would be representing New York in the new Federal Congress. Opponents of the constitution believed that citizens, specifically the yeomanry, should exercise authority over society through state legislatures composed of men much like themselves. It was in the legislatures, said Anti-Federalist leader Melancton Smith, that "the people have a full and fair representation." He argued that the "middling men," that is, the overwhelmingly Protestant rural yeomanry, would be bypassed for office under the new system. They would be replaced by wealthier merchants, perhaps such as Catholics like Dominick Lynch of New York City. Repeating his claim that the new government would be dominated by the affluent and wellborn, Smith warned that "Men of this class are increasing: they have influence, talents and industry. It is time to form a barrier against them." By prohibiting Catholics in New York from all federal and state offices, Smith and his allies in the state legislature earlier that year had at least "formed a barrier" against one such group–Catholics—from holding state office.[30]

Delegates at the New York Convention eventually ratified the federal constitution by a narrow margin. Most of the Anti-Federalists who remained opposed to ratification at the end were delegates from the more remote parts of the state. Among them were leading agrarians Matthew Adgate of Columbia County and three men who had been key figures in the state legislature over the past two years in the effort to restrict the political rights of Catholics: William Harper of Montgomery, John Williams of Washington, and John Haring of Orange counties. Seven out of the eight delegates from Ulster and Orange counties, locales that had supported all of John Jay's anti-Catholic measures in 1777, voted against the constitution. The pattern in New York fits the general trend on the connection between religion and politics among delegates to the twelve state ratification conventions held on the constitution. Members from evangelical Protestant denominations, who distrusted centralized religious and political authority, generally voted against ratification. Federalists were more likely to be found among those for whom religion was less important, or who belonged to more hierarchical denominations such as the Anglicans. Catholics, it would seem, fell into the latter camp, especially in New York.[31]

■ ■ ■

Virtually all Catholics in New York would have welcomed the adoption of the federal constitution, with its liberal naturalization standards and lack of religious test for public office. The constitution presented Catholics with an opportunity to be part of a broader, more inclusive polity than that offered by the Anti-Federalists in New York. New York Catholics were well aware, as their petition in 1783 to Congress demonstrated, that the restrictions on their political and civil rights did not apply to members of other religions. The 1788 law passed by the Anti-Federalists concerning the oath of allegiance became the most serious obstacle faced by Catholic men, as it effectively denied them access to public office, a key measure of citizenship in a republic.

In New York, a group of Federalists emerged as the lay leaders of St. Peter's Church in the 1780s. Catholics of ordinary or modest means did not necessarily accept this group's claim to leadership, however, as the dispute surrounding Father Nugent indicated. The lay leaders of Catholics in New York included foreign diplomats such as Don Diego de Gardoqui; his king, Charles III of Spain, extended his generosity to New York Catholics to help establish a Catholic presence in the capital of the United States. While Catholics were understandably grateful for this assistance, the visible royal presence at the early public Catholic ceremonies in New York City highlighted the unique and potentially troublesome position of Catholics in the new republic. A long-persecuted religious minority in New York, they were now easily the church with the strongest connections to Europe. Although no individual Catholic was a major figure in New York politics, there were several prominent Catholics nationwide, all of whom were Federalists. Thomas Fitzsimons of Pennsylvania and Daniel Carroll of Maryland were delegates to the Constitutional Convention of 1787 and strong Federalists. Father John Carroll, a Federalist from Maryland, was named the first Bishop of the Diocese of Baltimore in 1789, which included all of the United States. Carroll's appointment made clearer the lines of authority within the Catholic Church in the United States. As bishop, he could now act with the powers, prestige, and tradition of that office behind him. American Catholics had faced their own "critical period" in the aftermath of the revolution. In asking that the pope appoint a bishop for the United States, Carroll had cited the confusion in New York as one example of why a bishop was needed to establish clearer lines of authority within a small church struggling to establish itself in an overwhelmingly Protestant society. The decision to create an episcopate that would be invested with decisive authority had some parallels with the desire of the Federalists to forge a stronger national government.

New York Catholics were now part of a new diocese, and governed in part by a new national Constitution, which did not discriminate against them on the grounds of religion. Some of the concerns that they had expressed in their petition in 1783 to Congress had been allayed. The new federal government took some power away from the states and protected the rights of minorities, including Catholics. Most Federalists, however, also believed that political power was best left in the hands of men of wealth and distinguished social background.[30] The majority of Catholics in New York during the 1780s, despite the influential merchants and diplomats among them, were of modest means and social standing. These two realities created the possibility of future tensions between Catholics and Federalists. Even so, it was the Federalists at the time of the framing of the Constitution who were clearly more willing than their political opponents to include Catholics in the answer to the question that the historian Carl Becker argued was central to the American Revolution in New York: Who should rule at home?

# CHAPTER 4

# "Federalists and Tories Carrying Everything With A High Hand"

## Catholics and the Politics of the 1790s

That Catholics in New York had determined that their political interests at the outset of the republic governed by the new Constitution lay with the federal government, and not with the state of New York, was evident at the ceremonies marking the inauguration of George Washington as the first president of the United States. There was a noticeable Catholic presence at the festivities, as the leaders of St. Peter's Church moved easily among those who gathered in New York in April 1789. The European ambassadors to the United States, many of whom were Catholic, and Dominick and Joana Lynch, attended a ball held in honor of Washington. Charles Carroll of Maryland, elected as a U.S. Senator from that state to the first federal Congress, was on a joint House–Senate committee charged with arranging the inauguration. The residences of the Spanish and French ambassadors to the United States were brightly lit, and a French warship, the *Galviston*, welcomed Washington to the city. In the months following Washington's inauguration, there was more evidence of the close social ties between New York's lay Catholic leadership and members of the new federal establishment. In the summer of 1789, Daniel Carroll, a U.S. Representative from Maryland, became godfather to

Margaret Lynch, another of the children of Dominick and Joana Lynch.[1]

Dominick Lynch was among a group of prominent American Catholics, all supporters of the new federal government, who sent congratulations to George Washington after his inauguration as president. John Carroll did so on behalf of the Roman Catholic clergy of the United States, and four men joined with him as spokesmen for the Catholic laity. Three of them—Daniel and Charles Carroll of Maryland and Thomas Fitzsimons of Pennsylvania—were well-known political figures who had signed either the Declaration of Independence or the U.S. Constitution. Fitzsimons and the Carrolls had all been elected to the first Congress under the federal Constitution.

After reminding Washington of the support of Catholics for the American Revolution, the Carrolls, Lynch, and Fitzsimons told the new president that Catholics in some of the United States still faced discrimination. Among that group, only New York pointedly excluded Catholics, and Catholics alone, from state office. Although they did not mention any state by name, New York must have been prominent in their minds, as in Maryland and Pennsylvania, Catholics faced no legal restrictions on their political rights. Dominick Lynch, unlike Thomas Fitzsimons and Charles and Daniel Carroll, held no office, and under the laws of New York, he was not eligible for state elective positions. The New York Catholic and his colleagues told Washington that regarding political rights for Catholics, "we pray for the preservation of them, where they have been granted; and expect the full extension of them from the justice of those States, which still restrict them." During the American Revolution and shortly afterwards, several states mandated religious tests for office, which the United States Constitution did not. Georgia, New Hampshire, New Jersey, North and South Carolina, and Vermont all restricted state officeholding to Protestants alone, thus excluding Jews as well as Catholics. Pennsylvania and Delaware, with their strong Quaker roots, had no religious tests, as was the case with the frontier states of Kentucky and Tennessee. Massachusetts and Maryland (the latter had a significant Catholic minority) denied state office to all those who were not Christians.[2]

In his reply to the Catholic spokesmen, Washington acknowledged the efforts of Catholics on behalf of the revolution, and conceded that indeed, not all of the fruits of that victory were currently available to them. He offered only the vague hope that Catholics one day would be more fully integrated into American political life, proposing that "as mankind becomes more liberal, they will be more apt to allow, that all those who conduct themselves as worthy members of the community are equally entitled to the protection of civil government." Washington, who had been a strong supporter of the Constitution, saw Catholics as entering a probationary period of sorts; if they acted in an acceptable manner, then they could expect to reap the full benefits of citizenship. The same year in which he was named the first Catholic bishop in the United States, John Carroll also complained of the prohibitions that remained in effect "in some of the States" against those who were not Protestant, lamenting that members of minority religions were "most unjustly excluded from the advantages which they contributed to establish." A major reason why Catholics had supported the Constitution was their hope that the new federal government would help to alleviate existing state and local prejudices. They understood that their religion remained in tension between the expanded religious tolerance that the American Revolution produced and the political culture of the new nation that the revolution also generated.[3]

RELIGION AND THE MAKING OF AMERICAN
NATIONALISM

Just as in the 1780s, when Catholicism had been viewed with suspicion by rural Anti-Federalists, it was also at odds with the ardent nationalism of the early 1790s that was developing in New York and other seaboard cities. There was little in the ethos of the first popular movement, which in New York State emerged in Manhattan in the years after the Constitution took effect, that would have appealed to Catholics. A group of mechanics who prided themselves on their independence and on being native-born Americans established the Society of St. Tammany (Tammany being the name of an Indian chief who was said to have welcomed William Penn) in 1789. One of their primary goals was to counteract what they believed to be an undue influx of foreigners into New York. The Sons of St. Tammany saw themselves as successors to the revolutionary Sons of Liberty; they continued the struggle after 1789 against "the machinations of those agents and slaves of foreign despots." A founding member of the Tammany Society recalled that after the British evacuated the city in 1783, "hordes of foreign adventurers with pride, insolence and national vanity and prejudice, began to assume the native rights and priviledges (sic) of American freemen." Under the society's constitution, which it adopted in 1791, only men born in America were eligible to serve as officers. Tammany's founders also established their society to keep a watchful eye on the affluent merchants who were staunch advocates of the federal government. An early Tammanyite described the organization as "a political institution founded on a strong republican basis whose democratic principles will serve in some measure to correct the aristocracy of our city." The society's anti-clericalism was clear; its members in 1792 called for "extinction to all Kingcraft and priestcraft, the poisons of public happiness." In its first years, members dropped the prefix "Saint" from the name, becoming simply the Society of Tammany. One of the organization's influential early leaders, John Pintard, known for his antipathy toward Catholicism, said of the name change: "we have lately uncanonized him."[4]

Tammany's artisans and mechanics had a nativist critique of the changes in their city since the winning of independence. They chided immigrants who had "presumptuously organized foreign National

Societies; to wit, St. Andrew's, St. George's, St. Patrick's, with views deep and dark as the Holy Inquisition." The Society of the Friendly Sons of St. Patrick was a fraternal organization of property-holding men, both Protestant and Catholic. Among its members were Dominick Lynch and George Barnewell from the St. Peter's Board of Trustees. The merchants and prosperous lawyers who made up the Friendly Sons were hardly a threat to the social order, but the native-born Tammanyites looked upon them with suspicion because of their economic status, their foreign birth, and the Catholicism of some members of the Irish group. The avowedly nationalist Sons of Tammany were hardly welcoming to New York's Catholics. Yet historians of American Catholicism have claimed that William Mooney, an early leader, or "Grand Sachem" of the Society, was a Catholic. Mooney was born in New York City in 1756 and was raised as an Anglican. He fought in the American Revolution, became an upholsterer, and married Abigail Blake in 1777 in Trinity Church. Mooney and John Pintard were early among the society's first leaders. William and Abigail Mooney remained Protestants because their son, William, who died in 1801, was buried in St. Paul's Episcopal Church. There *was* a William Mooney on the St. Peter's board of trustees from 1785 to 1796, but he was one of the several men of that name living in New York City in 1790 when the first federal census was taken. Given the character of the Tammany Society in its early years, and the history of the Mooney family in the Anglican and then Episcopal churches over a fifty-year period, it is highly unlikely that Tammany's "Grand Sachem" in the early republic was an active Catholic.[5]

The artisans and mechanics who organized New York's various societies turned to the Protestant churches for venues in which to conduct republican and nationalist rituals. Several churches were open on the anniversary of American independence in 1794, and the members of the Tammany, Democratic, and Mechanics' societies proceeded together to Christ Church (Episcopal) and to the New Presbyterian Church. Two years later, the societies gathered at Christ Church on the fourth of July and sang an ode to American independence, which included the phrase, "Dumb superstition flies apace, and knowledge soon succeeds." Protestant Anglo-Americans understood "superstition" to mean the irrationality of Catholic rituals. On such occasions, members of the various societies listened to sermons on the dangers that ecclesiastical authority and grasping clerics posed to American republicanism. It was appropriate to hold these celebrations in churches because the birthday of the American nation was infused with the trappings of a high holy day during the early republic. Catholicism remained apart from the commingling of nationalism and Christianity; not once was St. Peter's Church on the Tammany Society's Fourth of July itinerary. Members of the societies considered even Episcopal churches (including Trinity, whose membership during the revolution included many Loyalists), which were just recently part of the Church of England, suitable places to commemorate American independence.[6]

## THE POLITICS OF THE FRENCH REVOLUTION

In addition to continuing the debate over the meaning of their own revolution, citizens of the United States in the 1790s were confronted with the overthrow of the French king and revolution in France. Most Americans initially supported revolutionaries in France for their rebellion against the Bourbon Monarchy. In 1792, the Tammany Society hailed events in France as signifying "the Defeat of Aristocracy and the triumph of Liberty." Bishop John Carroll also supported the desire of the French people for a "free government, and political happiness." Following the execution of King Louis XVI in 1793 and the beginning of the Terror, however, the French Revolution became more controversial in the United States. The opinions of political factions and parties in the U.S. of the French Revolution, and its implications for their own republic, helped to shape American politics in the 1790s. Federalists and Catholics, particularly the latter's clergy, came over time to object strongly to the French Revolution's attitudes and policies toward religion. Their common opposition had different sources: Federalists were chiefly concerned about the attacks on religion and Christianity in general; Catholics feared that their church itself had become the target of revolutionary zeal. As early as 1790, John Carroll decried the "lamentable catastrophe in France" in describing the attempt of the French government to bring the Catholic Church in France under its control. The French revolutionary state began to seize church property and initiated a campaign of de-Christianization. At the height of this drive, revolutionaries ransacked Catholic churches, held Feasts of Reason in church buildings, and held mock ceremonies in which they wore priests' vestments; in addition, thousands of priests and nuns renounced their vows in public ceremonies, and members of the Catholic clergy who resisted were executed.[7]

The antipathy that Bishop John Carroll and the Catholic clergy came to hold for the French Revolution and the affinity of some Republicans (as the opponents of the Federalists were calling themselves by the early 1790s) in the United States for the radical revolutionaries, or Jacobins, solidified the clergy's allegiance to the Federalists. Catholics in the United States certainly had an interest in seeing that American republicanism did not take the anticlerical route of its French counterpart. At St. Mary's Church in Albany, New York's second Catholic parish, Father Matthew O'Brien used the occasion of a memorial service for the recently deceased George Washington to tell his congregation that if France had been graced with a leader of Washington's virtue, it would have been spared the misery of "the impiety that has overturned her altar and her throne." Instead, license and anarchy in France had led inevitably to tragic circumstances in which the "stones of the sanctuary are poured out in the top of every street."[8]

Federalists were also vigorously denouncing the "irreligion" of the French Revolution by the middle of the 1790s. Most of them conceived of religion as indispensable to the common virtue needed to sustain a republic; they also believed that the Republicans encouraged both deism and unpredictable and dangerously egalitarian forms of Protestant Christianity. In general, Federalists preferred older, established denominations with clearly drawn lines of authority. In the northern states, including New York, at the same time that Protestant ministers sympathetic to the Federalists and other supporters of Washington's government were denouncing the de-Christianization campaign in France, Federalists were accusing Republicans in the United States of being hostile to religion. Prominent Federalist writer Noah Webster condemned what he called the Jacobins' "war against Christianity," which included placing signs outside of cemeteries attacking the idea of an afterlife by declaring that *"death is an everlasting sleep."* Federalists in the 1790s were careful to make their defense of Christianity in France in general terms. Out of political caution and their own convictions, they made sure that they did not become the American defenders of European Catholicism. Their critique of the French Revolution could have led them to make a de facto defense of Catholicism. Noah Webster, for his part, made it clear that he held no brief for the Catholic Church. The revolutionaries in France, he contended, had merely replaced what he termed "religious fanaticism"—Catholicism and its imagery, symbols, and rituals—with the "political fanaticism" of Jacobinism and its various secular trappings.[9]

Republicans in New York had a different interpretation of the drama that was unfolding in France. They conceived of French republicanism, as they did of American nationalism, as inherently *not* Catholic. An important part of the French Revolution's appeal to them was the displacement of the Catholic Church from its place of authority and privilege in France. A writer in Thomas Greenleaf's *New York Journal and Patriotic Register*, the leading Republican paper in New York City during the 1790s, defended the campaign against the Catholic Church in France as necessary in light of that nation's history. "France, by throwing off all pretensions to religion, and giving up that bigotry which priests inculcated, will lie open, at his [God's] pleasure, to receive the truth." Within the broad Republican coalition, Enlightenment deists and Protestant biblical millennialists alike hailed the French Revolution as transformative in that it challenged both civil tyranny, the Bourbon Monarchy, and its ecclesiastical counterpart, the Catholic Church. New York's Baptists, who were predominantly Republican, thought that "the emancipation of twenty four Millions of people from a nation under the reign of popish and royal despotism" was a sign of the Second Coming. Matthew Adgate, a New York agrarian Anti-Federalist stalwart in the 1780s and Republican politician in the 1790s, was also a millennialist. He believed that the aggressive campaign waged by French revolutionaries against the Catholic Church was a dramatic signal that the Christian millennium was at hand. In his interpretation of the apocalypse predicted in the Book of Revelation, Adgate thought that the American and French revolutions both advanced the cause of justice on earth. The latter he believed to be a continuation of the Protestant Reformation in that it overthrew a Catholic tyranny. Adgate condemned the pope as "Anti-Christ," the "man of sin," and the "grand adversary of God," who, standing against the great tide of history, "will be devoured." He was still praising the French Revolution as late as 1800, after much of the original American enthusiasm for it had dimmed considerably. Influenced by American republicanism and millennial Protestantism, Matthew Adgate concluded that the reduction of kings and popes in Europe was a boon to liberty; he supported these events as a crusade against despotism and for the rights of man.[10]

Urban Republicans in Manhattan also welcomed the French Revolution's assault on the Catholic Church. Reverend John McKnight of the New Presbyterian Church commended the French revolutionaries, saying that "whilst we lament the disorder and confusion which have taken place amongst them, and the great effusion of blood which their struggle for liberty has cost them, we wish success for the cause." McKnight was more circumspect than Adgate on the subject of religion, as he did not mention the Catholic Church by name. He did, however, offer a plea for the liberation of "those nations which are yet superstitious and inslaved." The Presbyterian minister implied that Catholicism, as a cornerstone of the old European order, was not easily reconciled with a republican future. McKnight, Adgate, and other Protestant Republicans hoped that a variant of reformed Christianity, and not atheism or deism, would eventually supplant Catholicism in France. Other Republicans admired the French Revolution for its championing of secular reason in the face of Catholic dogma. The Democratic Society of New York City declared in 1794 that "SUPERSTITION in a religious creed, and DESPOTISM in civil institutions, bear a relation to each other similar to that which exists between the children of common parents." Now that the American Revolution had in turn sparked a similar upheaval in France, some Republicans believed that the world was entering a new, post-religious era. Tunis Wortman, a deist and leader of the Democratic Society, implied that Catholicism, given its nature and history, had no place in this emerging epoch. A key to the transformation of human society, in his view, would be the demise of "that monkish and dishonorable doctrine which teaches the original depravity of mankind." All that which had kept people from realizing their freedom was to be swept away by the force of republicanism, Wortman confidently asserted: "Persecution and superstition, vice, prejudice and cruelty will take their eternal departure from the earth." "Monkish" and "superstitious" religions, especially Catholicism, would not survive in new societies that had as their pillars liberty and reason.[11]

## THE IRISH AND THE RIGHTS OF MAN

While the French Revolution was important in the forging of American politics in the 1790s, events in Ireland and American reactions to those events also proved to be very influential. Tom Paine was as vociferous as any in his criticism of traditional Christianity and the *ancien regime* in France. An avowed deist, he supported the French revolutionaries' campaign against the Catholic Church. Paine's conviction, however, that structures of discrimination should be dismantled everywhere had great appeal to Irish Catholics, a people who had been systematically denied religious and political liberty. His book, *The Rights of Man*, was greeted with wild enthusiasm in Ireland; more copies of it were sold there than in England and Scotland combined. Catholics in Ireland were particularly roused by Paine's denunciation of the British monarchy. All questions of theology aside, Paine's withering criticisms of inherited privilege and power made his political ideas relevant and attractive to Catholics across the Atlantic world. The broad appeal of his thinking was a first indication that Republicans, even the most radical among them, might find some political common ground with Catholics.

Paineite republicanism was a source of inspiration for the United Irishmen, including Catholics, who rose in rebellion in the 1790s against British power in their homeland. They sought to establish an Irish republic in which all religions would be respected on an equal basis. Even though that rebellion failed, Irish Catholics saw that they too might realize the promise of republicanism, even if they had to leave their native country to do so. Irish Catholics of the lower economic orders emigrated to the United States during the 1790s at higher rates than they had during the previous two decades, and their numbers in New York City began to rise noticeably. The commissioners of the almshouse in 1796 noted an "increase of the numerous poor imported from Ireland" over the past decade. Parishioners at St. Peter's that same year requested another priest to meet the demands of a "rapid increase" in the number of new members of the church.[12]

Many of these immigrants entered the city under grim circumstances. Those who arrived from Ireland at the docks along the East River in 1795 were forced to stay aboard ship because of the epidemic of yellow fever raging through the city. Not only were they considered potential carriers of the fever, the Irish had little money with which to pay New York City's high rents. When they did finally come ashore, most could afford to rent only basement apartments and cellars, with no windows to let in light; one visitor to those underground quarters commented that "it might literally be said of them that they were buried alive." Irish Catholics who came to New York City in the 1790s were poorer than those Catholics who had migrated earlier. Father William O'Brien, the pastor at St. Peter's, was shocked at the living conditions of the newest arrivals. When O'Brien visited the sick and administered the last rites to dead and dying Irish Catholics, he found that in "most places, they had not even a stool to sit on, nor a bed to lie upon." In the late summer and early autumn of 1795, nearly eight hundred inhabitants of New York City died of yellow fever; according to Father O'Brien, 462 were members of his parish. Most of the Irish who died in 1795 had not lived in New York long enough to join St. Peter's; Father O'Brien noted of the dead that "nineteen twentieths were totally unknown to me." Irish immigrants who survived the epidemic became part of New York City's impoverished and laboring poor. City officials wondered what the city ought to do about "these poor people huddling together in cellers and sheds, in and about the Ship-Yards."[13]

The rise in Irish Catholic immigration to New York coincided with the appearance of one of the most divisive issues in American politics during the 1790s. John Jay represented the United States in negotiations with Britain on several unresolved issues between the two nations, some dating from the American Revolution. The resulting agreement, which the two nations signed in 1795, was commonly known as the Jay Treaty. It quickly became the center of intense controversy, with opponents of the treaty condemning it as a surrender to British economic might and a shameful episode of American bowing and scraping to the British crown. The debate surrounding the treaty was one of the most important factors in the Republicans' and Federalists' opposition to one another. Except for some international merchants, who would have favored the continuance of American trade with Britain that the treaty guaranteed, most Irish Catholics in New York were not likely to support it. Republicans understood this and organized protests against the Jay Treaty in New York City. Many of the demonstrators were immigrants and workers, including the "Irish [patriot] laborer, his face powdered with lime, shirt sleeves torn or rolled up to his shoulders." When Republicans and opponents of the treaty burned a copy of it in effigy, "the Irishmen danced the *white boy's march,* and the Frenchmen sung, Dan sa la Carmanoll."[14]

The issues raised by the French Revolution concerning the relationship between republicanism and Catholicism, important as they seemed initially, continued to be eclipsed by conflicts much closer to home. Among the Irish immigrants who came to New York in the 1790s were Thomas Burk and Timothy Crady, who found work piloting ferries from Brooklyn to Manhattan. One day in late 1795, Gabriel Furman, a Federalist alderman (an elected member of the Common Council), arrived at the dock. Growing impatient, he demanded that Burk and Crady depart ahead of schedule and ferry him across the East River. When they refused, Furman arrested the two men, and he allegedly beat Burk and Crady as he led the two to jail. The case quickly became widely known, and William Keteltas, a young Republican lawyer, came to the defense of Burk and Crady. Keteltas had originally been a Protestant, but by the middle of the 1790s he was a deist who championed the "rights of mankind." At the trial, which was conducted by four Federalist officials and without a jury, Richard Varick, the Federalist Mayor of New York, warned the two ferrymen: "you rascals, we'll trim you, we'll learn you to insult men in office." Burk and Crady were convicted of vagrancy and sentenced to two months of hard labor; Crady also was given twenty-five lashes. The affair was significant not only as a dispute between persecuted laboring people and their defenders versus haughty Federalist overlords, but it also marked the initial defense of the Irish by Republicans. This may have not been their original intent. Republicans initially cast the two Irish immigrants as victims of Federalists who refused to accept the idea of social equality among citizens in a republic. They described Burk and Crady as refugees who "fled from the tyranny of their native land and sought a sanctuary in this nursery of freedom." Contrasting free republican citizens in America with the oppression and capriciousness that common people endured in the British Isles, Republicans asked, "If the aldermen are permitted thus to act arbitrarily, pray where is the difference between the board of aldermen in New York, and the board of aldermen in London and Dublin?" Republicans in New York were for the first time beginning to think in terms of the common adversary they shared with Irish Catholics: Anglo-Americans known as Tories in Britain and Federalists in the United States. As they were by a wide margin the largest ethnic group at St. Peter's, the Irish had a crucial role in determining the place of Catholics in the politics of early republic New York. The vast majority of Irish married within their ethnic group between 1785 and 1815, which enabled them to retain a strong sense of identity within St. Peter's parish.[15]

Having left behind religious and political discrimination in their native country, the Irish were eager for opportunities to exercise their republican liberties in America. A group of Irish immigrants and Irish Americans in 1796 formed a militia that they named the New-York Hibernian Volunteers. They were oriented more toward the nation as a whole than the state of New York; their goal was to "assist in the defence and protection of the United States, its Constitution and laws against all enemies foreign or domestic." The only requirements for membership were that the applicant be "an Hibernian or the Son of an Hibernian." Although the group had no religious test for membership, the name Hibernian in the late eighteenth century was understood to mean native, Gaelic Irish, that is, Catholic. The name and uniforms of the Hibernian Volunteers were all sym-

bolic of Catholic Ireland and its centuries-long struggle against English and Protestant domination. The use of green was a more recent
innovation, introduced by the United Irishmen. The Hibernian Volunteers paid special attention to the design of their uniforms. Each
volunteer was to wear a "grass green short coat" and "a shamrock
on the shirt." Their helmets featured green bands with green and
white feathers. During the 1790s, Americans often literally wore
their politics on their sleeves. Republicans sported red, white, and
blue cockades to demonstrate their admiration for the French Revolution; Federalists showed their support of the national government by
wearing black cockades. By wearing the green, the Hibernian Volunteers made their own politics very clear.[16]

On St. Patrick's Day in 1796, thirteen of the Hibernians met at a
coffeehouse for dinner. A delegation of them later went to a banquet
hosted by the merchant-dominated Society of the Friendly Sons of
St. Patrick. Several members of St. Peter's were Friendly Sons, including Dominick Lynch, Andrew Morris, John Kelly (a business
partner of Lynch and Stoughton), and Michael Bradford and Michael
Hogan, who ran an import business together. The Friendly Sons'
guest of honor that day was none other than John Jay, now the Federalist governor of New York. Jay noticed the Hibernians' green uniforms and asked to meet the next day with Robert Cox, the elected
captain of the militia. At that time, Jay told Cox that the state would
not commission the officers of the Hibernian Volunteers (thereby
denying it legal standing), due in part to what he considered the
provocative design of their uniforms. John Jay reasonably concluded
that the Hibernian Volunteers were not likely to have supported the
treaty with Britain that he had negotiated the year before. many
Federalist leaders in the 1790s, most prominently George Washington, took a dim view of "self-created" societies, that is, those founded
by people of middling (or lower) economic status with their own
political ideas and culture. John Jay must have evaluated the Hibernian Volunteers in this light as well. Although he agreed to break

bread with merchants of the Friendly Sons of St. Patrick, Jay was not willing to sanction a group whose aims on the face of it seemed not so much commercial and social as political—and a type of politics of which he did not approve. In light of both American domestic politics and international diplomacy, Jay found little reason to facilitate the Irish brand of American nationalism, with its apparent hostility to all things English. As the Hibernians' historian lamented, "Governor Jay forbade the wearing of the green." Two years later, in 1798, the Irish New Yorkers again tried to organize their own militia. This time, they went by the more politically neutral name of the "Washington Infantry." John Jay was still governor, however, and with the Federalist-dominated Council of Appointment, once more rejected the militia's choice of officers. Disappointed for a second time, the New York Irish were beginning to see new lines of division in American politics as they tried to make sense of their latest setback: "Federalists and Tories carrying everything with a high hand; a man who professes the rights of man had no chance."[17]

In the early 1780s, New York Catholics had looked to the national government for redress of their grievance against state laws on naturalization that they believed were discriminatory. By the late 1790s, however, the Federalist Party, which maintained its grip on that government, was determined to reduce the number of immigrants into the country. They increasingly looked on immigrants, a good number of whom were Catholics, as carriers of dangerous and radical ideas; John Jay told a colleague in 1798 that a federal law should be enacted to prohibit "any foreigner" from holding an elective or appointive office of the United States. His attitude toward immigrants was becoming typical of many in his party. Harrison Gray Otis, a Federalist member of Congress from neighboring Massachusetts, gave voice to this attitude most bluntly, saying that he did "not wish to invite hordes of wild Irishmen, nor the turbulent and disorderly of all parts of the world, to come here with a view to disturb our tranquility, after having succeeded in the overthrow of their own Governments." Federalist unease with immigrants reached its peak when Congress passed the Naturalization Act in 1798. President John Adams signed the bill, which extended the period of residency required for citizenship from five to fourteen years. Through this measure and the Alien and Sedition acts, Federalists sought to suppress dissent and reduce the influence of immigrants in American politics. Edward Livingston, a Republican member of Congress from New York City, argued vehemently against the Alien Act, which gave the president the authority to expel from the United States any immigrant who had not yet become naturalized and who was considered "dangerous to the peace and safety of the United States." In New York, relations between Irish Catholics and the Federalists worsened in the aftermath of the United Irish uprising of 1798. Many Irish were outraged by the conduct of Rufus King, United States minister to Britain, and a leading Federalist. King had persuaded the British government in 1799 not to allow captured United Irishmen, known as the Irish State Prisoners, to go into exile in the United States. The growing importance of the Irish question was beginning to change the way that Catholics and Irish in the United States understood American politics.[18]

The second Catholic parish to be established in New York during the early republic proved to be even more Irish (although there were French Catholics active at the outset) in its ethnicity than was St. Peter's. There were Catholics in upstate New York as well. In the Albany area, some of the wealthier Catholics had social ties with Federalists, much as did their counterparts in New York City. The Catholic laity in Albany was led initially by men of social and economic standing who were allied with the Federalists. Stephen Louis Le Couteulx, an exiled aristocratic French Catholic, played a major role in establishing a Catholic church in Albany. His name, describing him as one of two "founders" of St. Mary's parish, was inscribed on the cornerstone of the church. Le Couteulx, a friend and business partner of the Federalist financier Robert Morris, opened a store in

Albany, from which he sold goods to travelers passing through the city on their way westward. Thomas Barry's name was also on the cornerstone of St. Mary's. He owned a prosperous tobacco shop on the main street in Albany, was friendly with Alexander Hamilton and Bishop Carroll, and was pleased to see that Sunday Mass at St. Mary's attracted some of Albany's "genteel people." Barry referred to Le Couteulx as "the best friend I had in founding the Catholic Church in Albany." One of the wealthiest members of the parish, Barry noted that he had "spent a great deal of my time and money to establish a church in Albany." A Federalist, he was elected as the first President of St. Mary's Board of Trustees, and served in that post for many years. Another exiled French Catholic was Madame Henrietta-Lucy de La Tour du Pin, who, along with her husband, Frederic-Seraphin, and their children left for the United States after they had been persecuted during the French Revolution. They moved to rural New York, near Albany. The family was aristocratic; Madame du Pin had been a lady-in-waiting to Marie-Antoinette, and both her father and father-in-law were executed during the Terror. In New York, the du Pins' social circle included the Schuylers, the Van Rensselaers, and Alexander Hamilton.[19]

Catholics in Albany established St. Mary's, however, just at the time when the Federalists in New York (and nationally as well) were pursuing policies that were unpopular with Irish Catholics. By the late eighteenth century, the question of religious freedom for Catholics was settled in New York; there was no nativist opposition to Catholics establishing a church in Albany. Residents of Albany, in fact, congratulated themselves on the willingness of many in the city who were not Catholic to donate funds to St. Mary's building fund, a gesture that "bespeaks the tolerant and liberal disposition of the country." In that same spirit, the Albany Common Council unanimously granted the parish a suitable piece of property on which to build its church. Even though Federalists reacted to the French Revolution by defending religion, Catholics would have found that less important in the late 1790s than they would have a decade or so earlier, when Catholicism was resurfacing in New York after nearly a century of prohibition.[20]

And so the early merchant leaders of St. Mary's were not decisive in determining the political allegiances of Catholics in Albany. Thomas Barry notwithstanding, most of the Irish Catholics in Albany were more oriented toward the Republicans. An example was the Cassidy family, who emigrated from Ireland to Albany in 1790. Thomas and Margaret's Cassidy's son John became a leading Republican politician in Albany early in the nineteenth century. The Irish were even more heavily represented in St. Mary's than they were at St. Peter's. At least six of the original nine trustees of the church were Irish. Nearly all of a group of about thirty men who described themselves in 1799 as "the trustees and principal members of the congregation of the church in Albany" were of Irish birth or ancestry. Although the parish covered a large geographic area, more than half of the congregation was made up of people who lived in the city of Albany, which became the capital of New York State in 1797. This gave the parish a character that was more urban, such as it was, than rural.[21]

Catholics in New York State in 1800 were predominantly Irish, even more than they had been in the middle of the 1780s. The Irish question was quickly replacing the French Revolution as the most significant international issue for the majority of Catholics in the state. Federalists, who earlier in the decade had been aligned with the Catholic clergy in denouncing the antireligious character of the French Revolution, now were at odds with most of the Catholic laity on the question of independence for Ireland. They had also proven themselves to be hostile toward immigrants, whom they largely considered to be political malcontents, despite the religiosity of some of the newcomers.

CATHOLICS AND THE ELECTION OF 1800

Immigrants from Ireland and France had boosted the city's Catholic population to a higher percentage of the city's total in 1800 than it had been in 1790. By the middle of the first decade of the new century, the number of Catholics in New York City had been placed by observers, both Catholic and otherwise, as between ten thousand and fourteen thousand, with most of that increase coming in the 1790s. The population of the city as a whole was about sixty thousand in 1800; as many as one in seven or eight New Yorkers that year was probably at least nominally Catholic. As a growing percentage of New York City's population, Catholics were now beginning to be at least identified by the city's politicians as a potential voting bloc. New York was an especially important state in the intensely fought presidential election of 1800. Federalist John Adams had captured its electoral votes in 1796; Republicans calculated that if they could win New York in 1800, the result would almost certainly be the election of their ticket of Thomas Jefferson of Virginia and Aaron Burr of New York. The state legislature chose New York's delegates to the Electoral College. Burr, who led the Republican campaign in 1800, devised a strategy of which the key goal was winning New York City's Assembly seats away from the Federalists. To this end, he put together an exceptional slate of candidates for those offices, persuading a reluctant George Clinton, the former governor, and Horatio Gates, a hero of the revolution, to accept nominations for the Republican ticket.[22]

Burr essentially united the three main factions—his own and those associated with the Livingston and Clinton families—of the loosely organized Republicans in New York for the 1800 elections. He and his supporters, known as the "the little band," were the most energetic Republicans during the campaign that year. The Burrites compiled a list of all voters in the city and sent canvassers to visit each one personally. DeWitt Clinton, who was emerging as the leader of his family's political interest, was not especially active in 1800. Burr and his supporters were nationalist Republicans; many of them were members of Tammany and other societies that had nativist tendencies. The stakes were too high in 1800, however, for Republicans to alienate Catholic voters, especially in light of the opportunity created by the recent Federalist stance toward immigrants and the Irish. They wisely kept the focus of their campaign strictly on the questions of social equality and political liberty; they made no efforts to appeal to Catholics on religious grounds. Republicans made a direct appeal to New Yorkers of modest social status, and to immigrants as well; most Catholic voters would have been in those categories. The Republican strategy was to denounce Federalists as a "British junto" and as "Tories." They further charged that the freedoms and liberties gained during the American Revolution were now in danger from a faction devoted to "aristocracy [and] monarchy." And Republicans warned New Yorkers that if the citizenry did not turn the Federalists out of office, "you will wreck upon the shoals of aristocratic design the vessel of the state which includes in it the liberties and happiness of the people." The Federalists inadvertently contributed to the logic of the Republicans' strategy. One of the more well known members of a generally undistinguished list of their Assembly candidates was infamous among New York laboring people. The *American Citizen,* a Republican paper, asked its readers, "Who is unacquainted with the political character of Gabriel Furman? If any, let him inquire of the Fly Market ferrymen." Furman served the Republicans well as a symbol of a haughty and elitist Federalism.[23]

Despite this, Federalists were not prepared to concede the votes of devout Christians to the Republicans. They tried to introduce religion into the campaign by linking their opponents to deism and worse. In portraying their opponents, in particular Thomas Jefferson, as hostile to religion, Federalists claimed that the Republican nominee was "an enemy to all religious establishments," and asked "who will now dare to give his vote for this audacious howling atheist?" They pleaded with New Yorkers to vote to protect "the holy ordinances of religion" and warned that if the Republicans won, "the temple of the most High will be profaned by the impious orgies of the Goddess of Reason, personated as in France by some common prostitute." This was a clear attempt to revive the specter of the French Revolution, as Federalists sought to align themselves with Christianity and cast the Republicans as fundamentally opposed to it. Federalist campaigners also decried "Jefferson's *illuminated* philosophy." That was a reference to the Illuminati, a society that emerged in Germany in the late eighteenth century dedicated to combating supernatural and revealed religion through appeals to reason. To describe someone as "illuminated" was to accuse them of deism or atheism. Given their social and political policies toward immigrants and their stance on Ireland, Federalists understandably realized that religious themes were their best chance to win the votes of naturalized citizens and those who belonged to one of New York's many churches, including St. Peter's.[24]

Federalists had some potentially important allies in this effort. The Catholic clergy in the United States continued to be wary of the Republicans on the religious question. Father Matthew O'Brien (brother of Father William O'Brien of St. Peter's) delivered a sermon to parishioners at St. Mary's in Albany in early 1800 on a national day of remembrance in honor of George Washington, who had recently died. Considered one of the most eloquent Catholic priests in the country, O'Brien reminded Albany Catholics of the dangers that the French Revolution posed to their faith. He warned parishioners to "take lessons against the woes that irreligion must produce." O'Brien's sympathies were clearly with the Federalists. After praising Washington and the Federal Constitution, he advised the parishioners of St. Mary's to trust their national government, as "the presumption of the individual must be in favor of the administration." The priest counseled Albany Catholics, most of whom were Irish immigrants, to be grateful for all they had received in "your adopted country." O'Brien also cautioned against the Federalists' opponents, urging Catholics to avoid "political quacks who are scattered about our streets, and crammed into every drinking house," whom he feared would lead society to "dissension, to irreligion, and to anarchy." Father O'Brien endorsed a profoundly hierarchical and conservative vision of politics in the capital of a republican state: "Our holy religion informs us that all power is from God; that every soul must be subject to superior powers; that resistance against power is rebellion against Heaven." His attitude reflected that of Bishop John Carroll in this regard. Better to be governed by the Federalists, with their vision of a harmonious and hierarchical society and their proven record of religious tolerance, than risk the elevating the Republicans and their potential anti-Catholicism to power. For the dire consequences that could result from such a party gaining power, one only had to look to the beleaguered and demoralized Catholic Church in France. And in a warning that echoed the Federalists, the Catholic priest denounced the "methodical abominations of our modern illuminati."[25]

Despite the clear misgivings that the Catholic clergy harbored toward the Republicans, by 1800 members of that party were beginning to make inroads among the lay leadership at St. Peter's. Cornelius Heeney, a longtime Republican, was elected as a trustee of the parish in 1799. Heeney had emigrated from Ireland to Philadelphia, and was among the Catholics who had moved to New York City after the revolution. He was a merchant in the fur business with John Jacob Astor and John Gottsberger, an Austrian Catholic immigrant. Within a few years of opening his own fur shop, Heeney had become affluent. Despite his wealth, Heeney did not do as earlier prosperous Catholic merchants did and become a Federalist. Distinguishing himself as a Republican (and a Jeffersonian one at that) by his personal appearance, he was described by one friend as "the only gentlemen I ever knew who wore a pigtail." Heeney was among those particularly angered by Rufus King's actions against the United Irishmen. For Cornelius Heeney, Ireland's struggle for independence was of more importance to him in shaping his American political identity than was his economic status. And as a new lay leader of St. Peter's, Irish politics was a way for him to connect with the majority of Catholics in New York who did not share his material prosperity.[26]

Neither party raised directly the question of political equality for Catholics in 1800. Neither Federalists nor Republicans wanted to take the chance of alienating Protestant voters by linking themselves too closely to Catholics in New York. As their numbers grew, Irish Catholics were becoming a symbol of foreignness whose faith was an unwanted novelty to some in New York. On St. Patrick's Day in 1799, Protestant New Yorkers had paraded in the streets near the docks of the East River with effigies of St. Patrick that they called "paddies"; some Irish Catholics replied with fisticuffs. St. Patrick of Ireland had replaced English rebel Guy Fawkes as the Catholic image of popular ridicule in New York. Yet, at the same time, the Federalists and Republicans avoided any overt, anti-Catholic statements; religious bigotry of any sort may have backfired among the general electorate, and neither side could be sure how Catholics themselves might vote. Just before the polls opened, however, Federalists did tentatively broach the Catholic question as they sought to link Republicans with nativism and religious prejudice. They claimed in the pages of the *Daily Advertiser* that *"Exclusive Republicans"* were threatening to activate the provision of the New York State Constitution, which gave election inspectors the authority to require voters to take an oath of allegiance to the state. As with other oaths in the 1777 New York Constitution, it required those who took it to renounce "all foreign ecclesiastical authority." Although Federalists did not mention Catholics by name in their oblique criticism of Republican campaign tactics, it was obvious whom they meant as they declared that "the object of such threats cannot be mistaken." And their characterization of the oath as requiring "abjuration" was essentially correct; it would have forced any Catholic voter who took it to forswear a decisive element of his religious identity. But it is not entirely clear whether this isolated charge, coming as late as it did, had any basis in fact or was simply an act of desperation as Federalists sensed that defeat in New York was imminent. The diffidence with which Federalists raised this potentially explosive issue was typical of how, before 1800, they did not use newspapers as sharp, partisan weapons the way that Republicans did. Federalists believed that such tactics were inappropriate and would lower them to the level of their "Jacobin" opponents; not until after the shock of their defeat in 1800 would they begin to effectively employ newspapers as a political tool.[27]

Federalist efforts to retain New York City, in part by appealing to Catholic voters through this shadowy episode of the election oath, fell far short. Republicans won a clear victory in the 1800 state elections, and with it a majority in the New York legislature and control of the state's presidential electors. Key to the Republican triumph was their sweep of New York City, where they won decisively in the city's outer wards, home to immigrants and laborers. Historians have long maintained that one important contributing cause to the national Republican victory in 1800 was the vote for that party in those wards. One Federalist was convinced that the votes of the "U. Irishmen, & French & other Foreigners" in the sixth and seventh wards for the Republicans had made the difference in their victory. A Catholic priest in New York City noted in 1801 that it was "in the extremity of this city where most of the poor Catholics are thronged." The property and wealth requirements for Assembly elections were the lowest, opening up those contests to more voters of modest means. In 1800, over 60 percent of the members of St. Peter's parish lived in the city's poorest wards, the fifth, sixth, and seventh, which provided the Republicans with their margin of victory in the city. It would seem that a combination of the struggle of Ireland for independence and Federalist hostility to immigrants, both nationally and in New York, had delivered the majority of Catholic votes to the Republicans. The Federalists were discovering that religion, standing on its own, was not proving to be much of a political issue in a society of universal religious liberty. The politics of the French Revolution, too, were fading in importance, despite the continued misgivings of the Catholic clergy about the potential hostility of Republicans toward Christianity in general and Catholicism in particular.[28]

Building on their momentum from the 1800 elections, Republicans captured an overwhelming majority of delegates (86 out of 100) elected to a state constitutional convention in 1801. Aaron Burr, now vice-president of the United States, was elected president of the convention; DeWitt Clinton, his principal rival for the leadership of New York's Republicans, was not there. The Republican-dominated convention did not repeal or amend the oath of office that discriminated against Catholics. Neither did the 1801 convention address section eight of the 1777 Constitution, which gave election inspectors the right to require oaths of allegiance that might prohibit Catholics from voting. The Republican legislature retained, without debate, the 1788 oath of office law in their revision of the state code later that year. Governor John Jay, who had been openly hostile to the idea of religious and political equality for Catholics for twenty-five years, signed the bill, which effectively maintained the ban on Catholics holding any state office, civil or military, in New York.[29]

■ ■ ■

The 1790s were in many ways a formative decade in American political history. By the turn of the nineteenth century, two distinct political persuasions were emerging, each possessing a vision of how the republic should develop. Ordinary people, in addition to developing allegiances to the national parties and their leaders, had forged their own political culture, with its rites and rituals. The place of New York Catholics in this politics was singular. They had emerged from the revolutionary era endowed with new religious freedom and the right to vote (although the latter was not beyond challenge), at least for men who met the minimum property requirements. Yet, they were essentially barred from holding state elective office. At the advent of the new national government established by the federal Constitution in 1789, Federalists seemed positioned to become Catholics' political allies. They had defended the political rights of Catholics in the late 1780s. The impact of the French Revolution in the United States could have conceivably drawn Federalists and Catholics together on the basis of a shared religious sensibility and a common belief that American Republicans were essentially hostile to Christianity. Indeed, more affluent Catholics did join the Federalist ranks.[30]

This potential alliance was sidetracked, however, by the Federalists' unease with the changing and growing Catholic population. Of the Catholic immigrants of the 1790s, Federalists were most compatible with exiles from the French Revolution. They could hardly allow themselves, however, to become known as the defenders of Catholics, if Catholic to most New Yorkers meant foreign, royalist aristocrats. Federalists were demonstrably less sympathetic to Irish immigrants, whom they distrusted as a people whose long history of subjugation at the hands of, and resentment toward, the English had made them turbulent, prone to disorder, and ill-suited to life in a constitutional republic. And so over the course of the decade, the question of Irish independence, for which Federalists did not voice support, began to replace interpretations of the French Revolution as the leading international issue in American politics. This was a major reason why Federalists made little in the way of a systematic effort to win Catholics to their side.

Most Catholics in the election of 1800 appear to have voted for the Republicans out of displeasure with Federalist policies and attitudes that they deemed hostile to immigrants and laboring people. In the wake of the election of 1800, Catholics remained in a political space in New York between the two parties, although the foundations for building an alliance with the Republicans now seemed to be in place. The most avowedly nationalist faction of Republicans, however, led that disparate early party in New York. At the state Constitutional Convention, held soon after their dramatic victory in 1800, Republicans did not address those sections of the state constitution and statutes that kept Catholics in a position of second-class citizenship. The aversion, too, of some Republicans in that party to Catholicism was further evidence that any partnership between Catholics and Republicans would not be easy to forge or sustain. All of this left Catholics in New York as a religious body set apart by law and political culture as was no other such group in the state. Their religion remained ill-suited to the ethos of American nationalism, as it was developing. These considerations, along with the tortured history of Catholicism in New York, combined to keep Catholics on the margins of the state's political life.

# CHAPTER 5

# "In All Countries Such Distinctions Are Odious: In None More So Than This"
## Political Equality in the Early Republic

The 1800 elections did not mean an end to the tensions between the triumphant Republicans and their potential Catholic allies. Dennis Driscol, a former Catholic priest from Ireland, was a United Irishman who fought against British rule in the 1790s. By late 1800, he was living in New York City, where he was editor of a deist newspaper, The *Temple of Reason*. In the first issue of the paper, Driscol welcomed "the great number of Irish emigrants lately arrived in this country . . . those victims of tyranny and oppression [that] shun the bear-like hugs of John Bull." More of an Atlantic than a nationalist Republican, Driscol was an immigrant and did not define republicanism as something limited to the United States. His opposition to the British monarchy and to the Federalist party in the United States would have appealed to many Irish Catholic immigrants in New York. Driscol's undisguised hostility toward Catholicism, however, complicated his attempts to draw Irish immigrants further into the ascendant Republican coalition. The *Temple of Reason* taunted Catholics by invoking Jesus' exhortation to one of His apostles, on which the Catholic Church in part bases its claim to be the original Christian church: "Thou art Peter, and upon this rock I will build my Church, and the gates of hell shall not prevail against it." The paper also contended that the Catholic Church had less to fear from the proverbial "gates of hell" than "from the *pillars of truth*." It also ran a mocking, satirical history of the papacy, entitled "of the progress of Christian superstition and idolatry under the auspices of the popes of Rome." Driscol encouraged Catholics who had come to republican America to reject clerical authority (as he himself had done) so as to "cure our fellow-citizens of this destructive evil." After three months in New York, Driscol and the *Temple of Reason* removed to Philadelphia. The former priest's open contempt for his former church, however, illustrated that any developing political bond between Catholics and New York Republicans was susceptible to being undermined by the tensions inherent between them.[1]

## CATHOLICS, FEDERALISM, AND REPUBLICAN FACTIONALISM

After the success of the united front that Aaron Burr cobbled together for the 1800 elections, Republicans in New York soon fell to division and bickering. The three primary blocs in the Republican Party in the early nineteenth century—those associated with the Clintons, Aaron Burr, and the Livingston family—were, as one historian has put it, "three factions in search of a following." By 1803, the main division among Republicans was between supporters of the Clinton family and those led by Aaron Burr; the former had allied with the Livingstons in opposition to Burr and his "little band." Some of the rivalry was about patronage; there was also lingering resentment from the presidential election of 1800, in which Thomas Jefferson had ultimately prevailed over Aaron Burr in the House of Representatives. The Clintonian, or Atlantic Republicans, had favored Thomas Jefferson for the presidency. James Cheetham, a radical exile from Manchester, England, an ally of the Clintons, and editor of the *American Citizen*, charged that Aaron Burr had been dishonorable in seeking to dislodge Jefferson from the top of the Republican ticket in 1800 after the two had unexpectedly received the same number of votes in the Electoral College. The competitive politics of New York in the early republic, with its intense factionalism among the Republicans, and the sharp rivalry between Republicans and Federalists, created opportunities for outsiders such as Catholics. American politics, at least in New York, had not yet settled into a clearly defined, two-party system; it possessed a flexibility to address the needs of groups on the margins of public life. The fragmentation of the Republicans after 1800 redounded to the benefit of Catholics. The Federalists had pushed immigrants and Catholics away; nationalist Republicans had successfully sought their votes as part of their larger strategy of besting the Federalists in New York City. The latter, however, were not prepared to fight for political equality for Catholics.[2]

In the context of their rivalry with other Republican factions in the early nineteenth century, the Clintonian Republicans, whose faction included a strong international element, saw an opportunity in becoming the advocates of Catholics and immigrants. During the imperial crisis with Britain in the early 1770s, the young Assemblyman George Clinton of Ulster County had been as outspoken as any in his denunciations of the Quebec Act in 1774 for its favoritism toward Catholicism. Clinton emerged in the 1780s as the leader of the state's rural Anti-Federalists, who were clearly opposed to political equality for Catholics. After the revolution, however, the Clintons found it useful to stress their ethnic heritage; Ireland was the ancestral home of the Clinton family. Their family religion was Presbyterian, but Irish Americans were not necessarily divided sharply along religious lines in the early nineteenth century; the legacy of the United Irish movement of 1798 was one reason for this. DeWitt Clinton, for example, became a member of the Friendly Sons of St. Patrick in 1790. As a U.S. senator from New York in 1803, he led the effort to repeal the Federalist naturalization law that had required immigrants to wait fourteen years to become citizens. As a growing segment of the population, one that was concentrated in the state's two largest cities,

Catholics were now a potentially influential bloc of voters. St. Peter's parish had grown to the point where its pastor, Father William O'Brien, reported in 1801 that it had "vastly increased and even now would fill two churches."[3]

Catholics still lacked a committed advocate among the state's parties and factions, but the Atlantic Republicans were beginning to represent their interests in the contest with their intraparty rivals. Nationalist Republicans, at the same time, chose to make religion and Irish immigration two points of contention in this burgeoning rivalry. Spokesmen for the two main factions of Republicans wrote a series of dueling political pamphlets between 1802 and 1804. John Wood, aligned with the nationalists, charged in one of them that Atlantic Republicans were dominated by deists. He claimed to be in possession of a list of ninety-five members of that group, "every one of them, however, without exception, is in politics a Clintonian." There was some truth to the charges. Among those who fit that description was James Cheetham, who, like other English radicals of the late eighteenth century, was consciously *anti-trinitarian* in that he rejected the central tenets of Christianity. Upon arriving in New York, Cheetham and other exiles rejuvenated the New York Society of Theophilanthropists, a deist group, to which DeWitt Clinton had also belonged. Cheetham and his heterodox religious views were a favorite target of the nationalists. William P. Van Ness described the English deist as "an open blasphemer against God, a reviler of his Saviour, and a conspirator against the religious establishment of his country."[4]

The nationalists' invocation of religion and denunciation of their Republican rivals supposed that deism did not lead them to appeal to New York's Catholic population on the grounds of a common Christianity. This might have been an especially fruitful strategy to employ in the wake of Dennis Driscol's openly anti-Catholic *Temple of Reason*. Driscol was aligned with the Clinton faction; James Cheetham had assisted him in publishing his paper. Instead, the nationalists tried to make the case that the Atlantic Republicans were religious deviants in that their ranks included both deists and Catholics. John Wood sneered that without Cheetham's support, Driscol, a former priest, "probably would have been reduced to the necessity of again humming mass to a few superstitious Irish maids." Protestant men had long feared that women were particularly susceptible, given their emotional natures, to the irrationality and mysticism of Catholic ritual. Driscol, Wood further explained, "was only a few years since, a Romish priest, and possessed all the Jesuitical cunning, which the apostates from that order generally do." The ethos of nationalist Republicans was clearly Protestant. The leaders of that faction—Aaron Burr, Matthew Davis, Melancton Smith, William P. Van Ness, and John Swartwout—were descended from New York's early Dutch and English settlers or from others who were early immigrants to America. The pamphleteer John Wood differed from this norm, as he was an immigrant, albeit a Scottish Protestant. The nationalists prided themselves on being true Republicans, not dominated by a great family, as were the Clinton and Livingston factions, nor a party of aristocrats, like the Federalists. Many nationalist Republicans were also members of the Tammany Society, which remained unfriendly toward immigrants, especially Catholics.[5]

Nationalist and Atlantic Republicans clashed over Irish immigration to New York. John Wood charged that Tunis Wortman, the clerk of New York City who was aligned with the Clintons, knew that city's rapid naturalization of immigrants was not legal. Nonetheless, Wortman and the Atlantic Republicans proceeded to process the Irish as citizens, in the hopes, Wood claimed, of "rivetting forever their friendship to the Clinton family." The nationalist writer also alleged that Wortman and Richard Riker, another leading Atlantic Republican, were holding private meetings on a daily basis "for the purpose of laying plans in order to promote the Clintonian interest among the lower classes." And Wood made no secret that Irish immigrants were prominent among "the lower classes" that the Atlantics were allegedly wooing. The latter had supposedly directed a couple of the Irish immigrants to "run among the new imported Hibernians, in order to quiet their locaqious (sic) wants." Contemporary Irish politics also influenced New York's politics in the early nineteenth century. Although the bold effort of the United Irishmen to build a coalition of Protestants and Catholics failed to overthrow English rule in Ireland, it had managed to transcend the deep religious chasm that had plagued the country since the sixteenth century. The United Irish who sought independence for their country were determined to abolish the penal laws that systematically discriminated against Catholics in many ways. Some refugees from the movement came to New York City. Among these were Thomas Addis Emmet and William MacNeven, who were both in New York by 1805. Emmet was born into a Protestant family, and MacNeven was a Catholic. These Irish political exiles became Republicans in their new country, and they were among those immigrants in New York City who formed the Hibernian Provident Society in 1802. Its stated purpose was to provide relief for its members, most of whom, the society declared in the preamble to its constitution, were "forced by persecution, and the oppression of a tyrannic government to seek an asylum in the United States."[6] From the outset, however, the Hibernian Provident Society was more than a charitable group. Although there were no religious requirements for membership, the society insisted that all who joined be supporters of Irish independence. It pointedly did not welcome any "Irishman, who had willingly aided in continuing the dominion of Great-Britain over Ireland." American politics were also a consideration; membership in the society was open to all those who were "Democratic Republicans and of good moral characters." The Hibernian Provident Society aligned itself with the Atlantic Republicans from the outset. On St. Patrick's Day in 1803, its members toasted "Our Governor, George Clinton, the firm and undeviating republican." Toasts in the early republic were an important political ritual, carefully written out beforehand to reflect the views of those present, and later published in the partisan newspapers of the day. The pro-Clinton *American Citizen* published annually the Hibernian Provident Society St. Patrick's Day toasts. The Irish immigrants saluted other republican heroes on March 17, 1803, including Sam Adams, Tom Paine, and the president of the United States, Thomas Jefferson. Notably absent from the society's long rounds of toasting, however, was the name of Aaron Burr, one of the leading Republicans in New York, and the current vice president of the United States.[7]

The nationalists returned the disdain of the Irish, and then some. The New York City Common Council, dominated by Federalists, had passed an ordinance in 1803 making it a crime to drag or carry an effigy of St. Patrick through the city streets on March 17, St. Patrick's Day, or any other day, with the intent "to ridicule such titular Saint." The new law drew the ire of nationalist Republicans. On the day before St. Patrick's Day in 1803, the *Morning Chronicle*, the newspaper of their faction, published a satire purportedly written by St. Patrick himself. The Irish saint appealed to the Common Council for an expansion of the St. Patrick's Day law to keep his wife "Shelah" off the streets on March 17, lest she "exhibit herself around the city." This comment echoed the long English tradition of depicting Gaelic Irish women as particularly licentious and wild, sinning freely in the comforting knowledge that their priests would forgive them. It was the "young, ragged and sunburnt order of citizens in this city" who had conducted the mock St. Patrick's Day rituals, according to the nationalists. In their competition with the Clinton faction and the Federalists for the allegiance of New York's laboring people, the nationalist Republicans in this instance placed themselves on the side of the "sunburnt order," that is, those who worked outdoors, against both the Federalist Common Council that had sought to protect the image of the saint, as well as Irish Catholic immigrants to New York. Their satirist also compared the St. Patrick's Day law to a papal decree, adding that any *"bull"* found running loose on the streets of New York on March 17 would be slain and its meat given to the poor. That play on words, along with the general tone of the piece, illustrates the emphasis that nationalist Republicans placed on forging ties with native-born Protestant laborers. If this occasionally involved mocking St. Patrick and Catholicism and potentially alienating Irish Catholic immigrants, they were willing to do so.[8]

While the Republicans battled over religion and immigrants, the Federalists became the first political party in New York to nominate a Catholic for public office. Parties and factions in New York in the early republic often recruited candidates from underrepresented groups when their political fortunes were at a low ebb. In the aftermath of their overwhelming defeat in 1800, Federalists selected Andrew Morris as their candidate for assistant alderman from New York City's merchant-dominated first ward in 1802. Morris, in addition to being a trustee at St. Peter's, was also active in the larger community, serving as a governor of the New-York Lying-In Hospital. An Irish immigrant, he had ties to the city's artisan population, becoming a member of the Mechanics' Society in 1792. Morris was a prosperous chandler and soap maker, but he identified more with other prosperous Catholic Federalists and the leaders of the Catholic clergy than with members of his own craft. Bishop Carroll lodged with Andrew Morris and his wife Eleanor at their country estate on his visits to New York. The Morrises chose Thomas Stoughton, the Spanish consul and trustee of St. Peter's, to be godfather to their daughter Eleanor. Eleanor Morris had been born a Skinner, which is an English name, and she may have been a convert to Catholicism. Her husband's decision to marry outside his ethnic group, which suggests that he did not have a strong sense of Irish identity, was rare for Catholics in New York during the early republic.[9]

The Federalists' hostility to Irish immigrants as a whole did not dissuade them from recruiting Morris for office. With his victory in the charter, or city, election, Morris became the first elected official of his faith in New York City since the late seventeenth century.

The municipal post of assistant alderman did not require an oath of allegiance similar to that mandated for state officeholders, so Morris's religion was not an issue when he took office. Despite their nomination of Andrew Morris and their defense of the image of St. Patrick, Federalists were not prepared to bring Irish Catholics fully into New York City's politics. Republicans pressed for suffrage reform in municipal politics soon after the 1800 elections. Common Council elections for aldermen and assistant aldermen (the mayor was appointed by New York's governor) were restricted to those with significant property and wealth. The system was so heavily weighted in favor of property that only 5 percent of the city's population was eligible to vote in municipal elections, while some of the richest New Yorkers were able to vote in each ward in which they owned at least twenty pounds in land or real property. Federalists resisted Republican calls for reform, the most prominent of which was James Cheetham's pamphlet, *Dissertation Concerning Political Equality and the Corporation of New York*, in which he argued for lowering the property requirements for voting in city elections. In defending the status quo, Federalists employed nativist rhetoric, warning of the threat that *"Irish freeman"* posed to liberty, qualifying the insult by adding "no disrespect is meant to the respectable part of that nation."[10]

Despite having passed legislation making it illegal to mock the image of Catholic saints, and having furthered the prospects of prosperous, individual Catholics such as Andrew Morris, Federalists still resisted the prospect of being on equal political terms with poorer Irish Catholics. Morris, on whose support Federalists could depend, voted with the majority of the Common Council in rejecting a Republican petition to alter the city charter "so as to extend the right of suffrage." The Council contended that reform was unwise, as "perfection in human institutions is not to be expected." Morris and the others insisted they would, if necessary, "remedy *important* defects in the Charter." They did not consider extending the suffrage to those of modest means to be a question of major consequence. In 1804, however, the state legislature, in part due to the efforts of De-Witt Clinton, broadened considerably the body of eligible voters in New York City. Federalists were also alarmed over the growing immigrant population in New York City. Their anxieties were heightened by their belief, which they shared with nationalist Republicans, that the Clinton faction quickly naturalized immigrants in order to win their support at election time. One Federalist, writing as "An American," claimed that Edward Livingston, the mayor of New York City (appointed by Governor George Clinton) and City Clerk Tunis Wortman, an ally of the Clintons, were "employed at transmogrifying *Irish emigrants* into *American Citizens*," creating as they went "good Republicans, with votes in their hand."[11]

Federalists were also starting to lose ground to Republicans at St. Peter's, as the merchants' hold on the lay leadership of the party in the parish weakened. By this time, most of the diplomats who were so prominent in the late 1780s had moved on to the new capitals at Philadelphia and then to Washington, D.C. That dominance, first broken by the election of Republican Cornelius Heeney as a trustee in 1799, suffered another blow when Francis Cooper, also a Republican, followed Heeney onto the board in 1802. Patrick McKay was another prominent Republican at St. Peter's. A political leader in the heavily immigrant sixth ward, he was elected a parish trustee in 1805. Despite their growing influence at St. Peter's in the early nineteenth century, neither Cooper, Heeney, nor McKay was close to John Carroll, the bishop of Baltimore. In his letters to New York, Carroll would ask to be remembered to Federalist trustees Dominick Lynch, Thomas Stoughton, and Andrew Morris, but not to their Republican counterparts. The poorer Irish immigrants who came into the parish in the 1790s were beginning to make their influence felt in the politics of the city's Catholic parish as well. The election of Cooper and McKay as trustees was paralleled by the movement of Catholics toward the Republicans in the politics of the larger society. Most of the parishioners at St. Peter's were not reconciled to Federalism, despite the connections, dating back twenty years, between the trustees and the Federalists. That party's resistance to political participation by poorer Irish immigrants had curtailed any broad-based alliance between Catholics and Federalists; the connection remained limited to affluent members of St. Peter's. Nationalist Republicans remained ambivalent about Catholics. Atlantic Republicans, however, were becoming New York's primary advocates of Catholics and immigrants, and now prepared to make a systematic bid for the support of the main body of Catholic voters.[12]

DEMOCRATIZING NEW YORK: CATHOLICS AND THE
OATH OF OFFICE

The intense competition between Republican factions and the growing Catholic population, along with a new assertiveness on the part of Catholics themselves, combined to bring the question of Catholic political rights to the forefront of New York politics for the first time in nearly two decades. The wider political community now had to confront this question directly. Atlantic Republicans saw the political advantages in advancing the interests of a growing and potentially coherent religious body that was ready to assert its claims to political equality. One estimate made in 1806 placed the number of Catholics in New York at ten thousand out of a total population of seventy thousand. As a minority group seeking to move in from the margins of New York's public life, Catholics needed influential allies. The interests of each converged in 1805 when the Atlantic Republicans nominated Francis Cooper, a trustee at St. Peter's, and a close adviser and ally of DeWitt Clinton, as one of their candidates for the Assembly from New York City in 1805.[13]

Cooper was a sound choice to be the first Catholic nominated for state office in New York. He lived in the city's affluent second ward, which meant that many of the parishioners at St. Peter's from the outer wards would have known him not from their neighborhoods, but from church. In the early republic, religious services were for many people their most important and frequent occasion to be with others in a larger setting; and such gatherings, which served both sacred and social purposes, could have political importance as well. Born in Pennsylvania to German parents (his father served in the Pennsylvania militia during the revolution), Cooper came to New York City in the 1780s where he apprenticed as a coppersmith and was befriended by Cornelius Heeney, the first Republican trustee of the parish. In addition to his involvement at St. Peter's, Cooper was active in citywide secular organizations, joining the General Society of Mechanics and Tradesmen in 1793. Unlike Andrew Morris, who joined the society but never became active in it, Francis Cooper became a leader among the mechanics. He was elected their second vice president in 1801, the following year he was chosen as vice president, and in 1805 the artisans who comprised the society elected him as their president. The society was not as overtly nationalistic and nativist as Tammany. New York City's mechanics and artisans were affiliated for the most part with the Republicans; both nationalist and Atlantic Republicans recruited successful artisans for their tickets. Cooper's record of winning high office in the society demonstrated that his religion did not necessarily impede his advancement in organizations that included few Catholics. And Cooper, who was not personally controversial, was an American by birth and of German, rather than Irish, ancestry. All of this made him a relatively difficult target for nativists. The political circumstances of the moment were also in his favor. The Federalists were in disarray in 1805 and nominated no Assembly candidates of their own in New York City.[14]

Despite Cooper's uncontested victory at the polls, there remained the problem of the oath of office. Requiring those who took it to renounce "all foreign ecclesiastical authority," the oath had not been challenged since the state enacted it into law in 1788. The problem, however, was that Catholics understood themselves to be in communion with all those around the world who recognized the Bishop of Rome—the pope—as their spiritual leader. Catholics recognize the pope as the successor to the apostles, Peter in particular. For a Catholic in New York to take the oath as it was written in 1806 would mean denying their union with the pope and in essence reading themselves out of their own church. Had Cooper taken the oath as it was written, not only would he have damaged the unity of the Catholic Church, but he also could have set a significant precedent by putting American Catholics, at least in New York, on the path toward a national church, one independent of Rome. The oath question—an important moment in the relationship between Catholics and the American republic—quickly became larger than the political career of one individual. The Catholic clergy was alarmed at the prospect of Cooper taking the oath as it was. Father Michael Hurley, the pastor of St. Peter's, described it as "the most prolix and sanguine oath ever exacted from Catholics." The Catholic laity had already disregarded clerical warnings about aligning with the Republicans; their priests certainly did not want them to sacrifice a central tenet of their religious identity for political power. However, if Cooper had declined to take the oath and relinquished his seat in the Assembly, Catholics would have taken part in the strengthening of their status as second-class citizens.[15]

The decision of whether to challenge the oath, however, was not Cooper's alone to make. Three weeks before the state legislature was scheduled to meet in Albany, a large group of Catholics met in the schoolroom of St. Peter's to consider the question. The overwhelming decision of those present was to draft a petition to the legislature outlining their objections to the oath; thirteen hundred persons eventually signed it. Petitions in the early republic were often employed by those on the margins of the nation's political life, including women and African-Americans. Although Catholics may have been nominally marginal, they were also operating from a position of strength, having just elected one of their own to the legislature. In their determination to remove the offending words from the oath, Catholics united across partisan lines. Andrew Morris, the Federalist alderman, chaired the meeting, which sent the petition to the legislature under his name. This was a striking move in such a partisan era, as the purpose of the petition was to place a Republican in the legislature. This might result in the Republicans becoming the party of New York's Catholics, which Morris must have realized. Yet the prospect of Catholics dismantling the barrier to Catholics holding state elective office took precedence for him and other Catholic Federalists.[16]

Even as they transcended the political differences within their parish, New York Catholics also recognized that they could advance their interests through the competition between Republican factions. As Father Hurley explained to Bishop Carroll: "At variance with one another, and bent upon determined and open opposition, our Democrats will be the more likely to attend to our petition, and grant us the relief we sue for, to ensure to themselves the interest of the Catholic body, at the ensuing election." Hurley noted that his parishioners were already solidly in the Clinton camp, telling Carroll that even if the Republican-dominated legislature rejected the position, in his estimation it would not change "the political sentiments of a single individual among us." If the Atlantic Republicans were unsure as to how Catholics would react if they failed to change the oath, that was to the Catholics' advantage. As Father Hurley put it, "it is well for our purpose that the present ruling party entertains the apprehension: all that we have to do is to avail ourselves of their fears."[17]

Catholics, frustrated by their political status in early nineteenth-century New York, were intent on making the language in the oath of office a key test of citizenship. The 1777 state constitution, with its guarantee of universal religious freedom, had held out to them the promise of a general concord with the general citizenry. Instead of religious freedom leading to political equality, however, Catholics had instead seen the "cup of equalized rights dashed from their lips, by a subsequent determination, and an invidious barrier, surmountable only by perjury or apostacy." They objected to the oath on the grounds that it forced Catholics to choose between "a total exclusion from every office of honor, profit or trust, in the state, and a virtual abjuration of the religious principles of their forefathers and themselves." The Catholic petitioners argued their position unequivocally, maintaining that the oath denied them "the benefits of the free and equal participation of all the rights and privileges of Citizens" and that the "religious test, to which their consciences are opposed, operates upon them as an absolute disqualification."[18]

In seeking to be recognized as equals, Catholics asked that New York State reconcile its political system more fully with that of the national government. The state oath of office contradicted those rights "granted by the enlightened framers of the Constitution of the United States (of which it forms one of the most admirable features.)" The parishioners of St. Peter's assured the legislature that the state had little to fear from allowing Catholics to share power in New York. They pointed out that in the other American states "which adopted the liberal and just principle of the Constitution of the United States, [none] can exhibit an instance of any danger or inconvenience having resulted from non-existence of a religious test." New York's unique practice of excluding Catholics alone from political office, the petitioners argued, was an aberration that the legislature needed to correct. Moreover, the growing number of Catholics in New York was something that they could now use to their political advantage. The immigration of the past decade had made the percentage of Catholics in the city as high as 15 percent; Catholics reminded the legislature that they did now "compose a considerable portion of the population of this City." Those who signed the petition included a wide swath of the parish that stretched far beyond the Federalist trustees who had acted as spokesmen for St. Peter's in the 1780s and 1790s.[19]

The parishioners of St. Peter's were now mobilized as the "Catholic body" as they asked the state of New York to *de-politicize* their religion, once and for all. They were willing to allay the concerns of society at large about their relationship to Rome. Catholics maintained that even in the event of a hypothetical (and highly improbable) conflict that would force them to choose between their sectarian and secular loyalties, they would be found on the side of New York and the United States. They declared their willingness to "renounce and abjure all allegiance and subjection to every foreign power however titled in all matters not only civil but also ecclesiastical, as far as they may interfere with, or in the smallest degree affect the freedom, independence or safety of the state."[20]

New York Catholics wanted the legislature to think of the papacy as distant from American shores and a diminished institution, even in ecclesiastical affairs. In emphasizing the strict limits of papal authority, they admitted that while the "Bishop of Rome is the acknowledged supreme head of the profession of which they are members," his jurisdiction was confined to "matters purely and solely, spiritual." They pointed out that it was unlikely under any scenario that the pope would try to "interfere either with the civil or religious rights of their brethren of other denominations." In fact, the authority and prestige of the papacy was at a low ebb in the late eighteenth and early nineteenth centuries. The Catholic monarchies of Europe had long since wrested away much temporal and ecclesiastical power from the bishop of Rome. Pius VI had died an exile in 1799, forced to flee from Rome by the armies of revolutionary France. His successor, Pius VII, was subject to the whims of Napoleon and was hardly the picture of an absolute monarch.[21]

As planned, Francis Cooper refused to take the oath of office when the New York legislature convened, and was in turned formally denied his seat in the Assembly. He and his co-religionists had a powerful ally in DeWitt Clinton, who in 1806 was mayor of New York City and a member of the New York senate. Clinton presented the Catholic petition to the senate, and was appointed chair of the committee charged with considering it. His committee reported to the whole senate a bill that removed the word "ecclesiastical" from the oath of office, thus modifying it specifically to accommodate Catholics. The senate promptly passed the measure with only one dissenting vote. Federalists in the Assembly, however, opposed changing the oath of office. This was despite the plea that Catholics had made in their petition for New York to bring its practices in this matter into line with the United States Constitution and the national government. By 1806, however, Republicans had been in control of the federal government for five years. Federalists in the Assembly were abandoning the expansive nationalism that Hamilton and others, who, fifteen years earlier, had hoped would transcend centuries-old religious differences and bigotry that Americans had inherited from European history. Few issues, in fact, illustrated more dramatically the change in the Federalists from the 1780s to the early nineteenth century than their position on political rights for Catholics. As Federalists a few years earlier were unwilling to expand New York City's suffrage to those who were not affluent, they were now on record at the state level as opposing political equality for Catholics. They were becoming a party that feared greater democracy and inclusiveness at every turn.[22]

Republican Richard Riker of New York City, a leading Atlantic Republican and close personal associate of DeWitt Clinton (he acted as Clinton's second in an 1802 duel with nationalist Republican John Swartwout), spoke for the oath bill in the Assembly. For his efforts, he was *"ridiculed as an adherent of the Pope"* by Federalists. The antagonism of Federalist Assemblymen Abraham Van Vechten of Albany County and William W. Van Ness of Columbia County, southeast of Albany, surprised the trustees of St. Peter's, some of whom were Federalists themselves. There is a hint of betrayal in their tone as they reported to Bishop Carroll that the oath reform bill had met "a good deal of the old hacknied declamation against the Pope and popery by some *liberal* members of the lower house." Father Hurley of St. Peter's told Carroll that "I am sorry to say it met with the most decided opposition from the federal party, and that some of them indulged their illiberality so far as to cast upon us all the filthy dregs of . . . prejudice and animosity." In his view, "Van Ness and Van Vetchen were the two champions that entered into the lists of intolerance. The first I presume you have heard of before. His scurrility was of the lowest, his invective the most bitter." William W. Van Ness was the nearest thing to a successor to Alexander Hamilton that New York Federalists had in 1806.[23]

Van Ness and Van Vetchen have been classified by one historian as "Young Federalists" who borrowed the techniques of popular electioneering from their Republican rivals. Their political thinking, however, was not so innovative, as the two Federalist legislators revived anti-Catholic rhetoric that had not been heard from elected officials in New York since the revolution. The legislature in this instance was not facing an abstract question, as had been the case when the oath was written in 1788. The matter before the legislature in 1806 involved a man already chosen by the electorate for the office that he now sought to occupy. Federalists went on record as effectively repudiating the candidate duly chosen by the electorate. In their disregard for Francis Cooper's election (and by clear implication, for the political aspirations of Catholics across the state), they rejected the essence of republican government, which is the right of voters to choose their own representatives. Despite the Federalists' opposition, however, the Assembly passed the bill by a margin of sixty-three to twenty-six. Governor Morgan Lewis, a Republican, signed it into law. Francis Cooper immediately took the oath of office, revised with him in mind, and took his seat in the Assembly.[24]

The Catholics in New York to whom the Federalists were reacting differed from those whose rights they defended twenty years earlier. St. Peter's parish in the 1780s had counted among its number foreign ambassadors, diplomats, and merchants, along with others of more modest means. After the immigrations of the 1790s, the Catholic population of New York was comprised mainly of Irish immigrants, most of whom were laborers. The reputation of Catholics by the early nineteenth century had changed. When Elizabeth Ann Seton, who was born into a wealthy Anglican family, converted to Catholicism in 1805, her Federalist and Episcopalian friends and relatives were shocked. A daughter of wealth and privilege, she had lowered her social standing in becoming a Catholic. One early nineteenth-century observer described the Catholic congregation that Seton joined as "dirty, filthy, red-faced," and St. Peter's as a "horrid place of spits and pushing." Behind Francis Cooper, Federalists may have imagined, loomed hordes of unruly Irish who were on the verge of becoming their peers in terms of access to political power.[25]

For Atlantic Republicans, the passage of the oath bill represented something much different. They happily declared that "we congratulate the Church on the relief that has been granted." Cheetham's *American Citizen* took the Federalists to task, describing Van Vechten and Van Ness as *"patricia"* who "would make two excellent members of Parliament on the side of the English Church." His comment illustrates how this English radical saw politics in the United States. The Federalists were akin to the Tories in England; Catholics, who were not much of a political force in that country, were to Cheetham in New York a minority unfairly denied its legitimate republican rights. Thus, Cheetham argued in the *American Citizen*, the oath bill was not only a victory for Catholics, but for the state as a whole..

Given the history of the Republicans in New York, it is not surprising that they were not of one mind on the question of political equality for Catholics. The Federalists had hoped that their opponents would be so divided on the oath bill that it would fail to pass. The Atlantic Republicans themselves conceded that "several republicans have voted with them [the Federalists] from religious scruples," an apparent reference to those Republicans whose politics were influenced by their devotion to low-church Christianity. A few veterans of the old, rural, Anti-Federalist stripe were still active in New

York politics. Cornelius Humphrey of Seneca County, who had been among that group in the 1780s, voted in 1806 to retain the oath of office. It was the new urban coalition between Catholics and Republicans that was crucial in revising the oath; as the *American Citizen* reported, "Our City representation deserve credit for the zeal and ability which they have manifested on this occasion." Urban politics of a sort were at work in Albany County as well, as it became a hub of Federalist opposition to reforming the oath of office; all four of the county's Assemblymen voted against revising the oath of office. Albany was home to the state's second Catholic parish, St. Mary's. The resistance of Albany County's Federalists to liberalizing the oath suggests that the predominantly Irish Catholics in the city of Albany were also Republicans.[26]

Republicans in New York City had their own differences, however, on whether Catholics merited political equality. The nativism that the nationalist Republicans had exhibited toward Catholics resurfaced now that Catholics had aligned with their Atlantic opponents. Although Aaron Burr's political career had ended after the duel with Alexander Hamilton in 1804, there was still a group of Republicans in New York whom he had previously led. Their paper, the *Morning Chronicle*, did not report on the Catholic victory in the legislature. That same week, however, it did publish a satire of a fictitious Irishman, "Tague O'Liegain," who was depicted as a barely literate reader of the *American Citizen*. The exiled radicals from Britain who helped to form the Atlantic Republicans had some serious differences of their own with Catholicism. However, with the exception of Dennis Driscol, the former priest, they agreed as a whole that the more important concern in their adopted country was that no religious group in the United States be denied their rights as citizens. The efforts of radicals on behalf of the Catholic bid for political equality in the United States was also part of their larger struggle to realize the promise of the American republic. The new oath, as James Cheetham's newspaper characterized it, was "just, and such as no man exempt from religious prejudices can object to." The Atlantic Republicans declared that by eliminating the disqualifying measure against Catholics, the legislature had acted in the true spirit of American republicanism.. They added for emphasis that "in all countries religious distinctions are odious but in none are they more so than in *this*." The United States, as part of its work in distancing itself from the English way of politics, had to transcend the old European religious rivalries, much as Hamilton had urged two decades earlier.[27]

Historians have overlooked the connection between the exiled radicals' political program and their support for Catholics in New York. This may be in part because little has been written on the political history of Catholics in the United States in the early republic. Historians have also assumed, and not without reason, that Anglo-American radicals in the late eighteenth and early nineteenth centuries would have had little cause to promote the political fortunes of members of a church that they considered, in abstract and historical terms, to be a bulwark of reaction. The irony, then, was that English radicals such as James Cheetham, who had defined themselves as anti-trinitarian in England, found themselves in the United States fighting to remove political disabilities against Catholics. They and others in the Atlantic Republican camp concluded that the danger posed by the Federalists (whom, they feared, secretly hoped to establish a mixed government that would include a royal sovereign, after the English model) was now the true threat to American republicanism. That most Catholics in New York were Irish, a people with their own history of resistance to the English monarchy, made it easier for radicals to defend Catholic political rights. For Catholics in New York, what was most immediately important was that the barrier represented by the old oath of office had been dismantled, and Francis Cooper was now safely in his seat in the Assembly.

St. Peter's parish reaped immediate benefits from his place in the legislature and from the consolidation of their alliance with the Atlantic Republicans. At the turn of the nineteenth century, the state of New York provided direct funding for the schools in New York City established by the various religious congregations. In 1802, St. Peter's applied for funding from the state. The Assembly passed a resolution that year calling for the parish school to receive aid on an equal basis with other church schools, but to no avail. Simultaneously with the entreaty regarding the oath, the trustees of St. Peter's sent a second petition to the legislature asking that their school be awarded state funding. Father Hurley said of the petition that "if successful [it] will enable us to place this institution on a better footing than it has hitherto been." The parish had so many children apply to its school on the church grounds in lower Manhattan that it made plans to open a second school in the Bowery, toward the outskirts of the city. With much of the city's Catholic population living in the outer wards, a second school would "prevent the Catholic children from going to other schools in the winter, as they have done heretofore." The school petition in 1806 was referred to a committee chaired by Richard Riker and which included Francis Cooper. The legislature passed the bill without opposition, and St. Peter's was ordered to be paid a "like sum as was paid to the other congregations" for the purposes of education. Their new political stature enabled Catholics to draw on the resources of the state to educate their children as members of other churches had done previously.[28]

■ ■ ■

Commenting on the accommodation that the legislature had made specifically for Catholics in altering the oath of office, Father Hurley of St. Peter's said: "from this we may date the epoch of Catholic respectability in this state." Tempering his optimism slightly, the priest cautioned that "it only remains for us to deprecate most earnestly whatever might tend to retard its progress." The Catholic campaign to remove barriers that they found discriminatory was achieved with the support of a broad cross section of their number: clergy and laity, Federalists and Republicans, merchants and laborers.

Only a minority of Catholics in New York were positioned, however, to take advantage of this opportunity. Catholic women and enslaved people were still excluded from the formal political community for reasons that extended beyond their religion. Impoverished Irish immigrants, too, still faced enormous cultural barriers to gaining broad acceptance as citizens; Francis Cooper, after all, was of German, not Irish, ancestry. However, with Cooper's election the alteration of the oath of office to accommodate them, and the granting of state funds for their schools, Catholics in New York had overcome the legal and political barriers that had prevented their full participation in the state's public life. For the first time in twenty years, Catholics secured the support of influential allies who were willing to advance their interests in the political arena. They were also becoming part of an urban republicanism that was proving to be much different from the rural Anti-Federalists in regards to the political aspirations of Catholics. The growing alliance of Catholics with Atlantic Republicans illustrated how American politics had changed since the revolution and the debate over the federal Constitution. The fear of papal tyranny no longer motivated the state's more avowedly egalitarian party, or at least a leading faction of it.[29]

By the early nineteenth century, Catholics had also acquired new political foes. The Federalists, unable to conceive of poor Irish immigrants as their political equals, had employed a political strategy that, if successful, would have effectively denied the benefits of full citizenship to Catholics. Nationalist Republicans also harbored a current of resentment toward Catholics that was rooted in suspicion of all things European. Their rivals, the Atlantic Republicans, by championing the cause of Catholics, incurred the criticism of these more nativist Republicans. This disagreement over the role of Catholics in the state's political life would continue to be a source of division among New York's factious Republicans.

Catholics had overcome the ban on their holding state office with the assistance of exiled English and Irish Republicans, most of whom were from the Protestant tradition. They understood the exclusion of Catholics from public office, however, as essentially a secular problem. Their political ethos emphasized the building of a new political order that included a sharp division between church and state, one in which sectarian loyalties would be a private matter. Even as Pius VII retained his tenuous hold on the papacy, some of those most inclined to reject the very idea of a pope fought for the right of his co-religionists in the United States to be both uncompromised communicants of the Catholic Church and unbowed citizens of the American republic.

# CHAPTER 6

# "A Middle Party?"
## Catholics and Republican Nationalism

As the only Catholic Church among the many houses of worship in New York City, St. Peter's had enjoyed two decades of general peace since its founding in the 1780s. That period of quietude was interrupted quite suddenly at Christmas in 1806. Midnight Mass on Christmas Eve in the nineteenth century was the occasion for elaborate, public processions and ceremonies in predominantly Catholic nations. In New York City in the early nineteenth century, however, such open displays of Catholicism were not held, "lest the novelty, by attracting crowds at an untimely hour of the night, might terminate in broils and riots." This reticence on the part of Catholics did not prevent about fifty members of a gang of native-born Protestants, known as the Highbinders, from gathering at St. Peter's around midnight on Christmas Eve in the hopes of seeing Catholic rituals for themselves. The Highbinders, disappointed to find that no part of the service at St. Peter's was to be held outside, demanded noisily that the doors of St. Peter's be opened so that they could see what was happening inside the church. Some of the parishioners became alarmed and called for Andrew Morris to come immediately. Morris, who had just been reelected as an assistant alderman from the city's first ward a month earlier, was able to persuade the gang to disperse without harming person or property.[1]

The next day, on Christmas, a number of Irish Catholics, fearing that the Highbinders might return, armed themselves and surrounded St. Peter's. Come back the Highbinders did, and a melee ensued in which Catholics fought with the Highbinders "from the door of the church to Irish town." "Irish town" was the sixth ward, where many poor immigrant Irish Catholics lived. During the brawl, one of the Irish Catholics apparently stabbed to death Christopher Newfanger, a member of the city watch. This enraged the Highbinders, who roamed through the sixth ward destroying Irish grogshops. Order was only restored when a large contingent of the city's watch, led by Mayor DeWitt Clinton, arrived on the scene. Ten Irish Catholic men were subsequently arrested for riot and assault, all of whom were residents of the sixth ward. John Brown, John McCosker, and Patrick Waters were grocers; Patrick Curran, John McGown, Michael Dunn (acquitted of the charges), and Luke Whim (convicted) were laborers; John Hanley, also acquitted, was a mason; Michael Conner was a mariner and Thomas Henry was a cordwainer.[2]

The various political factions and parties in New York responded to the fracas in ways that reflected their relationship to Catholics. DeWitt Clinton's initial reaction was to take the Highbinders to task for "insulting the congregation of the Roman Catholic Church." Clinton also offered a reward to anyone who identified the "leaders of the disturbances at the Roman Catholic Church." The disturbance at St. Peter's came less than a year after Clinton had been instrumental in changing the oath of office in the state legislature. Catholics now recognized him as an ally; one parishioner of St. Peter's, Elizabeth Seton, remarking on the threat to St. Peter's and Clinton's reaction to it, said that "they say it is high time the Cross is pulled down, but the mayor has issued a proclamation to check the evil." As Mayor, Clinton had responsibilities to the larger community as well, and so he denounced the killing of Christopher Newfanger, the watchman, and offered a reward for any person naming the guilty parties. Nationalist Republicans, however, refused to point the finger of blame at the Highbinders, noting cautiously that "many rumours are in circulation with respect to the causes of these disgraceful and bloody tumults," and that "it is perhaps impossible to ascertain the true state of facts." That faction, whose leader was once Aaron Burr, now had a new chief in Governor Morgan Lewis. He had been elected in 1804, with the help of the Clinton faction, over Burr, who ran as a Federalist. Disputes over patronage and the chartering of banks led to a rift in which, as one Federalist observer put it, "the Clintonians have excommunicated him (Lewis) from the democratic church." The Atlantic Republicans now referred to this faction as Lewisites, or occasionally the Quids (as in Quidum Tertum, "the third way"); nationalist Republicans preferred to call themselves the Independent Republicans.[3]

Despite their claims to be the champions of religion in American life, New York Federalists did not condemn the mob's menacing of St. Peter's that had sparked the bloodshed. They were more concerned about the threat to civil peace that they saw arising from the Catholics who organized to defend their church. They observed that "the blood of lower class Irish (great numbers of whom are Catholic) . . . was fired," adding that at one point in the melee, "nearly a hundred Irishmen appeared at a certain signal." The Federalists' concern for religion in the abstract was overridden once more by their fear of Irish Catholics as a poor and disorderly people who threatened the well-being and stability of society. The disturbances surrounding the midnight Mass at St. Peter's showed that Catholics remained under the threat of open hostility to their faith. The now outlawed parading of the effigy of St. Patrick in the street of Manhattan had turned into something more serious. It must have been disappointing to the parishioners at the city's lone Catholic Church that only one political faction was willing to condemn the infringement of their religious liberty on Christmas Eve. Antipathy toward Catholicism, despite all the progress toward religious and civic equality over the past twenty-five years that Catholics had enjoyed, stubbornly remained a part of New York's political culture.[4]

## THE AMERICAN PARTY AND THE ELECTION OF 1807

In the aftermath of the riot, the Federalists and nationalist Republicans together tried to make a political issue of both the violent Catholic reaction to the menacing of their church and a general fear of the growing influence of foreigners and Catholics in New York politics. The two took the step in 1807 of forming the "American" party in New York City around nationalist and nativist themes. In most states that year, the growing tension between the United States and Britain, which included serious talk of an embargo on all American goods, was the primary issue. In New York in 1807, the embargo had to compete with the question of the place of immigrants and Catholics in the politics of the city and state. Historians have generally located the emergence of Catholics as a major force in public affairs in the antebellum period; one scholar has argued that Irish Catholics in the middle of the nineteenth century gave "American politics its fundamental structure." Catholics became the focus of electoral politics much sooner in New York, in part due to the volatile history of Catholicism there.[5]

The Independent Republicans, as the Republican wing of the new party called itself, turned to nationalist and nativist appeals in their efforts to win the support of Protestant New Yorkers. In criticizing the alliance between DeWitt Clinton and Catholics as an imbalanced, patron-client arrangement that was improper for a republican society, they declared that "It is time to distrust those whose every word and action is in accordance with the wishes and views of a man upon whom they are entirely *dependent*." Nationalist Republicans emphasized that an inordinate number of those associated with Clinton and the radical émigrés were themselves immigrants who needed to be schooled in the ways of American republicanism. "It is full time for native Americans to teach the refuse of Europe, . . . that we are equal to the task of preserving those liberties which our fathers have secured to us with toil and blood." Boasting that the core of their support was "our old tried patriots—and our independent yeomanry," the nationalist Republicans argued that in stark contrast to the faction led by DeWitt Clinton, they represented New York's legitimate Republicans. The Republican "Americans" stated bluntly that the central question of the campaign was "whether we are to govern ourselves, or whether we are to be governed by persons under foreign influence?" They appealed to native-born voters by asking if the citizens of the American republic would be forced "tacitly to bow down before an *Irish representation?*" In singling out Irish Catholic immigrants, they accused them of drunkenness and fighting, of stocking "our state prison with convicts," and of being favored by DeWitt Clinton with licenses for cartmen at the expense of "respectable and industrious Americans." They also politicized the melee at St. Peter's the previous Christmas by taunting Catholics: "What class of people disturb the public peace with riots and murder our watchmen? The Irish." This last remark must have been particularly offensive to Catholics in New York, as the parishioners of St. Peter's believed themselves to have been protecting their church at Christmastime after it had been menaced by a mob.[6]

Federalists employed their own patriotic rhetoric in support of the new American Party coalition. Their clear intent was to divide New Yorkers into two camps; one native born, the other consisting of immigrants and Catholics. They declared of their effort that "We expect every true AMERICAN, to whatever party he may belong, to come out and give it his support." Federalists denounced the Atlantic Republicans as a "*conspiracy of foreigners,* leagued with an unworthy faction of our own," opposed by themselves, the "*Americans* and the sons of *Americans,* who achieved our independence."[7]

Although Federalist and nationalist Republicans had united to present a joint ticket to the New York City electorate for state legislative offices, they each pursued different strategies toward Catholics. The Federalists' approach was more complicated. Unlike their Republican allies, they actively sought the votes of Catholics. They placed

Andrew Morris, the Federalist alderman and trustee at St. Peter's, on the American ticket as a candidate for the Assembly, marking the first time that Federalists had nominated a Catholic for state office. Federalists then drew attention to Morris's candidacy in the hopes of attracting his co-religionists to the American ticket. They presented Morris's nomination much as they had his candidacy for city council, as less an endorsement of Catholics as a whole than as the promotion of an accomplished individual to higher office. And New York's Irish Catholics, Federalists suggested, should have been grateful for this act of largesse. Federalists pointed out with approval those Catholics who they claimed had shown the proper gratitude for Morris's nomination: "They value as they ought the distinction which has been shewn to their respectable countryman Andrew Morris, by placing him in one Ticket with the selected men of the county for worth, talents and integrity." Federalists told Irish Catholics that "you cannot be insensible to the honour done to your old country by the nomination of Mr. Morris." One longtime Catholic resident of New York refuted the notion that Federalists had been hostile to Catholics: "I never remember to see or hear any bad done us by the Federalists; on the contrary they were always good and kind to us." The tone of his remarks were of one who thought of the Federalists not as equals or partners, but rather as patrons or benevolent superiors.[8]

For the first time, Federalists customized their traditional advocacy of Christianity specifically for Catholics. Their goal here was to encourage Catholics to view politics primarily through the prism of religion. If Catholics did so, Federalists expected, and with good reason, that it would redound to their benefit. They especially wanted to use religion to drive a wedge between Catholics and radical, more secular Republicans, including United Irish exiles. One Federalist decried these Republicans as "men who had abandoned the Crucifix, the Bible and the Christian Altar to keep Paine's Rights of Man, and Age of Reason." Another Federalist, writing under the name of "A Real Roman Catholic" to "the Roman Catholics," emphasized the irreligious nature of the Atlantic Republicans, denouncing them as "Deists and Atheists, who fly in the face of God, deny Jesus Christ, laugh at the Cross, and have abjured all religion—openly too, *except at election times*, when the Devils of Hell (for the Clintonians are) want to get your votes." He maintained that the dark secret of the Clintons and their radical allies was their atheism. DeWitt Clinton himself was a member of the "Illuminati," the allegation continued. The Catholic Federalist also took the opportunity to remind his fellow Catholics of one Atlantic Republican who had been openly hostile to their church. "There was a runagate [renegade] Priest of the name of Driscoll, an Irishman, very deep in the business: He published a book called 'The Temple of Reason;'—Just as bad, almost, as Tom Paine's Age of Reason." The Catholic Federalist concluded his invective against the Atlantic Republicans by urging his co-religionists to reject the party of "infidels, atheists, deists, antichrists." They should instead support "Andrew Morris—and turn your back upon the devil and all his works, and so may God, and his Blessed Son, that died for our sins, bless you." Federalists also reminded Catholics of the positive connections between them, pointing out that Andrew Morris had chaired the meeting at St. Peter's at which Catholics wrote their petition to the legislature the previous year. They urged the parishioners of St. Peter's to follow the lead of their clergy and support the Federalist ticket, as "Bishop Carroll and all regular and most respectable Dignatories of your church are federalists." Federalists asked Catholics "would your most esteemed and reverend pastors connect themselves with those who were, as the *Citizen* describes Federalists to be, your 'oppressors and persecutors?'" This would seem to be an effective line of argument, as Federalists here fairly described the way most of the Catholic clergy understood American politics in the early republic.[9]

Turning to the more distant past, Federalists said that when Andrew Morris had been leading the drive to raise funds to build St. Peter's in the 1780s, "his federal friends subscribed liberally and

largely towards it." One prominent individual who was not so generous at the time, Federalists claimed, was George Clinton, then governor of New York. "Governor Clinton is a man of immense wealth,
and yet he refused to give a penny towards so laudable an object."
Such reluctance on Clinton's part would have been in keeping with
the politics of the party he led, the popular Whigs, who formed the
core of Anti-Federalism in the 1780s. Federalists tried to make a
major issue of George Clinton's stinginess twenty years in the past,
when they put this question to Catholic voters: "And this Clinton
party now dare address themselves to you and represent themselves
as your exclusive friends and the Federalists as your oppressors and
persecutors?" It is not likely, however, that many Catholics would
have found this particular line of argument persuasive. The Clintons
and others had undergone a dramatic transformation in their attitude
toward Catholics since the 1780s; and as the oath debate in the legislature demonstrated quite clearly, so had the Federalists.[10]

Casting their lot with nationalist Republicans and the American
Party, however, made it harder for the Federalists to woo Catholics
away from Atlantic Republicans. They also undercut their own efforts to do so by employing ethnic stereotypes against Irish Catholics. Federalists in 1807 satirically portrayed Gaelic Irish immigrants
as prone to violence and disorder and bent on disrupting American
elections: "The *Alien Regiment* is under orders to be aiding and as-
sisting with their SHELALAHS." Shillelagh was a Gaelic word that
entered the English language in the late eighteenth century as a syn-
onym for cudgel. Federalists also accused "Irish democrats," of
fighting with "a small bit of white paper in their hats to distinguish
one another by" during their brawls. They described the Atlantic
Republicans as "Irish Jacobins" and "French Sansculottes" who were
preparing to seize America for themselves.[11]

The Federalists' fear of disorder, colored by a certain class bias,
made it difficult for them to accept Catholics as full members of the
polity. The case of Elizabeth Ann Seton, who was born to an affluent

Episcopalian New York family and later married into another, illustrated these tensions between Federalists and Catholics. As a young widow, she attended Mass at St. Peter's, where Andrew Morris invited her and her children to join him in the family's pew. Despite the relatively high social standing of a few members of the parish, one of New York's "most respectable" inhabitants told Seton that "a person might frequent the house of a professed Deist, but to consort with Catholics was perfectly horrifying." While her conversion to Catholicism was met by her family and social circle with surprise and puzzlement, it was Elizabeth Seton's role in her sister-in-law Cecilia Seton's decision to join the Catholic Church that caused her more serious problems. Seton's own family denounced her as a "masked missionary, a disturber of the peace of families, a female Jesuit." Upon Cecilia's conversion, Elizabeth Seton was cut out of the wills of two of her wealthiest relatives. She was now seen by her family and Protestant friends not as a widow making wrong choices out of grief, but rather as a dangerous woman who was persuading others to follow her lead. And women, the Setons and others feared, were especially vulnerable to the allure of the Catholic Church's mysticism and superstition.[12]

Although many of them probably had a stronger aversion to Catholicism on strictly religious grounds than did the majority of Federalists, Atlantic Republicans put aside those misgivings about Catholicism once more in 1807. In seeking to retain the support of Catholics, they emphasized not religion so much as politics, ethnicity, and history. Atlantic Republicans matched the new American coalition's nomination of Andrew Morris by again placing Francis Cooper on their ticket. In their own public letters addressed "To the Roman Catholics," Atlantic Republicans dismissed the nomination of Morris by their opponents as a cynical ploy, one born "in the hope of dividing your votes, and not from respect for you." They acknowledged Morris's personal virtues, but expressed disappointment that he would allow his name to be placed "on the Tory ticket." The Atlantic Republicans warned Catholics that "the federal party, that party whose candidate Mr. Morris is, are your oppressors and persecutors."[13]

Atlantic Republicans wanted Catholics to envision a re-Federalized America in which some variant of Protestantism was established by law and given a prominence over and above their own faith. The model of such a grim society was readily available: England. New York Republicans sought to draw parallels between the relationship of Catholics to the Protestant establishment in England with that of Catholics to Federalists in America, whom they derided as the "British ticket." To drive home that point, they included in their appeals to Catholics an extended excerpt of the English anti-Catholic penal laws from Blackstone's *Commentaries*. The Atlantic Republicans also accused the Federalists of favoring a state religion, adding that "it is unnecessary to say what religious denomination would have been established." But as a result of the Republican victory of 1800, in which, Atlantic Republicans told Catholics, "you bore an honourable and distinguished part, cut up by the roots church ascendancy *as established by law,* and placed all religious sects upon an equal footing." The Atlantic Republicans wanted Catholics to see them as their natural allies in the ongoing battle to preserve a genuine republicanism, one that included freedom from religious coercion. They used other examples from Europe to encourage Catholics to believe that religious and political tyranny in America could become linked in the way that they had been in Ireland.[14]

The battle just the year before in the state legislature over the oath of office gave Atlantic Republicans credibility with Catholic voters. They reminded them that "your petition was introduced into the Senate by Mr. Clinton, a name dear to freedom and its advocates." They contrasted Clinton's advocacy for reforming the oath with Federalist opposition. Not only had their rivals *"opposed and voted against it!* They did more; they treated your church—your ministers, and yourselves with marked disrespect. They represented you as wretches unfit to live in civil society—as rebels against God and man." The Atlantic Republicans sought to persuade Catholics that despite the Federalists' claims to be the champions of religion, when the key moment came they had disregarded Catholics on those very grounds. "Catholics! For your religion the Federalists rejected you from seats in the legislature of this state. The Republicans abolished the law by which you were rejected." As the Atlantic Republicans would have it, "the FEDERALISTS abused your RELIGION—vilified your Reverend Ministers—spoke of you as cut throats, and roundly asserted that your religion taught you to bathe your hands in the blood of your fellow citizens!" This latter reference may be to the riots that arose from the menacing of St. Peter's at Christmastime 1806, which had in fact come after the debate in the legislature over the oath of office. Even so, Atlantic Republicans wanted Catholics to think of Federalists as fearing and mistrusting them to the point where they would revive old fears, ones that were especially old in New York, about whether Catholics could be trusted to be legitimate members of the body politic.[15]

Atlantic Republicans continued their efforts to get Irish Catholics to see politics in New York as a continuation of the history of the land of their birth. "Catholics! A TORY is a TORY all the world over. In the abuse and persecution of your religion here by the FEDERALISTS, you see the principles and the cruelty of the BRITISH GOVERNMENT." Without their efforts, the Atlantic Republicans claimed, the political restrictions against Catholics enacted in the 1770s and 1780s would have become permanent. "They [the Republicans] have destroyed the invidious distinction which existed, and which the *Federalists* sought to perpetuate against you." Although they basically represented themselves as Catholics' *political* allies, the Atlantic Republicans also invoked religion at the end of the campaign. They asserted that by giving Republicans their votes, Catholics were acting on behalf of their faith. "Irishmen! Catholics! In opposing the BRITISH PARTY, you support the cause of Republicanism,

of Religion, and of God." The Atlantic Republicans left Catholics to
their religion, neither seeking to convert them to Protestantism nor
trying to lure them away from Christianity entirely and make deists
of them.[16]

Federalists were clearly on the defensive due to their opposition
the previous year to changing the oath, and they had little choice but
to respond specifically to some of the charges made against them.
They contended that in the case of Ireland, most of the penal laws
had been repealed and the rest are "never rigidly executed." In light
of the loyalty of Irish Catholics and their priests to the papacy, and
the constant designs of France and Spain to "introduce a Roman
Catholic Government" to England, Federalists maintained that the
repression of Catholics in Ireland was not entirely unreasonable.
They also pointed out that the English had relaxed the penal laws
after the demise of the Catholic Stuarts. All this may have been true,
but the immediate political point was that the Federalists found
themselves in the difficult position of defending English rule in Ireland. This made it all the more difficult for them to win many Catholic votes in New York because so many of them were Irish. United
Irishman William Sampson moved to New York in time for the 1807
campaign and promptly joined the Atlantic Republicans. He wrote
his wife, Grace Clarke Sampson, that "the Irish are extolled by the
Republican party and abused by that which looks toward England."
Closer to home, Federalists had to concede that two members of their
party had led the opposition to changing the oath of office in 1806.
That opposition was based on legal principles rather than religious
bigotry, they contended. The two "lawyers," as the Federalists referred to William W. Van Ness and Abraham Van Vechten, had spo-
ken against DeWitt Clinton's bill reforming the oath because they
"doubted whether it could pass, consistent with our constitution."
This was slightly misleading, however, as the bill was designed to
overturn a statute that had not originally been in the New York Constitution, although that same language had appeared elsewhere in the
document.[17]

Both wings of the new American Party were intent on limiting the influence of radical exiles in New York politics. Nationalist Republicans linked James Cheetham with proverbial Catholic treachery by describing him as a "Guy Faux of a conspirator," a subtle reminder of the political connections between Catholics and the Atlantic Republicans. They also accused Thomas Addis Emmet, a leader of the Hibernian Provident Society, of converting that charitable organization into a front for radical émigré politics. A member of the Hibernians had introduced a resolution demanding the expulsion of any member who voted for Andrew Morris, who in joining the Federalists, "had forfeited all pretensions to their esteem." Nationalist Republicans linked the Hibernian society to Catholic authoritarianism simultaneously as they defended Morris: "We find it denouncing our most honorable and patriotic citizens; nay, more, issuing its Bulls of excommunication to whoever shall support or adhere to them." One Catholic Federalist urged his co-religionists to "rescue your national character from the foul aspersions to which the *Provident Hibernian Conspiracy* have done."[18]

The legacy of Irish politics was at work in other ways in New York in 1807. Rufus King was on the American ticket, and Thomas Addis Emmet and William MacNeven, two former United Irishmen, objected strongly to his candidacy. Atlantic Republicans made public a letter that Emmet had written to King that spring. The Irish exile revived the accusations that King had been a pro-British ambassador during the 1798 uprising and had tried to prevent Irish rebels from finding sanctuary in the United States. King did not respond publicly to the charges, now nearly a decade old, although he denied them in private. The Atlantic Republicans linked King with English tyranny in Ireland, describing his actions toward the United Irishmen as "unpatriotic, cruel and wicked." At the same time they portrayed the United Irishmen as noble freedom fighters for *all* the Irish people, both Protestant and Catholic.[19]

Federalists contested this characterization of the United Irishmen. Far from being martyrs for the cause of Irish freedom, they claimed, the United Irishmen who were executed by British authorities were nothing more than traitors to their country, guilty of "the most horrid crimes against social order itself." These rebels, Federalists insisted, had roused a contented Gaelic peasantry, proclaiming "reform and *Catholic emancipation* while in reality they meant *separation and democracy.*" If by separation they meant Irish independence from England, Federalists were not ready to support for the Irish that which Americans had fought for and won just thirty years earlier. They also argued that without the demagoguery of the United Irish in 1798, the long-suffering Irish people would have been spared this latest calamity. "Mr. Emmet found the peasant and the citizen at peace beneath their roots; Mr. Emmet harangued them into a belief of grievances." Therefore, the claims of Emmet, MacNeven, and others to speak for the Irish nation were a fiction, one that the Federalists implied that the Atlantic Republicans were only too eager to perpetuate on American soil for their own purposes. Federalists did seek the support of those they described as "worthy, respectable *Anti-Jacobin Irish,*" and proclaimed themselves to be liberal toward "foreigners of good private character and correct views."[20]

On the Sunday before the election, Atlantic Republicans handed copies of their campaign appeals to Catholics attending Mass at St. Peter's. They also placed several of the letters on the pillars at the entrance to the church. Federalists professed shock at this mixture of politics and religion, asking, "Is the Sabbath thus to be profaned and the Roman Catholic Church turned into a Beer House?" They said that such an outrage had never occurred before in the city, and expressed the hope that Catholics "will meet it with that just indignation it merits." Federalists tried to get Catholics to concentrate on the Atlantic Republicans' presumptive disrespect for their religion in this instance, rather than the political content of the letter in question. Their Republican allies echoed this theme, asking if the Atlantic Republicans had displayed the proper "reverence for divine laws or shew a due respect towards that day of Holy Rest?"[21]

The American Party's case that religious considerations should make Catholics the enemies of the Atlantic Republicans was a difficult one to make. The alliance of most of the Catholic laity with these Republicans had not resulted in any large-scale defections from the faith, as Catholic priests had feared might happen during the height of the French Revolution in the 1790s. Although Father Anthony Kohlmann was initially discouraged at the seeming indifference of Catholics in New York toward their religion when he arrived to become pastor of St. Peter's in 1807, two years later he counted 16,000 Catholics in the parish. Pope Pius VII, acting on the recommendation of Bishop John Carroll of Baltimore, named New York as one of four new dioceses in the United States in 1808, with New York City as its seat. Soon after that, moreover, Father Kohlmann reported to his superiors that Catholicism was now flourishing: "The communion-rail daily filled, though deserted before."[22]

In contrast to the clergy's fear of irreligion in the 1790s, Father Kohlmann was an early Catholic critic of American materialism. He spoke of a successful merchant, who with great regret, came to the realization that "til now I have been a man of great business but neglecting the only business for which I am in this world." "Men of business" were among those he listed as society's greatest sinners. This was a subtle critique of Federalism, as most wealthy merchants, including those at St. Peter's, belonged to that party. At the same time, the Republicans' successful efforts to change the oath of office had made it easier for ambitious Catholics to remain in the church. Ethnic and class politics in the end counted more than religion in 1807. The alliance between the Federalists and the nationalist Republicans failed in New York City, where the Atlantic Republican Assembly ticket was elected. Across the state, their candidate for governor, Daniel Tompkins, defeated Morgan Lewis, who had been supported by the nationalists. Jubilant Irish immigrants extended the campaign to the streets in celebration of the victory by their Republicans. A crowd of them went to the homes of defeated Federalist candidates Rufus King and Andrew Morris, knocked on the doors and windows, denounced the occupants, and raised three cheers for *"Emmet* and Liberty!"[23]

Federalists angrily blamed their defeat on the votes of immigrants. They claimed to have overheard one Clinton ally boasting of the large numbers of them who had been naturalized in the months leading up to the election. Republicans conceded that between January and May of 1807, the New York City courts had indeed naturalized about 2,000 Irish immigrants. "Half the voters in one ward Foreigners!" was one complaint typical of Federalist disgust. They feared that the United States was already a different nation, racially and ethnically, from that which it had been at the time of its founding. The nation, Federalists lamented, had been transformed into a "multifarious heterogenous compound—a Gallo-Hibernico-Hispanico-Corsicano race, living where once lived Americans. Oh, rare Americans!" They found the Irish celebrations of the victory, with their *huzzahs* for Thomas Emmet, particularly vexing. "A foreigner of three years standing is brayed up to the skies, while your Washington and your Hamilton are forgotten." Federalists further sensed that their influence in New York City was slipping away, and even forging an alliance with one faction of Republicans had done little to stem the tide. They had a ready explanation for how the political character of the young nation was changing. "Let it be remembered, that had Americans alone voted, the result would have been as it ought to be." Because of a concerted effort by the growing number of Catholics and immigrants to claim political equality for themselves, the problem for the Federalists and their Republican allies was that their definition of just who was an "American" was becoming too narrow. The Atlantic Republicans were not free of prejudices, however, and those prejudices influenced their own analysis of the elections. In characterizing their opponents as a "Quadruple alliance" consisting of "the Feds, Burrites, Lewisites and Negroes," they used race as one way to define themselves in opposition to the Federalists.

Their commitment to protecting the political rights of Catholics did not extend to Americans of African ancestry. At this early moment in nineteenth-century American politics, Irish Catholics and African-Americans were already on opposing sides of New York's partisan divide.[24]

Atlantic Republicans continued to denounce the Federalists as irredeemably hostile to Catholics even after the balloting was over. Gloating over their victory, they boasted that the Federalists had nominated Andrew Morris in the hope of securing the votes of Catholics, but that "not one of whom, and it is mentioned in their honor, gave him a vote." Although this was surely an exaggeration, the Atlantic Republicans were right in believing that their own strategy regarding Catholics had succeeded. They were also happy to point out that Morris had received the fewest votes of any candidate on the American ticket, taunting the Federalists by asking if this was because "he was a *Catholic*?" As it happened, however, Francis Cooper received the lowest vote total of the nine winning Republican candidates, an inconvenient fact that the Atlantic Republicans overlooked. In any event, most Catholic voters were now even more firmly linked to the Atlantic Republicans. Given the history of their religion in New York, Catholics were fortunate to have such allies.[25]

THE WIDENING SCHISM BETWEEN CATHOLICS AND REPUBLICANS

After the Atlantic Republicans' sweeping victory in 1807, Catholics by most measures would seem to have become an important part of the Republican coalition. The next year, the party, now led once again by DeWitt Clinton, re-nominated Francis Cooper for the Assembly. He and his Republican colleagues in New York City won another easy victory. In the rest of the state, however, the Federalists won most of the counties. That party was enjoying a revival, especially across much of New England and New York. This resurgence stemmed in part from widespread opposition to President Thomas Jefferson's drastic embargo policy, under which no goods could be exported from the United States. After the 1808 elections, Federalists contrasted the electorate in New York City with that of the rest of the state, declaring that an immigrant "mob consisting principally of day laborers, . . . now govern the city of New-York in its elections. Farmers! It is on you the country must depend for our political salvation." Federalists also attributed their defeat in New York City to corruption, alleging that the Atlantic Republicans continued to naturalize Irish immigrants improperly, and that at the polls, some Irish immigrants had voted with citizenship certificates that belonged to others. After the elections in 1808, Irish Republicans and Federalists fought in the streets of New York; one melee cost two men their lives.[26]

The alliance that Catholics had forged with the Atlantic Republicans had secured them a greater measure of political equality; it had also, however, won them the enmity of nationalist Republicans and the Federalists. That this was a problem became more apparent when the Atlantic Republicans lost control over the party to their Republican rivals in New York City in the fall of 1808. The attitudes of this faction of Republicans toward Catholics threatened to drive the majority of them out of the party and toward the Federalists, or perhaps even lead them to form their own party. One of the key issues of contention between the competing factions of Republicans was the Atlantic Republicans, continuing support for the political aspirations of Irish Catholics. At the decisive meeting of the Republican General Committee in September of 1808 at Martling's Tavern, nationalist Republicans yelled "*turn out the Irish*, down the damn'd Irish— hustle the Clintonians." The latter complained afterwards that "the Republicans of Irish birth have, as usual, partaken largely of the abuse lavished on the Republican party by their enemies the Quids." This was hardly a surprise, said one sympathetic Republican to Irish Catholics, as "known as you are to be friends of Gov. Clinton, you are thus for being so scandalously attacked by the adherents of Mr. Madison."[27]

National politics played its part in this latest round of the Republican rivalry. George Clinton, the aging vice president, was the choice of those in the party associated with his family, while their Republican opponents were for the eventual nominee, James Madison. Both factions claimed the title of Republicans. Beginning in 1808, the Atlantic Republicans referred to their opponents as Madisonians or Martlingites, after Abraham Martling's tavern, where they met. Supporters of DeWitt Clinton chided Madison as the beneficiary of a "cabal nomination," one which could only be secured in a secret caucus and that was incapable of being "directly procured in the great Republican wards of the city" where their faction enjoyed strong support, especially among immigrants and Catholics. The supporters of Madison's candidacy included many who had previously been in what the Atlantic Republicans had labeled the Burrite, Livingston, Lewisite and Quid factions. One key to the success of the nationalist Republicans was the growing strength of the Tammany Society in the politics of New York City. The native-born Protestant braves and sachems of Tammany continued to be cool toward the political aspirations of Catholics and immigrants. Reflecting this ethnic and religious tension, Francis Cooper denounced Tammany as secretive and unrepublican, saying that he "thought it disgraceful for any man to be a member of it." The Atlantic Republicans also alleged that another Tammany leader, Abraham Stagg, had sworn that he was *"determined to exert himself to put down the Irish,"* for they were "a turbulent set of beings," and that he would personally "blackball" any Irishmen who tried to join the society.[28]

The change in leadership of the Republicans did not bode well for Catholics. The Atlantic Republicans compared the Republicans supporting James Madison to the Federalists: "In Federal days, in the reign of terror, when British persecution seemed to pursue you even here, you were termed hordes of 'Wild Irish.' In the name of Mr.

Madison, you are insultingly called the 'half-clothed regiment of Pat McKay!' What is the difference between Federalism and Madisonianism?''

Nationalists had singled out Patrick McKay, a leading Irish Catholic Republican in New York City. Jacob Vandervoort, a supporter of Madison and a Tammany leader, said that "Pat McKay and his followers might go where they chose; that Republicans [meaning the nationalists] could do without them; and that if they were like McKay, it was no matter where they went.'' The supporters of George Clinton defended McKay, a grocer in a neighborhood where many Irish immigrants lived, as a "respectable citizen and substantial freeholder, [who] has uniformly been and is now one of the most useful, zealous and discriminating republicans among us.''[29]

Those Republicans who had supported the successful candidacy of James Madison emphasized patriotic and nationalist themes the following spring in the 1809 campaign. Having won control of the Republican party, the nationalists now turned their rhetoric on their erstwhile Federalist allies. The nationalists presented their candidates as the "Republican Eagle and Seventy-Six Ticket" and characterized the Federalists as the "Tory, Federal, Lion and Unicorn Ticket." They also urged immigrant and Irish Catholic Republicans to rally to their side, urging them to recall the Federalist "reign of terror" when Richard Varick was mayor of the city and the Irish could not "then get a license to keep a tavern or drive a cart." In selecting candidates for state office, however, the Republicans followed the nationalist path. They did not nominate Francis Cooper or any other Catholic for office in 1809. For the first time in five years, there was no Catholic, not even a native-born citizen like Cooper, on the Republican ticket.[30]

The frustration that immigrants, especially Irish Catholics, felt over their exclusion from office reached a peak in 1809. A citywide meeting of the "Adopted Republican Citizens" passed a resolution lamenting that the party had passed them over once again. "Look at the ward committees, read over their names and Lo! how entirely, and with what caution you have been excluded." The "adopted Republicans" protested that "we have been systematically excluded from the general Republican committee." After years of associating Federalism in America with British and Protestant authority in Ireland, some Irish Catholics in New York decided that the nationalist Republicans now leading the party were no better than either. One concluded sadly that "whether tyranny approaches in the form of a Lord Lieutenant, or under the garb of a Republican demagogue, its result is slavery still." Despite their own hostility to Federalism, and their record of supporting Republican principles and candidates, the immigrants complained that "we are denominated foreigners and treated as slaves" within their own party. "Fitzgerald," an Irish Republican, denounced the nativism of the party's current leaders, charging that the Republican nominating committee had brazenly declared that "a *foreigner* had no business on an American committee."[31]

Francis Cooper's terms in the Assembly and the reform of the oath of office three years earlier notwithstanding, Catholics in New York, especially the Irish, still considered themselves as political outsiders. Immigrant Republicans in two of New York City's wards passed their own resolutions in support of the one that the citywide meeting had crafted. In the ninth ward, where Patrick McKay was now a leader, immigrant and Catholic Republicans made clear their determination "not [to] support, at the approaching election, the ticket nominated by the committee." The heavily Irish sixth ward adopted a similar resolution. Immigrant Republicans at a general meeting declared that "we will not support a ticket, in the formation of which we have been excluded." They bluntly told their fellow immigrants that "you will be called on to vote for the Republican ticket. *Vote not at all.*"[32]

Catholics and immigrants made good on their threat not to turn out for the Republican ticket in 1809. Their boycott nearly cost the

the party control of the city's Assembly delegation that year. The citywide margin for Republicans plummeted from 1,094 votes the year before, when the Atlantic Republicans controlled the party, to only 125. Most of the losses were in the immigrant wards, where the majority of the city's Catholics lived. Irish Catholic voters had not turned to the Federalists in their anger at the Republicans, but instead had simply stayed away, in large numbers, from the polls. For encouraging the Irish to do so, Patrick McKay earned special enmity from the nationalist Republicans. They blamed their troubles on a "Clintonian division—a Cheetamite division—a Pat McKay division," and appointed a special committee to investigate the matter.[33]

The fissure between Catholics and Republicans remained open the following year as the nationalists continued to control the party in New York City. To complicate matters for Catholics, DeWitt Clinton made his peace with nationalist Republicans in New York City to safeguard his interests around the state. As part of the deal, Clinton agreed to the demands of his Republican rivals that James Cheetham be stripped of his patronage as a state printer. Having been essentially purged from the Republican ranks, Cheetham plotted his revenge. Part of his plan to weaken the Republicans politically was to drive Catholics away from them. When Francis Cooper received only seven votes out of seventy from the nationalist-dominated Republican nominating committee in 1810, the *American Citizen* charged that Cooper had been rebuffed so decisively "because he is a Catholic. There is no other cause, for a more honest, faithful, and upright man never lived." Cheetham also alleged that a leading nationalist Republican had gone so far in his hostility to Catholicism that he proclaimed that "it was a pity that ROMAN CATHOLICS were allowed to build a church in this city!" Not all of the disaffected immigrant Republicans were Catholic, but the schism became increasingly sectarian. The *American Citizen*, at its inception a decade earlier a radical Republican paper, had now become the political voice of Catholics in New York City. It publicized a remark by John Hopper, a

Republican. He was asked how, given his well-known dislike of the Irish, he could support the candidacy of Robert Swanton, a native of Ireland and the only immigrant on the Republican ticket in 1810. "O, that is another thing—Swanton is a Protestant," he replied. Cheetham denounced Swanton in turn as "having abandoned the rights of his countrymen and become the dupe of their oppressors, he is unworthy of the name *Irishman.*"[34]

Nationalist Republicans tried to heal the rift by nominating Cornelius Heeney, the wealthy Irish Catholic Republican, for the Assembly. But Heeney refused the honor, declaring that he would not be "made a tool of by any party for the purpose of deceiving my countrymen." In exasperation, the Republicans complained that if they successfully recruited an Irish Catholic for the ticket, the candidate was denounced by Cheetham and his allies as a "traitor to his nation and a sycophant to undue influence"; if they nominate no Catholics, they are then rebuked for making "an insult to the great body of adopted citizens." The prior record of the current nationalist Republicans and their predecessors was such that they had trouble convincing Catholics of their sincerity.[35]

Patrick McKay and James Cheetham tried to keep the Catholic issue at the center of the campaign in 1810. McKay wrote an open letter in the *American Citizen* in which he complained that Republican election inspectors were humiliating Catholic voters at the polls by placing paper crosses on the Bibles on which they were sworn in. The thinking behind this tactic, which Cheetham called "an insult which was offered to the Catholic religion," was that Catholics could not be trusted to make a true oath on the Bible alone, and thus the symbol of the cross became necessary to insure their honesty. Party leaders did not respond directly to this charge, although they did concede that "a few republicans have manifested an unbecoming jealousy of the 'adopted citizens.'"[36]

The Republicans were clearly concerned about losing the votes of Catholics and immigrants. They admitted that by remaining neutral in large numbers during elections the previous year, the Irish and others "gave to the Federalists that partial ascendancy" upon which they were now trying to build. Despite their current problems with Catholics, the nationalist Republicans presented themselves as the defenders of *all* European immigrants. They hearkened back to the late eighteenth century, to a time when Republicans had been less divided, reprinting a speech by Edward Livingston, then a Republican member of Congress, against the Federalist alien law. Republicans also reminded New York's "adopted citizens" that Samuel Mitchill, currently on the party's Assembly ticket, had been instrumental in repealing that notorious law in Congress. Nationalist Republicans warned Catholics and immigrants to reject any efforts, whether led by Federalists, Cheetham, or McKay, to organize them into "a middle party" between the two principal ones. Proposing that the Irish had suffered throughout their history due to differences among them, especially religious ones, Republicans writing as "Hibernian" and "Hibernicus" pleaded with Irish New Yorkers to avoid that fate in their new country. They asked the Irish to consider the history of the Republicans and Federalists in the United States. If they did, it would become obvious to them "which party has been the uniform friend and which is the uniform enemy of the emigrants." And to defend themselves from James Cheetham's earlier insult of "Orangeism," they insisted that there is "not an Orangeman in America who is not a Federalist."[37]

With the three most prominent Republican members of St. Peter's—Francis Cooper, Patrick McKay, and Cornelius Heeney—disaffected from them, Republicans could not afford to ignore the feud between themselves and Catholics. They became frustrated at their inability to end the schism, and thought they had discovered the problem, asking: "does Mr. Patrick McKay possess such an undue influence, such an unbounded ascendancy over his countrymen that he can treat them as his vassals?" The Republicans tried to debunk the idea that McKay spoke for the majority of Catholics in New York

City. They circulated handbills publicizing his recent defeat as a candidate for trustee at St. Peter's, and they also attempted to link McKay's failure in the trustee elections to his efforts to lead Catholics away from the Republicans. One writer in the Republican press, signing himself a "Catholic," claimed that McKay had been defeated in his bid for re-election as a trustee because the parish as a whole recognized that he had become "the companion and the dupe of the apostate Cheetham" and "had formerly been a friend, but is now a foe to republicanism, [and] every patriot, every Christian who belonged to our faith, answered Amen." In response, James Cheetham characterized the Republicans' injecting a private, ecclesiastical matter into the public domain for political advantage as "base and unbecoming" and profoundly disrespectful to Catholics and their "ancient place of worship." The *American Citizen* also denied that the trustee election reflected the wider politics of Catholics in the city or state, saying only that it was decided "for reasons with which we are not well acquainted." Cheetham's paper noted that McKay, Francis Cooper, and Cornelius Heeney and the other Republican trustee candidates at St. Peter's were bested by "gentlemen . . . attached to the Federal Party."[38]

The trustee elections at St. Peter's in 1810 paralleled the political comeback that the Federalists were making in New York, as in the previous year they had regained control of the city's Common Council and scored important victories in the state legislative and congressional races. There also remained a Federalist core of lay leaders at St. Peter's that had not lost its influence within the parish. That group still included Dominick Lynch, Thomas Stoughton, and Andrew Morris, all first elected in the eighteenth century; they were joined in 1810 by Michael Roth, a merchant. In their impressive victory that year, the three leading Federalist candidates collected over three hundred votes; none of the Republican candidates, including Cooper, McKay, and Heeney, received even one hundred. The trustee elections was another possible indication that the parishioners at St.

Peter's were turning away from the Republicans and back toward the Federalists. Earlier in the decade, Catholics who were Republicans had won election to the board of trustees; the pendulum now appeared to be swinging in the other direction.[39]

At the end of the civic campaign, Republicans spoke directly to Catholics. Their argument was that "Republicans are the true decided natural friends of Catholics. They have always contended for the free enjoyment of religious opinions, coupled with a perfect equality of civil rights." Nationalist Republicans associated themselves with the effort led by their Atlantic Republican rivals at the time, asking, "who altered the oath to be to be taken by members of the legislature, so that conscientious Catholics might take their seats without a scruple?" They also invoked the name of their long-standing but apparently erstwhile foe, DeWitt Clinton. James Cheetham was no friend of Catholics, they argued, because he was now attacking Clinton, the man who "broke down the barriers which excluded Roman Catholics from the honors of this country."[40]

The Federalists expended little effort to exploit this latest division between Republicans. They did make a rather tepid attempt to win over disaffected immigrant Republicans by appealing to an older sense of unified politics that would bring together New Yorkers of all religions and ethnicities. However, they did not nominate any Catholics in 1810, and unlike in 1807, when Andrew Morris was on their ticket, Federalists made no direct appeals to Catholics. Once again, Federalists were slow to take advantage of an opportunity to win Catholics to their party. Despite the Federalists' seeming indifference toward Catholics, Republicans had become convinced that the Cheetham–McKay faction was in effect supporting the Federalists. In contrast to the year before when they had urged Catholics and immigrants to stay home at election time, Cheetham and McKay called on them to "now ACT" and to "Rush to the polls, and vote down the tyrants." Their meaning was clear, even if they did not mention the Federalists by name: Catholic Republicans could advance their cause only by defeating the nationalists who were currently in control of the party. If that meant supporting the Federalists to do so, then so be it.[41]

The dissident Republicans were partially successful in their effort to damage the party's fortunes. The Federalist congressional candidate won the fourth and ninth wards; Federalist Assembly candidates won the fourth ward and did better in the other largely immigrant wards than Federalists had done previously. Six of the city's eleven-member Assembly delegation were now Federalists; the Republicans blamed their narrow losses in part on the Catholic schism that had divided Republicans. Catholics in a sense had become a "middle party" between Federalists and Republicans, albeit one without power or prestige. They were also once more not represented by any of their own in the state government.[42]

■ ■ ■

After the elections of 1807, it began to seem as if "Catholic" might disappear as a political category among Republicans, and that individual Catholics would become more or less indistinguishable from others in that party. The religious affiliation and foreign birth of most Catholics might, it seemed, no longer set them apart. However, the following year, overtly nationalist Republicans, who counted nativists in their ranks, gained leadership of the party in New York City. Their attitude toward Catholics becoming their political equals ranged from skepticism to outright hostility. And only a minority of Catholics (albeit influential at St. Peter's) were openly identified with the Federalists, a party that feared the poorer Irish Catholics who had immigrated to New York since the revolution.

DeWitt Clinton, Catholics' most important ally during the early nineteenth century in New York, had given priority to improving relations with the nationalist Republicans who led the party in New York City. As a result, the efforts of Catholics to achieve genuine political equality and be accepted as full citizens suffered. Several months after the spring elections of 1810, James Cheetham, the radical exile from England who had become an improbable champion of Catholics in New York, died. He had been prominent among those radical political exiles who had called for Catholics to have the same access to political office as members of other religions, which amounted to a major victory for Catholics. Even so, Catholics remained vulnerable to the effects of the widely held idea that the foreign birth of many of them, combined with the unrepublican character of their church, made it right that they remain political outsiders. Indeed, it may have occurred to parishioners sitting in the pews of New York's Catholic churches in 1810 that despite some important steps forward in the drive of Catholics to be accepted as full-fledged American citizens, they were yet susceptible to the machinations of Tories. In New York, the Tories could appear in the guise of both Federalists and Republicans.

# CHAPTER 7

# "The Great Chain of National Union"
## Catholics and the Republican Triumph

In a brief summary of the history of Catholicism in New York, written in 1810 by an anonymous writer in a distinctly self-congratulatory tone, the ambiguous political status of Catholics in the state went unmentioned. The occasion was the printing of a second edition (the first was published in 1744) of Judge Daniel Horsmanden's *The Trial of John Ury*. During the slave conspiracy of 1741, Ury had been executed as a Catholic priest. In the 1810 preface to Horsmanden's account of the trial, the writer remarked that "after a lapse of nearly three quarters of a century, we look back with astonishment at the panic occasioned by the negro plot, and the rancorous hatred that prevailed against Roman Catholics."[1]

The animosity toward Catholics at that time stemmed not only from Europe, the writer noted, but from New York's unique history. "Our Dutch forefathers, glowing with all the zeal of the early reformers," the writer continued, were encouraged in their antipathy toward Catholics by "the policy of the English government" in the province. The colony's "exposed situation" on the frontier of British America, the proximity of the French ("the natural and ever enduring enemy of England") to the immediate north, and the appeal of Catholic rituals and mysticism to the "senses of the rude savage" all contributed to anti-Catholicism in New York having a special inten-

sity. New Yorkers "born and educated before the American revolution, will recollect how religiously they were taught to abhor the
Pope, Devil and Pretender."[2]

Living in the "more favored and enlightened" era that followed
the American Revolution, as the writer had it, New Yorkers had now
supposedly transcended their earlier hostility to Catholicism. Not all
Catholics agreed, however, that New Yorkers had progressed so dramatically in their attitudes toward their religion. Joseph Coppinger
complained in 1813 that there remained many "illiberal Protestant
ministers (who) sought to keep the flames of superstition alive" and
did so by deriding Catholicism from their pulpits "with all the low
buffoonery of holy ridicule." Optimism about the present was most
credible when the standard for the status of Catholicism in New York
was the hysteria that prevailed in 1741. Just a few years before the
republication of Horsmanden's book, however, a mob had menaced
St. Peter's Church. And in politics, there was still a price to be paid
for being a Catholic. Although the horror of 1741 survived only as a
memory, the legacy of Jacob Leisler's crusade against Catholics had
not yet passed entirely into history.[3]

CATHOLICS AND THE WAR OF 1812

In large part due to the divisions among Republicans, the Federalists
won a decisive victory in 1812 in New York City. At the outset of
that year, in which the second war between the United States and
Britain broke out, Republicans in New York remained at odds. In
addition to the usual disagreements, DeWitt Clinton, with Federalist
support, was challenging Republican incumbent James Madison for
the presidency. For the first time in New York City, Atlantic and
nationalist Republicans each put forward their own slates of candidates. The former nominated Francis Cooper and Thomas Addis
Emmet for the Assembly; the latter put up no Catholic or Irish candidates.

Two rival camps of Republican "adopted citizens" also emerged that year. The competing immigrant groups met in different venues; the nationalists gathered at Martling's Tavern, long a pro-Tammany establishment, while the Atlantic group favored Andrew Dooley's Long Room. Religion was one of the primary ways in which they divided. The Atlantic faction was led by William MacNeven and Dennis McCarthy, both Catholics and members of St. Peter's; the other faction supported the nationalists and was dominated by Protestants, including Robert Swanton, an Irish immigrant. The latter accused William MacNeven of splitting the immigrant vote and thereby helping the Federalists, maintaining that the former United Irishman was as "active in his adopted country to divide Republicans, as he was in his native to unite them!" The Atlantic "adopted citizens" promoted their ticket in the pages of the *Shamrock*. Edward Gillespy, an Irish immigrant who advocated Irish independence and Catholic emancipation, had founded the newspaper that same year. It was in effect a national newspaper for literate Irish immigrants, with readers in several cities, including Albany. With the battling Republican factions spending considerable energy in denouncing each other as Federalists in disguise, they were losing elections in New York City to the real article. Republicans were more successful in the state's rural counties, where there were few immigrants and Catholics to exacerbate the differences among them. Although in New York, with war looming, nationalist Republicans were now embracing Irish immigrants. Religion remained a factor, however, as they promoted Protestants and not Catholics.[4]

The centrality of local and state politics were soon overtaken by the United States's growing conflict with Britain. During the war, the relationship of Catholics to society and the state helped to solidify their claim that they (the men, that is) were entitled to the benefits of full citizenship. Unlike the American Revolution, when Patriots and Tories actively sought to recruit Catholics for their armies, there was little doubt where the loyalties of New York Catholics lay in

1812. The *Shamrock* provided a sounding board for the views of Irish immigrants on the growing crisis with Great Britain. Edward Gillespy's paper was an early advocate of a second war between the U.S. and its former colonial master. One writer in the *Shamrock* said before the fighting had broken out that every Irishman should "exult at the possibility of doing England an essential injury." Although most Irish Catholics probably needed few reminders, the *Shamrock* encouraged them to think of the British as the "natural enemy of Irishmen, of Americans, of republican institutions."[5]

Irish immigrants easily adapted their rituals to a wartime footing. The Hibernian Provident Society held a Fourth of July celebration in 1812 at which revelers carried a banner, decorated with a shamrock and a liberty cap, which was draped over a harp, a symbol of Irish nationalism and culture. The banner read: "The harp: tuned to national spirit: War with Great Britain, the tyrant of the ocean." After the war began, the *Shamrock* changed the symbol on its masthead. Instead of a harp alone, it now featured an American eagle, one festooned with shamrocks in its mouth, an Irish harp on its chest, and arrows and olive branches in each of its claws, after the national symbol of the United States.[6]

The War of 1812 had a considerable impact on domestic politics. Although the *Shamrock* had promised initially that it would be "freed from party bickerings," by 1815 it was printing Republican essays condemning the Federalists for their lukewarm support of the war. One point of contention between the United States and Great Britain that had helped to precipitate the conflict was the British navy's practice of seizing American sailors, many of whom were Irish immigrants, on the grounds that they were rightfully subjects of the British crown. This issue, understandably, was particularly important to Irish immigrants living in the United States. Some Federalists essentially agreed with the British that these sailors were deserters from their homeland with no legitimate claim to American citizenship. This view was in keeping with the Federalists' long-standing ambivalence about the claims of Irish immigrants to be their equals in a republican society. Republicans across the nation and in Washington, conversely, led the United States into the war. In New York, nationalist Republicans were the loudest in calling for another war of independence against Britain.[7]

For Irish Catholics in the United States, the War of 1812 became a struggle to preserve their religious and political freedoms. As the *Shamrock* put it, the Irish in America had "found what was unfeelingly denied us at home." One Irish immigrant, identifying himself a "Catholic Lieutenant" in the U.S. army, appealed to Irish immigrants to join the military for both religious and ethnic reasons. He exhorted the "Sons of Hibernia" and "Irishmen of America" to be "proud of being one of yourselves" and to be grateful for their new home, in which "no religious persecution *here* tramples you in the dust" and where Catholics "could serve your God after the custom of your fathers." Irish Catholics in the United States had special reason to fear a British victory and the possible loss of American independence. The *Shamrock* asked its readers to contemplate the Protestant ascendancy in Ireland, in which the "disenfranchised Catholic [was] required to bend the knee." Such a fate, as British impressment of Irish Americans ominously suggested, could also befall the United States.[8]

The War of 1812, much like the American Revolution had done, gave Catholic men the opportunity to establish their patriotic credentials. In 1807, a decade after Governor John Jay had refused to certify an Irish militia, a visitor to New York remarked on an Irish regiment, outfitted in green, that was taking part in the celebration of Evacuation Day. This holiday commemorated the British departure from the city in November of 1783 and which was a particularly important nationalist festival in New York. By the War of 1812, there were Irish "Republican Green Rifle Companies" in both New York City and Albany. Captain James Mahar, a Republican who had been allied with DeWitt Clinton and who was a prominent member of St.

Mary's Church, led the Albany company. Albany's Republican Greens distinguished themselves during the war by capturing the town of Little York, just over the Canadian border. New Yorkers of all religions and ethnicities in turn appreciated the efforts of the Irish militia. A soldier in the Republican Greens recorded that while en route from New York City to Albany, their contingent was "paid every respect and attention." The accolades given to the Irish during the war were not limited to members of the military. In August of 1814, DeWitt Clinton, now mayor of New York City and fearful of an attack by the British, called for volunteers to buttress Fort Greene, just outside the city. Responding to his summons, fifteen hundred Irish men and women marched through the streets of Manhattan and Brooklyn, "cheered by the citizens" as they made their way out to the fort. The city's Committee of Defense later praised New York's "Patriotic Sons of Erin" for their aid in this regard.[9]

The "Second War of Independence" between the United States and Great Britain went a long way toward creating a new relationship between nationalist Republicans and Catholics in New York. The Tammany Society, in a pivotal change, extended its hand to Irish and Catholics as part of a new and more inclusive nationalism. At the Hibernian Provident Society's Fourth of July celebration in 1812, a delegation from Tammany toasted the Hibernians, declaring that both societies were now "distinguished for their united exertions in support of the measures of the present Administration of the General Government, and the Cause of our Common Country." The Hibernians returned the respects the next year, hailing Tammany on St. Patrick's Day for "*opposing* the seductive arts of Faction, and *supporting* the great chain of National Union." John Rodman of Tammany told a Fourth of July celebration in 1813, which was attended by members of both the Hibernian Provident and Tammany societies, that British impressment of naturalized U.S. citizens was "the grossest indignity that can be offered to us," and that "we cannot surrender (to Britain) the poor but gallant seaman." Emphasizing the expansive nature of American republicanism, Rodman applauded those who had suffered religious persecution in their native lands and then found refuge in the United States, where "no test acts exclude them from the honors and offices of their country." In its 1814 celebration of Evacuation Day, Tammany honored Commodore Thomas Macdonough, a Catholic officer, for his crucial role in the American naval victory at Plattsburgh, New York. Soon after the war ended, Tammany adopted a resolution honoring Captain James McKeon, a Catholic native of Ireland, for his heroism during the conflict.[10]

Both the new stance of nationalist Republicans toward immigrants and the logic of the war itself benefited New York Catholics. During the war, the state legislature changed the oath that election inspectors could require potential voters to take at the polls. Citizens could now be asked only to renounce "all allegiance and subjection to the King of Great-Britain, and to all and every other foreign king, prince and potentate and state whatsoever." Most Irish Catholics would have been eager to repudiate formally and publicly all ties to the English monarchy, especially during the war. As was the case with the oath of office after it was reformed in 1806, voters would no longer be asked to renounce foreign ecclesiastical authority, that is, the papacy. This law eliminated any potential distinctions between Catholics and other voters in New York in terms of their presumed loyalty to the state. Republican governor Daniel Tompkins, who had originally been elected with the support of the Atlantic Republicans, but was now aligned with the nationalists, signed the measure into law.[11]

Catholics also enjoyed a strengthening of their religious freedom during the War of 1812. This resulted from a court case in which civil authorities formally acknowledged the inviolability of the secrecy of the confessional. Because penance, or confession, is a sacrament in the Catholic Church, this was an important aspect of their religious freedom and equality. The case began when Father Anthony Kohlmann of St. Peter's was asked by New York City authorities in 1813 to name the penitent who had given him some stolen jewelry, which the priest in turn had handed over to the city. Kohlmann refused to reveal the identity of the person on the grounds that the section of the New York Constitution guaranteeing religious liberty protected his right to keep secret what he heard in the confessional. The case eventually reached the Court of General Sessions, over which Mayor Clinton presided. Clinton and the city at first sought to avoid an unseemly religious controversy by offering to drop the case altogether. Father Kohlmann and the lay leaders of St. Peter's, united on this issue and sensing the importance of the case for Catholicism in New York, pressed to have their day in court. Federalists Andrew Morris and Don Thomas Stoughton, the Spanish consul, were especially eager for a trial. Dennis McCarthy, a Republican, acted as spokesman for the parish in this matter. Their thinking was that a favorable verdict in the case would "ensure to all Catholics, in common with the rest of mankind, and according to the words of the constitution, the free exercise and enjoyment of their religious profession and worship." Once again the goal that Catholics in New York sought was equal treatment from the state, in matters both religious and secular.[12]

William Sampson, a prominent New York Republican and once a United Irishman, joined the case as a friend of the court (Thomas Addis Emmet was supposed to join Sampson, but he was called away to another case) on behalf of Father Kohlmann. Acknowledging that Roman Catholics accept the spiritual supremacy of the Pope, Sampson argued that it was also true that "politically, or as connected with government, or civil society, they acknowledge no supremacy whatsoever in the pope." Making a clear distinction between political and religious allegiance, Sampson echoed the same central point that Catholics had emphasized in the oath of office controversy seven years earlier. The Republican lawyer also called the attention of the court to the record of Catholics acting in defense of their new country: "our Catholic brethren have never hesitated to take up the sword with us, and to stand by us in our hour of danger." He also invoked George Washington's words of gratitude to American Catholics in 1789 for their military service in the revolution. Given that Catholics were at that very moment fighting for the United States in large numbers against the British invaders, no one could plausibly question their loyalty to the nation; this added much strength to Sampson's argument.[13]

The Irish birth or ancestry of most Catholics in New York was also to their advantage during the wartime trial, and William Sampson made use of that fact. "Who they are that compose the bulk of the Roman Catholics in this city," he said of the Irish, "would not join an English invasion of the city even if the troops of his holiness himself" were fighting with England. His Holiness was safe in Rome, and all religious fealty to the pope aside, Irish Catholics in New York would put their duties as republican citizens first. They would take up whatever weapon they could find, Sampson insisted, including their "old sanctified shillelah," to defend American soil from any foreign invaders, even those that might be led, fantastically enough, by the pope himself. Invoking this preposterous scenario had been part of the defense that Catholics had made in 1806 of their loyalty to the United States, and suggests something of how desperate Catholics were to be accepted as loyal citizens of the republic. Sampson also made new rhetorical use of the venerable shillelagh. Several years earlier, Federalists described it as the very symbol of Irish lawlessness and brutality; Sampson turned it into a uniquely Irish-American patriotic weapon, one that Catholics would wield with republican fervor in defense of the nation. The Republican lawyer warned that there was one thing, however, that might threaten the loyalty of Catholics to their adopted country. That would be if New York authorities "put their clergyman in prison for not betraying the most holy of engagements towards God or man." If the state had the power to require priests to reveal what they had learned from penitents, it would seriously damage Catholicism in New York, Sampson maintained, asking "who would afterwards go to confession?" To avoid such a troubling result, the city and state need only to respect the wishes of Catholics for a "pure and perfect equality. Hands off on all sides," he urged.[14]

As they had earlier, Catholics benefited from the support of United Irish immigrants such as William Sampson. The Irish exile said that any law that gave preeminence to Protestantism over Catholicism would be a "moral monster, incongruous and amorphous." For Sampson and other United Irish, the American republic had explicitly *not* been established as a Protestant entity. Their experiences in Ireland, where they had devoted themselves to bridging sectarian divisions, made that idea especially reprehensible to them. This motivated Sampson to help American Catholics achieve, across the board, equality with Protestants. He took this charge so seriously that he began to refer to Catholics in New York as "us." Sampson unabashedly declared, "I am a friend to Catholics," and commended how steadfast they had been in the United Irish struggle against English rule in Ireland, an important cue for an American court during the War of 1812. When it came to political and civic equality for the majority of the Irish people, including those in the United States, Sampson said simply, "I am a Catholic."[15]

Richard Riker was another prominent Republican champion for Catholics at the trial. Riker, the longtime ally of DeWitt Clinton and advocate for Catholics in the New York legislature in 1806 during its debate on the oath of office bill, was supposed to present the district attorney's case. He was also persuaded that Catholics were on the right side of the law, and he took the unusual step of excusing himself from the prosecution so that he could join Sampson as a counsel for the defense. Riker said that the delegates to the New York Convention in 1777 understood that "auricular confession" was an important practice within Catholicism; nowhere in the constitution was it stipulated that liberty of conscience should not protect it. What is probably closer to the truth was that the convention that had met thirty-five years earlier did not go that far in its thinking about Catholicism and its sacraments. Riker was surely correct, however, in arguing that no specific limitations or restrictions had been placed on the exercise of the Catholic faith at the time, other of course that its adherents in no way threaten the safety of the state.[16]

The prosecution responded, careful to make its case largely on grounds that were constitutional and not religious. District Attorney Barent Gardenier argued that if the government conceded the right of Catholic priests to remain silent before legal authorities in all circumstances, then it would in effect place the safety of the state in their hands. Such an outcome would not be consistent with the original intent of the framers of the state constitution with regard to religious liberty. Gardenier said that the citizens of New York at the time that their representatives wrote the state constitution were a "Christian, Protestant People," which seemed to make the religious liberty of Catholics probationary. Acutely aware, however, of the dangers posed to genuine religious liberty by establishing any one church, the framers of the New York constitution made sure that no single denomination would become "superior to any other," Gardenier argued. Hence, the state could not grant immunity to Catholic priests if they had information relevant to criminal cases without violating that principle of equality before the law. Doing so, the prosecution contended, would be giving special status to Catholicism. This claim was somewhat disingenuous, as no other religion in New York included private confession among its practices.[17]

In issuing his decision, Mayor Clinton reiterated that under the canon law of the Roman Catholic Church, Father Kohlmann was absolutely prohibited from revealing what had been said in the confessional. Clinton spoke to the consequential nature of this case for Catholics: "This is an important enquiry: It is important to the church upon which it has a particular bearing." He praised the state constitution for its liberality, which was especially important for Catholics facing the "narrow views and bigotted feelings, which prevailed at that time so strongly against the Roman Catholics." In this particular case, any action by the state that infringed upon the practice of a sacrament, including confession, would be wrong, he continued, as "secrecy is of the essence of pennance." Objections to Catholic confession had traditionally been based on dogma rather than politics, Clinton maintained, arguing that "the confession of sins has ever been considered as of pernicious tendency, in any other respect than it being a theological error." The heart of this case was religious, not political. "Although we differ from the witness and his brethren, in our religious creed, yet we have no reason to question the purity of their motives, or to impeach their good conduct as citizens." A Presbyterian who was becoming increasingly pious later in life, Clinton also conceded that in the past the Catholic Church had threatened religious freedom in other societies and asserted that New York authorities would block any attempt "to establish the inquisition" in the state. With that caveat, one that was by now almost routine, Mayor Clinton ruled emphatically that Catholics were fully protected by the "laws of and constitution of this country," and dismissed the case against Father Kohlmann. With this decision, Clinton added another chapter to his history as the most prominent champion of equality for Catholics in New York. Catholics had won an important legal victory, one that set a precedent for courts in other states on questions of this kind.[18]

The consecration of New York's second Catholic church also demonstrated how city leaders, including for the first time nationalist Republicans, appreciated Catholics in a new way. St. Patrick's Cathedral became the seat of the diocese of New York in 1815. Among those in attendance at the church's formal opening were the new Republican mayor John Ferguson, a member of Tammany, and of course DeWitt Clinton, who had recently been deposed as mayor by the state government, at Tammany's insistence. In the pews of the new cathedral were also "the best families of New York." The opening of St. Peter's thirty years earlier had been marked by the distinct international flavor that Catholic diplomats gave to the ceremony. The dedication of St. Patrick's in 1815, however, had much more of a nationalist and localist aspect to it, one which reflected a growing wartime acceptance of Catholics in New York by the city's political and social leaders.[19]

The differing experiences of two groups of nuns also illustrated the positive difference that the War of 1812 had made for Catholicism in New York City. Soon before the war began, several Irish sisters of the Ursuline order moved into New York City in the hopes of establishing a convent school for "young ladies of all denominations." The Ursulines were an activist order, whose nuns often worked in cities in a variety of educational and charitable enterprises. Their initial effort to establish a school in New York City failed, however, as the sisters were unable to recruit enough students, especially those who were not Catholic. After three years they returned to Ireland. One observer, who was not Catholic but thought that the Ursulines' venture a worthy one, believed that one reason for its demise was that "our Protestant prejudices did not allow a fair chance to these experiments." Two years after the War of 1812 ended, however, three nuns from Elizabeth Ann Seton's Daughters of Charity convent in Maryland, Felicita Brady, Rose White, and Cecilia O'Conway, moved to New York City. The new bishop of the diocese, John Connolly, in 1817 had asked them to start an orphanage, and Catholic politician Francis Cooper aided the sisters in establishing one. Leaders of the Catholic laity in New York, impressed with the results, requested that the nuns next start a school. The achievements of the sisters in her native city were especially gratifying to Elizabeth Seton, who had left New York City a decade earlier to establish her religious community in a place more hospitable to Catholicism.[20]

The War of 1812 mostly benefited Catholics in their struggle to be accepted as full citizens of the republic, but there were also some disquieting moments. Patrick Byrne, an Irish immigrant and a volunteer in an American regiment (not the Republican Greens), was convicted of mutiny. He was led to the edge of a grave, where he was shot and quickly buried. Afterwards, some of his comrades received permission to dig up his remains and bring them to the graveyard at St. Patrick's Church in New York City, where they reinterred them. The reaction of many Irish Catholics in New York to Byrne's execution was intense. "Upwards of *nine hundred* of his countrymen went to his burial." There was a feeling among them that Byrne had been unfairly singled out, and that his Irish Catholicism had been a contributing factor in his conviction and execution. The *Shamrock* tried to dispel that suspicion, arguing that "it will also be a consolation to find contrary to the opinion of many, that nothing of malice or revenge had any share in accelerating his fate." The paper added that Byrne's case would be the subject of "a strict investigation." Even so, the reaction of many Irish Catholics to the execution shows that despite their latest service to the country in time of war, they continued to believe themselves vulnerable to ethnic and religious prejudice.[21]

## CATHOLICS AND THE REPUBLICAN DEFEAT OF FEDERALISM

Federalists in New York had generally supported the war more so than did their counterparts in other states. That allowed them to survive there, at least for a while, and they even managed to elect their Assembly ticket in New York City in 1815. Among their winning candidates that year was Andrew Morris, who became the first Catholic Federalist to serve in state office. During the campaign, Federalists taunted their Republican opponents for not nominating any Irish or foreign-born candidates. They claimed that when the name of Thomas Addis Emmet was put forward at the Republican nominating committee, one Republican rose in opposition and declared that "no Irishman or other foreigner should now or hereafter be nominated on the ticket; that it was sufficient privilege for them to be permitted to vote for others." The Republicans denied the charge, saying that "as to putting or not putting an Irishman on our ticket, we have got friends of Irishmen on it, and that is more than the Federalists can say." This was an apparent criticism of Andrew Morris for his continued involvement with Federalists and of Federalist policies and attitudes toward Catholics and immigrants. If Federalists had their way, Republicans speculated, "they would vote to send out of the country sooner than put in office any of them who were political friends to the mass of Hibernians in the state." The Federalists were motivated by political expediency, according to Republicans, as they asked, "How long is it since the Federalists felt such yearning for persecuted Irishmen?"[22]

Although the War of 1812 had seemingly changed the relationship between nationalist Republicans and Catholics, the political divisions between Irish Catholic immigrants and African-Americans emerged from the war stronger than ever. Republicans continued to portray Federalists as corrupt and elitist for their support of the political rights of African-Americans. They also contrasted the differing Federalist attitude toward the two groups, claiming that while Federalists demanded that Irish immigrants produce evidence of citizenship, they willingly "take a black man's word" that he was eligible to vote. In a play on words, Republicans said that *"Irishmen* may swear until they are black in the face without being allowed to vote unless they produce a *certificate!"*[23]

Determined to reverse their surprising defeat in 1815, Republicans united the next year to regain power from the Federalists. Now led by Tammany, Republicans in New York City presented a single, united ticket to the electorate. One of their tactics was to continue to link Federalists to the British in the minds of voters. The Federalist candidate for governor in 1816 was Rufus King. Republicans lambasted King for his stance toward the United Irish during the 1798 uprising. Irish Americans encouraged each other to "Refuse King." The *Shamrock,* now under the editorial control of Thomas O'Conor,

helped to mobilize Irish and Catholic voters against the former ambassador's candidacy. "A Son of Erin" proclaimed that "Mr. King's
political friends would drive every Irishman out of the land of liberty,
were the political tenets of the King party to prevail. You would this
day be aliens." The *Shamrock* reprinted a letter that King had written
in 1799, in which he complained that "a large portion of emigrants
from Ireland, and especially in the middle states, has, upon occasion
arranged themselves on the side of the *malcontents*," meaning the
Republicans. This was the latest effort by Republicans to portray
King, and by implication all Federalists, as disdainful of the aspirations of Irish Catholics, both in Ireland and the United States.[24]

Tammany Republicans complemented their anti-King strategy in
1816 by nominating Cornelius Heeney for the Assembly. This time,
the wealthy Irish immigrant accepted. Heeney became the first Irish
Catholic to run on the ticket of the party that had enjoyed the benefit
of the votes of Catholics and Irish immigrants for so long. His nomination, which came more than ten years after the Atlantic Republicans had initially recruited Francis Cooper to run for the Assembly
and subsequently challenged the restrictive oath of office, also
marked the first time that nationalist Republicans had put forward
any Catholic for state office. One contemporary described Heeney as
an "Irish Benjamin Franklin," and visitors to his estate on Long Island "would either bow or curtsey to him." A man of great wealth
and high social standing and a Republican in part due to his support
for Irish independence, Heeney was particularly interested in defeating Rufus King in 1816. At the same time, the Federalists once again
were making it difficult for themselves to win the votes of many
Catholics and Irish. Their list of legislative candidates that year included Richard Varick, a figure notoriously unpopular among New
York's Irish laborers dating back to the ferrymen affair of the 1790s.
Along with King, who one Republican described as "the hater of
Irishmen," disdain for Varick helped to unite the Republicans. William MacNeven argued that King had been threatened by the pros-

pect of massive Irish immigration to America because, simply, "Irishmen are republicans." King, MacNeven predicted, "will not have a single Irish vote." The Irish Catholic émigré remained an ally of DeWitt Clinton, but in 1816, befitting the improved relationship between Catholics and Tammany, MacNeven also supported Governor Daniel Tompkins and the rest of the Republican ticket. Cornelius Heeney and the other Republican candidates won a clear victory in 1816. The heavily Irish sixth ward in particular delivered an overwhelming vote against King and the Federalists. Andrew Morris's career in the Assembly ended after only one year, and the Federalists as a political party suffered a serious setback as they struggled to remain a viable force in New York politics.[25]

With the war over and their common domestic political opponent fading from the scene, Republicans in New York once again turned on each other. After their crushing defeat in 1816, Federalists the following year were unable to field a ticket of candidates in New York City or across the state. During the 1817 campaign, Republicans gathered at Tammany Hall to select candidates, with "one party generally taking the left, the other the right." A melee broke out at the meeting between the Atlantic and nationalist Republicans in which several persons were injured, and much of the furniture at the venerable hall was destroyed. Nationalists blamed Irish Republicans for the rumpus, claiming that they became enraged when Thomas Addis Emmet was passed over for an Assembly nomination. At their next meeting, nationalist Republicans referred to the incident by saluting "the City of New York—her latest triumph over a drilled mob is the triumph of national feeling and national principle." Suggesting that DeWitt Clinton was behind this latest fracas, Tammany called for "a speedy end to corrupt politicians."[26]

The divisions between the Republicans in 1817 became so pronounced that it drove them "into two adverse parties, designated as 'adopted' and 'native' citizens." Immigrant republicans held a large public meeting with between two thousand and three thousand in attendance. William MacNeven chaired the meeting, and Dennis Mc-Carthy of St. Peter's acted as secretary. The mainly Irish immigrants, both Catholic and Protestant, voiced their support for DeWitt Clinton's gubernatorial candidacy; he entered the race to succeed Daniel Tompkins when the incumbent resigned to become vice president under the new Republican president, James Monroe. The "adopted" Republicans then endorsed their own candidates for the Assembly, including former United Irishmen Thomas Addis Emmet and William Sampson. It may have appeared that once again, Irish Catholics were lining up neatly on the side of DeWitt Clinton and against the nationalist Republicans of Tammany. One observer described the supporters of Clinton in 1817 as "the Irish & that class who were brought in by the Democrats to break down Federalism." Supporters of Clinton themselves encouraged this thinking, disparaging the Tammany "Martling" ticket as hostile to immigrants.[27]

The reasoning of the "adopted" Republicans was complicated, however, when Tammany Republicans renominated Cornelius Heeney for another term in the Assembly. Unlike Andrew Morris, for example, Heeney emphasized ethnic politics, with his firm advocacy of Irish independence and staunch opposition to Rufus King and his brand of Federalism. As a member of the Assembly in 1817, Heeney helped to persuade the state legislature to pass two measures of incorporation for the benefit of Catholics in New York City. One was for St. Patrick's Cathedral, and the other was for the Roman Catholic Benevolent Society. The Atlantic Republicans became angry that Tammany was now openly competing for the votes of Catholics; they denounced "with *indignation* all attempts to mingle religious doctrine with political contests, and reprobate the idea that any man can be more acceptable to us than another on the mere score of his sectarian opinions." Given the prior relationships of nationalist and Atlantic Republicans to Catholics, this comment was rich in irony.[28]

Despite some of his political tactics and maneuvering, Clinton himself remained personally popular with Catholic Republicans.

During his campaign for governor in 1817, he celebrated the Irish holiday on March 17 with the St. Patrick's Society of Albany. Most of the leading members of the society were Catholics from St. Mary's, including John Cassidy, William Kearney, and Captain James Mahar. Cassidy, a grocer, was also a member of Clinton's statewide committee of correspondence. Joining Clinton from New York City at the festivities in Albany were Cornelius Heeney and William MacNeven. Albany's Irish Catholics hailed Clinton as a "man of the people." His campaign for governor drew wide support from Catholics in New York City as well. Clinton's committee of correspondence there included Dennis McCarthy, Dennis H. Doyle, Dennis Doyle, Patrick Monahan, Owen McCabe, Bernard Kennedy, Captain James Mahar, Philip Duffie, James Flinn, and a veteran of Republican politics, Patrick McKay. Clinton's appeal went beyond established Catholic political leaders; it also encompassed Irish laborers and recent immigrants. They favored his plan to build a canal from Lake Erie to the end of the Hudson River; this ambitious project held the promise of jobs to those willing (or having little other choice) to do such difficult work. Clinton's Republican opponents were initially skeptical of the ambitious enterprise; his supporters in turn made an issue of this hesitancy, denouncing Tammany as the "anti-canal" ticket.[29]

Clinton overwhelmed a weak Tammany candidate and was elected governor in 1817. He was, however, unable to transfer his popularity to the Republican legislative ticket that supported him. The Tammany Assembly candidates, including Cornelius Heeney, were elected easily, defeating Sampson, Emmet, and the other candidates even in the Irish immigrant wards. This was despite the prominence of some Irish Catholics among the Republican "adopted citizens" and the continued popularity of Clinton himself among many Catholics and immigrants. The nationalist Republicans' new, more inclusive attitude toward Catholics was beginning to work in their favor.[30]

This pattern held over the next two years. The Tammany Assembly ticket, featuring Cornelius Heeney, defeated their immigrant Republican rivals and their Catholic candidate, Dennis McCarthy. The anti-Clinton Republicans around New York State were by 1819 becoming known as the Bucktails, and the Tammany men were a crucial base of their support; Martin Van Buren of Kinderhook, in Columbia County near Albany, was emerging as their statewide leader. The Tammanyites won New York City's immigrant wards in 1818–19. The long-standing alliance between DeWitt Clinton and New York City's immigrant and Irish Catholics was weakening. Tammany wooed immigrants by maintaining a drumbeat of criticism of Clinton as an aloof and profoundly unrepublican aristocrat. It also dropped its earlier opposition to the Erie Canal, which better positioned it to compete with Clinton for the support of poorer Irish Catholics.[31]

For his part, DeWitt Clinton had begun to win members of the disintegrating Federalist Party around the state to his side, and let his own alliance with Catholics and immigrants crumble. This strategy paid off in 1820; Clinton was reelected Governor in a narrow decision over Republican Daniel Tompkins, although he fared poorly in New York City. Tompkins, running with a successful New York City Tammany Assembly ticket that once again featured Cornelius Heeney, carried the wards where Catholic voters were most concentrated. Clinton's party in New York City, where many former Federalists had found a political home, bemoaned Heeney's latest election. It had also not put any Catholics on its ticket in New York City, and hailed a presumptively Protestant "yeomanry triumphant" as now constituting its core of support in the state.[32]

Given the history of their religion in New York and the relative poverty of many of them, it is not surprising that most Catholics supported efforts to make New York's politics more democratic. Bucktail Republicans agitated for liberalizing the state constitution in 1821, especially the suffrage requirements. Tammany had initially been fearful of universal white male suffrage, thinking such reform would mean more Irish votes for Clinton. Their own new inclusive attitude toward immigrants and Catholics, and Clinton's embrace of the remnants of Federalism, now led Tammany to believe that they had more to gain by expanding the suffrage. The state legislature passed a bill calling for a referendum on holding a constitutional convention in 1821. Voters endorsed the measure by a comfortable margin, with strong support for it coming from the immigrant Catholic wards of New York City and Albany. There were not any Catholic delegates elected to the convention. Even so, Tammany and the Bucktail Republicans pursued reforms at the convention that virtually all Catholic voters would have favored. Delegates affirmed what the legislature had done during the War of 1812, as it omitted the language from the 1777 constitution that gave election inspectors the right to require voters to renounce foreign ecclesiastical authority. The convention in 1821 also mandated that the only oath for any public office in the revised constitution simply required those taking it to affirm their support of the constitutions of New York and the United States. This ratified the action taken by the New York legislature in 1806 in revising the 1788 oath of office to accommodate Catholics.[33]

With the 1821 constitutional convention came the formal end of any potential political and legal discrimination against Catholics that was based only on religion. After 1821, "Catholic" was effectively no longer an effective political category in New York. It was also true that the liberalization of voting requirements for white males directly benefited poorer Catholic men. Before 1821, most white men (78 percent) were eligible to vote in elections for the Assembly. The lower house of the legislature, correspondingly, was the only state office for which Catholics were nominated by Federalists and Republicans. (In 1820 and 1821, Republicans in Albany nominated their first Irish Catholics for public office, as Captain James Mahar and John Cassidy were elected to the city's Common Council.) As a result of the 1821 convention, however, the percentage of white men who were eligible to vote for governor went from thirty-three to eighty-four. In political terms, Irish Catholics in New York were never considered anything other than "white"; it was their religious heritage, their reputation as a rebellious people, and New York's unique history regarding Catholicism that lay behind legal measures designed to limit their participation in public life. Now those legal and constitutional barriers, every last one, had been removed.[34]

The political fortunes of African-Americans, with their Federalist benefactors no longer much of a recognizable political party, had begun to ebb by 1821. Bucktails and Tammanyites faced little opposition in disenfranchising, through steep property and wealth requirements, all but a small fraction of African-American men in the state. With the demise of the Federalists, most free African-Americans had become allied with DeWitt Clinton, but his party was unable to stop the Bucktails, who controlled the convention. The latter party, now becoming known as the Democrats, embraced white Catholics as it simultaneously pushed African-Americans, all questions of religion aside, even farther to the margins of the state's political life. Catholics, especially the Irish, and free African-Americans had for the most part been on opposite sides of the Federalist / Republican partisan battles of the early republic. The differences in the political status between Irish Catholics and African-Americans had now widened. Poor laboring Africans and Irish Catholics during the eighteenth century had forged social and political ties across racial lines; colonial authorities at times had considered them a joint threat to the security of New York. By 1821, however, the two groups were now squarely on opposite sides of an important political and legal divide. Five years later, the legislature amended the constitution further by dropping all property requirements for white men, thus establishing in New York the "universal white male suffrage" that historians have long associated with Jacksonian America.[35]

## DEFEAT OF THE FEDERALIST TRUSTEES OF ST. PETER'S

Differences in social and economic status influenced parish politics at St. Peter's in ways both similar and different to how the majority of

Catholic voters regarded reform of the state government. While most Catholics in New York supported efforts to expand democracy in the public sphere, changes at St. Peter's at that time resulted in increased authority for the bishop and less influence for the laity. As the Federalists disappeared from New York politics, it made less sense for the trustees who had long been associated with that party to continue to wield such considerable influence at St. Peter's. However, as they understood the history of Catholicism in New York City since the American Revolution, they had guaranteed through their own financial generosity the building and expansion of the church there. Over the decades of the late eighteenth and early nineteenth centuries, and increasingly so in recent years, Federalist leaders had been joined in the pews of the church by, as they put it, the "Irish, and almost all of them are poor, uneducated, and drunkards." This comment reflected some of the frustration and anxiety that Federalists as a whole had with the development of American society at large; the republic envisioned by Federalists in the late eighteenth century, one governed by the genteel and affluent, was being rapidly supplanted by a more raucous, and less refined, polity.[36]

The Federalist trustees faced a strong challenge to their leadership at St. Peter's between 1818 and 1821. New York, first made a diocese in 1808, was without a bishop-in-residence until John Connolly arrived in 1815. The first bishop of New York, Luke Concannon, had died before he was able to leave Europe for the United States, and John Connolly's departure for New York was delayed until after the end of the Napoleonic Wars. His presence eventually contributed to a dispute between the bishop and laity over who had the authority to appoint priests. The conflict was precipitated by a whirl of controversy that surrounded one Father Charles Ffrench, a native of Ireland who came to New York via Canada. The long-standing trustees had at St. Peter's had little use for Ffrench. The priest appealed, in their view, to the "worse class of Irishmen," gathering with people of that description "in the saloons even on Good Friday." A visiting Catholic prelate reached the same conclusion. Conceding that Ffrench had the

support of most of New York's Catholics, Bishop Joseph Plessis of
Quebec insisted that "this majority is composed of the Irish rabble
which Father Ffrench knows so well how to arouse and lead." The
trustees of St. Peter's, including Andrew Morris and the Lynch and
Stoughton families, accused Ffrench of encouraging the congregation, especially the poorer Irish, to oppose their party in the trustee
elections. Ffrench and some of his Irish supporters disrupted a trustee
election meeting in April of 1819, seizing the chair from Thomas
Stoughton and forcing the Federalist lay leaders to flee "even
through windows." Stoughton and others in his party compared
Ffrench's conduct in this case with that of a "sansculotte." The trustees suspended Ffrench's pay and demanded that he cease his priestly
duties in New York. The partisans of Father Ffrench denounced this
action, maintaining that only the bishop had the right within the
Catholic Church to appoint and dismiss priests. The trustees later
withdrew their financial support from St. Peter's because of Father
Ffrench, saying they no longer wanted "to be exposed to the insults
of a revolutionary."[37]

Ethnicity also shaped this latest dispute at St. Peter's. The established trustees described their party as including "some Irish, honest,
Frenchman, Italians, Spaniards and Dutch, [who] make the better
class of Cthcs in this congregation." This group admitted that they
were not "a mathematical majority," but claimed to speak for those
Catholics who were "religious and sensible." One French Catholic
described the majority ethnic group of the parish as "*malheurex Ir-
landais* . . . [unhappy Irish], intriguers [who] are Catholics in name
only and aspire only to the honor of being trustees." The number of
Irish in New York's Catholic population, always a majority, rose even
further after the end of the Napoleonic Wars in Europe. In 1815–16
alone, twenty thousand Irish came to North America; there was also
a famine in Ireland in 1817 that drove some Irish to America. Many
of these Irish immigrants were Protestant, but certainly not all.
Bishop John Connolly, who was himself an Irish native, noted the

increase. He said in 1818 that "at least ten thousand Irish Catholics arrived at New York *only* within these last three years," with most leaving for other destinations in the United States, but about a third remaining; this brought the number of Catholics in New York to about sixteen thousand, or a sixth of the population of the city. Many of those opposed to Father Ffrench and the "Irish rabble" were of French ancestry, primarily from what was then Santo Domingo.[38]

The class tensions between the competing factions of the laity became especially clear at a civil trial that stemmed from the conflict regarding Father Ffrench. Lewis Willocks, an affluent Federalist trustee and the son-in-law of Andrew Morris, and James Stoughton, son of the Spanish consul, sought to discredit Ffrench. They gathered information from Canada indicating that the priest was guilty of sexual misconduct and embezzlement while serving there. Ffrench responded by suing Willocks for slander. William Sampson, the former United Irishman who represented Ffrench at the trial, denounced Willocks as a "wealthy manufacturer" who scorned both the traditions and hierarchy of the Catholic Church and the views of the majority of parishioners at St. Peter's. Willocks and the other longstanding trustees, the former United Irishman continued, "who have ruled that church" should "look into their own hearts, and see whether wealth and worldly prosperity have not usurped the place of charity." Sampson contended that the affluent Federalist trustees "would not be the first whom fortune has corrupted, for man is weak and pride of purse makes insolence of heart." By refusing to bring their complaints against Father Ffrench directly to the bishop, as the laws of the Catholic Church required, the trustees had proven themselves "to be grandees who loved to sit in the high places, and receive greetings and salutations in the marketplace. They arrogated to themselves the right which no men have."[39]

Sampson tried to link the arrogant behavior of Willocks and his allies in ecclesiastical matters at St. Peter's with their inordinate influence in the society at large. Their wealth and privilege had compromised their ability to be virtuous citizens of the republic; their haughtiness had also caused them to be disobedient members of the Catholic Church. His point was rich in irony. Sampson, a committed Republican who was not Catholic, invoked the primacy of the clerical hierarchy of the Catholic Church over the claims of the American laity to some measure of influence within their church. He used the tradition of clerical authority within the Catholic Church to denigrate men who had been his political opponents in the larger society. The court, however, ruled against Ffrench, saying that under state law, which was based on Protestant traditions of church governance, the trustees did have the right to investigate Catholic priests. The decision notwithstanding, supporters of Father Ffrench gathered afterward to celebrate at Andrew Dooley's tavern, the site of earlier meetings of immigrant and Catholic Republicans. As they understood it, the trial had "fully justified" Father Ffrench's character. They applauded William Sampson's forceful defense of the authority of Catholic prelates. The supporters of Father Ffrench and Bishop Connolly maintained that "hierarchy is the ancient fundamental principle of the Roman Catholic Church, and power to appoint resides in the bishop." They stated that "We look upon all such attempts at disorganization as symptoms of dangerous ambition which it is our duty to resist." Although the court's ruling was not a complete victory for the bishop, as it continued to grant the trustees a formal role in the affairs of the church, it did not challenge his ability to appoint and dismiss priests.[40]

The changing of the guard on the board of trustees at St. Peter's occurred in 1819 and 1820, when a pro-bishop, all-Irish slate of candidates easily defeated their opponents in successive elections. Among the victors in 1820 was Cornelius Heeney, the Republican state legislator. A few weeks later, Heeney was reelected to the Assembly on the Tammany ticket. Although not a candidate for trustee, Francis Cooper also sided with Bishop Connolly during the dispute. Cooper and Heeney, two of New York's leading Catholic Republicans, defended the prerogatives of the bishop against a party that they had long opposed, both within and outside of St. Peter's. The predominantly Irish party that supported Father Ffrench had more reason to celebrate in 1821. They met again at Dooley's tavern after a failed effort by the old Federalist trustees to reinstate a priest, Father William Taylor, from whom Bishop Connolly had withdrawn his approval. Affirming their obedience to Connolly, the pro-bishop Irish declared: "We disclaim any interference with the sacred duties of the Episcopacy. We are sensible that the strongest barriers separate us from the Sanctuary." The Irish immigrants of modest means were not interested, at that point, in making more democratic the Catholic Church in New York; their goal was to defeat those in the laity who considered them to be their social and economic inferiors. In this, just as in their support for democratic reforms in the governance of New York State, they had been successful.[41]

■ ■ ■

Nationalist Republicans had initially shunned Catholics once again after gaining control of the party immediately before the War of 1812. This appeared to give the Federalists one final opportunity to win the support of Catholics, who were clearly growing weary of the nativism of the Tammanyites. Federalists could not overcome their class and ethnic biases toward Catholics, their defense of religion in general notwithstanding. As the Federalist Party disintegrated in the aftermath of the war, many of its members gravitated toward Clinton, who had run for president as a de facto Federalist in 1812. This allowed nationalist Republicans to denounce Clinton as the front man for aristocracy and made it easier for them to appeal to Catholics. The second war between the United States and Britain also led the most nationalist faction of Republicans to drop their public misgivings about the ability of Catholics to be loyal American citizens, allowing them to forge a new relationship with the majority of Catholic voters. DeWitt Clinton, who for many years had been the champion of

Catholic political interests in New York, remained personally popular with Catholics longer than did his party. He had a long record of breaking relations with his political allies, however, and although the partnership that he and Catholics made had been beneficial to both, it had faltered by 1821. By then, most Catholic voters were aligned with the Tammany and Bucktail Republicans.

Catholic support for democratic reforms in the wider polity, coincided, paradoxically, with the desire of most of the Catholic laity to place greater decision-making power in the hands of the bishop, who was appointed by the pope. The start of the third decade of the nineteenth century marked a confluence of these two streams. As white Catholic men, including of course the Irish, gained greater political rights in the republic, they were able to reconcile more easily the diminished role of the laity within their church. That the lay leaders they displaced were predominantly members of the discredited Federalist Party made this change all the more agreeable to them.

# Conclusion
## "A Most Democratic and Republican Class"

A decade after the New York Constitutional Convention of 1821, the French aristocrat Alexis de Tocqueville began his tour of the United States. His itinerary in New York State included New York City and Albany, where Catholics had established their first churches during the late eighteenth century. Tocqueville, who was born and raised a Catholic, remarked on the state of his religion in the United States in *Democracy in America* as he sought to persuade his French readers that religion and democracy were not incompatible. Tocqueville believed that religion encouraged morality and virtue and also acted as a bulwark against two of democracy's vices, namely materialism and individualism.[1]

Tocqueville boldly declared, just as another period of nativism against American Catholics was commencing, that Catholics "constitute the most republican and the most democratic class in the United States." His argument was that Catholic lay people were essentially equal in that they were all, each one of them, subject to the authority of the clergy. Tocqueville contended that while Protestantism encouraged independence, it also fostered inequality. Catholicism, conversely, left its lay adherents on one plane within their Church. The defeat of the affluent and socially prestigious Federalist trustees at

St. Peter's in 1819 had helped to insure that equality among the Catholic laity in New York City.[2]

The "social position" of American Catholics, as Tocqueville described it, also explained much about their politics: "Most of the Catholics are poor, and they have no chance of taking a part in the government unless it is open to all the citizens." The government in New York was by no means a model of representative democracy after 1821, but after the reforms that the state constitutional convention made, most male Catholics of European origin were able to exercise their right to vote. That the majority of Catholics were laborers of modest economic status shaped their political outlook as well. Tocqueville perceived that Catholics, as a religious minority, understood that "all rights must be respected in order to ensure to them the free exercise of their own privileges." Catholics were opposed to the slightest hint of a religious establishment or religious discrimination, something which radical Republicans in New York had understood a quarter of a century earlier. The desire of Catholics for political and religious equality, Tocqueville argued, "induce them, even unconsciously, to adopt political doctrines which they would perhaps support with less zeal if they were rich and preponderant."[3]

Tocqueville did not emphasize ethnicity as a factor in shaping the politics of Catholics in the United States. In New York, however, it was important. Irish Catholic immigrants had left their native land, in part, because of religious and political discrimination; they were resolved to resist any efforts to relegate them to second-class citizenship in their adopted country. That so many Catholics in New York during the early republic were Irish had a significant influence on how both Federalists and Republicans related to Catholics.

The other conditions that Tocqueville believed influenced the politics of American Catholics were especially true in New York. Fear of Catholicism had been a central feature of colonial New York's political culture, as members of New York's various denominations and ethnicities forged a pluralistic society that was at the same time essentially Protestant. They systematically defined Catholics and Catholicism as outside of the province's legitimate religious and political life. Although its own brand of anti-Catholicism could be dormant at times, colonial New York remained singularly inhospitable to Catholics. Hostility toward Catholics did erupt periodically, most vividly during the slave conspiracy of the 1740s. At that time, traditional fear of Catholicism, combined with racism and the English imperial rivalry with France and Spain to produce a bizarre and ghastly episode, one that was every bit as disturbing as that of the infamous Salem witchcraft trials a half century earlier.

This legacy made anti-Catholicism a more dominant political issue in post-revolutionary New York than it was elsewhere. At the outset of the American Revolution, the Patriots used anti-Catholic rhetoric to denounce the English king and his supporters in New York as crypto-papists bent on destroying the liberty of the colonists. By the end of the Revolutionary War, however, their alliance with France and the support of most Catholics for the American Revolution had transformed the Patriots' attitude toward Catholicism. Loyalists, as the last defenders of the old order in New York, seized in desperation on anti-Catholicism, thereby discrediting the ancien régime even further. After the war, the state legislature overturned the old statute that had outlawed Catholicism, and Catholics began building St. Peter's Church in Manhattan.

Despite winning religious freedom as a result of the American Revolution, New York Catholics did not emerge from that crucible as full citizens of the new republic. A party of chiefly rural legislators, who had been staunch supporters of the Revolution and who would soon oppose the federal Constitution, were apparently threatened by the emergence of a Catholic community in New York City. The leaders of these Catholics were a group from various European backgrounds who had much in common with New York's social and economic gentry. The agrarians tried to disenfranchise Catholics in 1787, only to be thwarted by a faction led by Alexander Hamilton that championed a strengthened national government that they believed would ultimately transcend ethnic and religious differences. The following year, in the midst of New York's impassioned debate on the proposed federal constitution, Anti-Federalists did succeed in effectively banning Catholics from holding state office by means of an oath that required them to renounce their spiritual unity with the papacy.

As they began to make the most of their newly secured religious freedom, Catholics remained on the periphery of New York's political life in the turbulent, formative decade of the 1790s. It was at that time that two distinct political persuasions, the Republicans and the Federalists, emerged in New York and around the country. On religious grounds alone, Catholics clearly had more in common with the Federalists, who in the decade after defending Catholic political rights now claimed to be the defenders of traditional Christianity. At the same time, there were Republicans in the 1790s who went so far as to support the French Revolution for its campaign against the Catholic Church. Federalists considered the French revolutionaries a threat to religion in general, and the Catholic clergy in the United States feared that American Republicans would adopt their French counterparts' deism and hostility to traditional Christianity.

Federalists, however, both in New York and nationally, began to exhibit a profound resentment of immigrants and Catholics, many of whom were poor laboring people from Ireland. This began to push Catholics toward the Republicans, who in the 1790s became the defenders of the aspirations of ordinary New Yorkers in the face of Federalist arrogance toward laborers and immigrants. Although most Catholics supported the Republicans in the crucial 1800 election in a reaction to Federalist nativism, the party was not yet willing to embrace Catholics as full-fledged members of their coalition.

Republicans in New York during the early republic were only occasionally a unified and coherent party. There were nationalist Republicans in New York City, who, along with much of the rural yeomanry, remained suspicious of Catholics and immigrants. In the early nineteenth century, however, Catholics found allies in DeWitt Clinton and his Republican faction, which included radical émigrés from the British Isles. In the context of the fierce rivalry within the party, it was these Atlantic Republicans who took the lead in over-turning the ban in 1806 that kept Catholics from holding elective state office. At the same time, Federalists in the early nineteenth century had become so alarmed by the growing number of poor Irish Catholic immigrants into New York, most of whom were Republican, that they fought in the legislature to deny Catholics the right to serve there. This strategy failed because the state changed the oath of office to accommodate Catholics. Nationalist Republicans did not overtly object to this reform, although they clearly were much less enthusiastic about it than were their Atlantic Republican counter-parts. The following year, in 1807, nationalist Republicans and Feder-alists united around a fear of Catholics and immigrants to form the "American Party," an effort that failed to push Catholics back to the margins of New York's political life.

The support of Republican émigré radicals for Catholics had its ironies. Deists such as James Cheetham, who opposed both the doc-trines of Christianity and its relationship to established power, be-came energetic advocates of political equality for Catholics in the United States. Cheetham and other immigrant radicals, including United Irish exiles, saw Catholics in the United States as long-stand-ing victims of English oppression. Their nationalist Republican rivals, conversely, viewed Catholics as potentially disloyal and not fully committed to the principles of American republicanism. It took un-qualified Catholic support for the War of 1812 for these Republicans to change their position and embrace Catholics as full members of their party.

When New York's political leaders met in convention in 1821 to revise the state's constitution, the question of whether the state could entrust Catholics with full religious liberty had been answered in the affirmative. Half a century earlier, during the writing of the state's original governing document, Patriots had nearly decided to keep in place the colonial prohibitions against Catholics legally practicing their religion. In 1821, Jonas Platt, a former Federalist and a delegate to the convention, referred to this in passing as he spoke in defense of voting rights for African-Americans. Advances, he said, were possible on race relations as they had been in other realms: he asked the convention "to consider the astonishing progress of the human mind, in regard to religious toleration" that the state had enjoyed in the decades since the American Revolution. The progress of Catholicism was the most important change in the religious character of New York since the colonial period. Platt's plea for similar generosity toward African-Americans failed, however. Republicans now excluded them from the rights of citizenship in a fashion similar, and even more extensive, to what the Anti-Federalists had done to Catholics in the 1780s. Moreover, Catholics themselves were by 1821 well on their way to becoming "the most Democratic class" in a strictly partisan sense, a political identity that did have a racial aspect to it.[4]

The Catholic Church in New York, and indeed in the United States, had come through the revolutionary era with its traditional system of authority intact. The influences of republicanism had not transformed it, as Bishop John Carroll had feared it might, into an independent, democratic church. The Catholic laity in New York, by their support of the prerogatives of Bishop Connolly over those of the Federalist trustees, helped to bolster the authority of the clergy. The increasing numbers of Catholics who had gained legal recognition as full citizens would take their democratic hopes into the wider arena of American politics. Catholics as a whole had concluded by the 1820s that the democratic impulses of the American Revolution, which had given Catholicism in New York new life after nearly a century of persecution, could not be extended to the sanctuary of the church without compromising the essentials of their ancient faith. State and society in New York did not interfere with the right of

Catholics to choose that unique path. That restraint was also an undeniable part of the legacy of the revolution.

Class, ethnicity, and religion all combined to shape a particularly Catholic political ethos during the early republic in New York. The growing separation of church and state in the United States was turning religion into something of a secondary political issue. Respect as equal citizens and access to political power were more important to Catholics than rhetoric about the importance of religion, as the early Republicans understood. By 1820, all factions of that party had sought Catholic votes and had nominated Catholics for state office. New York Catholics established two patterns that would generally apply for many years to their co-religionists across the country. They favored democratic politics in the wider polity (with race as an important exception to this general rule) and also retained traditional deference to the authority of the clergy within their church. As Tocqueville understood, this paradox could be explained. New York Catholics, particularly the laboring poor, chose the authority of priests and bishops over the leadership of a social and economic lay elite. In the wider polity, as they made clear, Catholics would settle for nothing less than to be full and equal citizens in a republic committed to protecting their religious liberty, and their church, so long as that republic might last.

# Notes

Introduction

1. The most important recent work is John McGreevy's masterful *Catholicism and American Freedom: A History* (New York, 2003) in which he traces the changing and yet enduring tension between Catholics and mainstream American political culture from the middle of the nineteenth century to the present.

2. The long affiliation of most Catholic voters with the Democratic Party, which arguably lasted from the Jacksonian period until the late twentieth century, has eroded in recent decades. For a view that emphasizes a drift among Catholics to the Republicans, see William B. Prendergast, *The Catholic Voter in American Politics: The Passing of the Democratic Monolith* (Washington, D.C., 1999).

3. See Ronald Formisano, *The Transformation of Political Culture: Massachusetts Parties, 1790s–1840* (New York, 1983), 297, 334–35. Michael F. Holt, *Forging a Majority: The Formation of the Republican Party in Pittsburgh, 1848–1860* (New Haven, 1969), 215–17. Harry Watson, *Liberty and Power: The Politics of Jacksonian America* (New York, 1990), 194.

4. Robert Kelley, *The Cultural Pattern in American Politics: The First Century* (New York, 1979), 173.

5. Lee Benson, in his pioneering study, *The Concept of Jacksonian Democracy: New York as a Test Case* (Princeton, 1961), describes French Catholic support for the Democrats in the 1840s as the continuation of a tradition first begun by Catholic Irish and Germans who had been "long mustered under Tammany banners," 175. Kerby Miller claims that Thomas Jefferson was elected in 1800 with "overwhelming Irish-American support" (*Emigrants and Exiles: Ireland and the Irish Exodus*

to *North America* [New York, 1985]), 189. William Shannon also made this assertion without providing much in the way of evidence in *The American Irish* (London, 1963), 7. Patrick Carey has cautioned, however, that "the political allegiances of Catholics in New York are difficult to determine" in *People, Priests, Prelates: Ecclesiastical Democracy and the Tensions of Trusteeism* (Notre Dame, 1987), 137. Shannon and others may have possessed an eagerness born of filiopiety to associate Irish Catholics with the Republicans, who have a more favorable historical reputation than do the Federalists.

6. Robert Kelley, in *The Cultural Pattern in American Politics* (126–27), relied on the work of Alfred F. Young in *The Democratic Republicans of New York* (Chapel Hill, 1967), for evidence that Catholics favored the Jeffersonians in the early republic. Young himself, however, admitted that in regard to New York, "There is very little scholarship on important nationality and religious groups, let alone what role they might have played in politics" (615).

7. Simon P. Newman, in *Parades and the Politics of the Street: Festive Culture in the Early American Republic* (Philadelphia, 1997), focuses on how ordinary Americans created their own politics quite apart from the world of Jefferson and Hamilton. David Waldstreicher (*In the Midst of Perpetual Fetes: The Making of American Nationalism, 1776–1820* [Chapel Hill, 1997]), emphasizes the role of print and newspapers in creating a national political culture that was designed to celebrate national unity at the expense of engaging issues that might have divided the country. Jeffrey L. Pasley, in *"The Tyranny of the Printers": Newspaper Politics in the Early Republic* (Charlottesville, Virginia, 2001), illustrates how newspaper editors, many of whom were radicals, played a crucial role in the development of American politics. Joanne B. Freeman focuses on political culture among the upper echelons of leadership in *Affairs of Honor: National Politics in the Early Republic* (New Haven, 2001). For the initial efforts of women to become full citizens, see Linda K. Kerber, *Women of the Republic: Intellect and Ideology in Revolutionary America* (Chapel Hill, 1980).

8. Charles and Mary Beard describe Catholics in the United States as entering the country in significant numbers "at the beginning of the middle period"; see *Rise of American Civilization* (New York, 1935), 2: 409. Perhaps even more typical is this account: "the number of Catholics grew dramatically during the 1840s as a result of the huge immigration of Irish"; see Bruce Levine, et al., *Who Built America: Working People and the Nation's Economy, Politics, Culture and Society* (New York, 1989), 1: 308. Also see Bernard Baiyln, et al., *The Great Republic: A History of the American* People (Lexington, 1985), 315. For a textbook that does mention widespread discrimination against Catholics in colonial America, see Pauline Maier, et al., *Inventing America: A History*

*of the United* States (New York, 2003), 61, 206, 428. Also see Timothy Walch, "New Tools for American Historical Research: A Review Essay," *U.S. Catholic Historian* 3 (Fall/Winter 1983): 201, and Leslie W. Tentler, "On the Margins: The State of American Catholic History," *American Quarterly* 45 (March 1993): 104–27, quotation on 106.

9. Historians employing a variety of approaches and methodologies have not included the political history of Catholics in their analyses of the early republic. Stanley Elkins and Eric McKitrick, *The Age of Federalism* (New York, 1993), and James Rogers Sharp, *American Politics in the Early Republic: The New Nation in Crisis* (New Haven, 1993), for example, study politics from the perspective of national leaders and events. Simon P. Newman in *Parades and the Politics of the Street* focuses on how ordinary Americans created their own politics quite apart from the world of Jefferson and Hamilton. David Waldstreicher, too, in *In the Midst of Perpetual Fetes*, emphasizes the role of print and newspapers in creating a national political culture that was designed to celebrate national unity at the expense of engaging issues that might have divided the country.

10. Two notable exceptions to this absence of Catholics in the literature of the early republic are Dale B. Light, *Rome and the New Republic: Conflict and Community in Philadelphia Catholicism between the Revolution and the Civil War* (Notre Dame, 1996), and William H. Warner, *At Peace with All Their Neighbors: Catholics and Catholicism in the National Capital 1787–1860* (Washington, D.C. 1994), which are valuable studies of the Catholic communities in Philadelphia and Washington, D.C. For the survey, see Jay Dolan, *The American Catholic Experience, A History from Colonial Times to the Present* (New York, 1985), 102. Joseph Agnito found similar harmony and mutual understanding between the colonial and antebellum periods; see "Ecumenical Stirrings: Catholic–Protestant Relations during the Episcopacy of John Carroll," *Church History* 45 (1976): 358–73.

11. Sean Wilentz, *Chants Democratic: New York City and the Rise of the American Working Class, 1788–1850* (New York, 1984), 77–78. Alfred F. Young, "Afterword: How Radical Was the American Revolution?" in *Beyond the American Revolution: Explorations in the History of American Radicalism*, ed. Alfred F. Young (De Kalb, 1993), 322.

12. David Roediger, *The Wages of Whiteness: Race and the Making of the American Working Class* (London, 1991), 134.

Prologue: "Disorder to None But Papists": Leisler's Rebellion and the Making of Anti-Catholicism in Colonial New York

1. Edwin G. Burrows and Mike Wallace, *Gotham: A History of New York to 1898* (New York, 1999), 98–99. "Dying Speeches of Leisler & Mil-

bourne," in *The Documentary History of the State of New-York* (hereafter *Doc. Hist. N.Y.*), 4 vols., ed. Edmund B. O'Callaghan (Albany, 1848–51) 2:378. "Leisler's Last Words on the Gallows, May 16, 1691," in *The Glorious Revolution in America: Documents on the Colonial Crisis of 1689*, ed. Michael Hall (Chapel Hill, 1964), 120.

2. "The Rights and Privileges of New Yorkers," May 13, 1691, in *The Glorious Revolution in America*, 123. *Documents Relative to the Colonial History of the State of New York* (hereafter *N.Y. Col. Docs.*), 15 vols., ed. Edmund B. O'Callaghan and Bernard Fernow (Albany, 1853–87), 3: 689.

3. John Raimo, *Biographical Directory of American Colonial and Revolutionary Governors, 1607–1789* (Westport, 1980), 243.

4. Edmund S. Morgan, "Bewitched," *The New York Review of Books*, January 9, 1997, 4.

5. "A Declaration of the Inhabitants and Soldiers belonging to the Several Companies of the Traine Band of New York," June 3, 1689, Leisler Papers, New York University. David Voorhees, "The 'fervent Zeale' of Jacob Leisler," *William and Mary Quarterly* (July 1994): 450–55, 457. John Murrin, "The Menacing Shadow of Louis XIV and the Rage of Jacob Leisler," in *Colonial America: Essays in Politics and Social Development*, ed. Stanley Katz (Boston, 2001), 384, 416. Randall Balmer, "Traitors and Papists: The Religious Dimensions of Leisler's Rebellion," *New York History*, 70 (October 1989): 344, 345, n. 10. "The New York City Militia Explains Its Actions, June 1689," in Hall, *The Glorious Revolution in America*, 109.

6. Peter R. Christoph, "The Time and Place of Jan Van Loon: A Roman Catholic in Colonial Albany, Part II," *De Halve Maen*, 60 (December 1987): 9, 10. Rev. Henry Selyns to the Classis of Amsterdam, October 28, 1682, in *Ecclesiastical Records of the State of New York* (hereafter *Eccl. Recs. N.Y.*), 7 vols., ed. Hugh Hastings (Albany, 1901–6), 2: 830. *N.Y. Col. Docs.*, 3: 415.

7. Murrin, "The Menacing Shadow of Louis XIV and the Rage of Jacob Leisler," 401, 406–7. "A Narrative of the Grievances and Oppressions Caused by Jacob Leisler and His Accomplices," *Eccl. Recs. N.Y.*, 2: 984. "Abstract of Colonel Bayard's Journal," *Eccl. Recs. N.Y.*, 2: 965. "Leisler's Proclamation Confirming the Election by the Citizens of the Mayor, Sheriff, Clerk and Common Council of New York," October 14, 1689, *Doc. Hist. N.Y.*, 2: 35.

8. "To the Towns of Long Island," June 12, 1689, and Jacob Leisler to William Jones, July 10, 1689, Leisler Papers, *Doc. Hist. N.Y.*, 2: 58. *N.Y. Col. Docs.*, 3: 614–15. Francis D. Cogliano, *Anti-Catholicism in Revolutionary New England* (London, 1995). Jacob Leisler to the Governor of Barbados, November 23, 1689, *Doc. Hist. N.Y.*, 2: 41.

9. Christoph, "The Time and Place of Jan Van Loon, Part II," 10. Raimo, *Biographical Directory*, 243. Stephen Van Cortland to Captain Nicholson, August 5, 1689, *N.Y. Col. Docs.*, 3: 609. Jacob Leisler to Simon Bradstreet, October 13, 1689, Leisler Papers. Leisler to the Governor of Barbados, *Doc. Hist. N.Y.*, 2: 40–42. Leisler to the Maryland Assembly, September 29, 1689, Leisler Papers.

10. Cadwallader Colden, *The History of the Five Indian Nations Depending on the Province of New-York in America* (1727; repr., 1980), 101–2, *Doc. Hist. N.Y.*, 1: 293, 2: 71. Nathan Gold and James Fitch to Capt. Leisler, June 26, 1689, *N.Y. Col. Docs.*, 2: 17.

11. Jerome Reich points to the failure of the Canada expedition as the beginning of Leisler's demise. See *Leisler's Rebellion: A Study in Democracy* (Chicago, 1953), 87–105. *New York Considered and Improved, 1695 by John Miller*, 68; "Loyalty Vindicated," in *Narratives of the Insurrection, 1675–1690*, ed. Charles Andrews (New York, 1915), 386, 110. Deposition of Andries and Jan Meyer, September 26, 1789, and Jacob Leisler to William Jones, July 10, 1689, Leisler Papers.

12. *N.Y. Col. Docs.*, 3: 601–2. Captain McKenzie to Captain Nicholson, August 15, 1689, *Eccl. Recs. N.Y.*, 2: 972.

13. Deposition of Pieter Godfried, July 22, 1689, Leisler Papers. Balmer, "Traitors and Papists," 347. *Doc. Hist. N.Y.*, 2: 431.

14. Burrows and Wallace, *Gotham*, 99. Balmer, "Traitors and Papists," 347, 348, n. 16. From their initial justification for seizing the fort, the Leislerians used these dramatic terms. See *Doc. His. N.Y*, 2: 55–58. Nicholas Bayard was accused after Leisler's death of "being as inveterate as any Papist against the Revolution." From *Loyalty Vindicated: Collections of the New-York Historical Society* (hereafter *N-YHS, Collections*), 35 vols., 1 (1868): 376.

15. Murrin, "The Menacing Shadow of Louis XIV and the Rage of Jacob Leisler," 396. "Affidavit of Kiliaan Van Rensselaer," *N-YHS Collections*, 1: 330.

16. Reich, *Leisler's Rebellion*, 114. *Doc. Hist. N.Y.*, 2: 366.

17. Jack Greene, *Interpreting Early America: Historiographical Essays* (Charlottesville, 1996), 184. "Proclamation Enjoining Good Order, Virtue and the practice of Religion," September 1, 1692, New York Council Papers, New York State Archives, Albany, microfilm #11, 38, 174. Burrows and Wallace, *Gotham*, 107; *Eccl. Recs. N.Y.* 2, 1012. "Declarations of Opposition to Church Doctrines," Albany County Hall of Records, Albany, N.Y.

18. *Doc. Hist. N.Y.*, 2. 182; Christoph, "The Time and Place of Jan Van Loon," Part 2: 10, 11. *Dictionary of American Biography*, ed. Allen Johnson and Dumas Malone (New York, 1930), 3: 364. *Annals of Albany*, 10 vols., ed. Joel Munsell (Albany, 1850–59), 3: 201.

19. Benjamin Fletcher to the Board of Trade, June 10, 1696, *N.Y. Col. Docs.*, 4: 159, 160, 166, June 11, 1696, New York Council Papers, 7: 193. Brockholls soon moved across the Hudson River to New Jersey. See Raimo, *Biographical Directory*, 243. Caleb Heathcote to Gilbert Heathcote, 1701, in *The Glorious Revolution in America*, 137. Burrows and Wallace, *Gotham*, 112. *The Colonial Laws of New York*, 5 vols. (Albany, 1896), 1: 453.
20. *Catholics in Colonial Law*, ed. Francis Curran (Chicago, 1963), 77, 78.
21. See Milton M. Klein, *The Politics of Diversity: Essays in the History of Colonial New York* (Port Washington, N.Y., 1974). Patricia Bonomi, *Under the Cope of Heaven: Religion, Society and Politics in Colonial America* (New York, 1986), and Richard Pointer, *Protestant Pluralism and the New York Experience: A Study of Eighteenth Century Religious Diversity* (Bloomington, Indiana, 1988).
22. Robert Middlekauff has said of the middle colonies, "There a genuine religious pluralism prevailed by the mid-eighteenth century." See *The Glorious Cause: The American Revolution, 1763–1789* (New York, 1982), 43. Mary Lou Lustig said that New York was a "prototype of modern American society" because of its religious and ethnic diversity and its pluralistic character. See *Privileges and Prerogatives: New York's Provincial Elite* (Madison, New Jersey), xi.
23. However, Milton Klein's conclusion that "in religion too, colonial New York set an example for the American Republic of the virtues of creedal competition in a state where the government acted the role of neutral" is overdrawn. See Klein, *The Politics of Diversity*, 120. Similarly, Richard Pointer acknowledges that Catholics were denied religious and political liberty amid complete freedom for Protestants, but by beginning his study in 1700, he avoids the particulars of how that systematic exclusion came about. See Pointer, *Protestant Pluralism and the New York Experience*, 34.
24. Carl Becker claimed in his classic study of early New York politics that between 1700 and 1769 elections for the provincial Assembly "did rest upon a suffrage that was uniform" but overlooked the denial of the vote to Catholics. See *The History of Political Parties in the Province of New York, 1760–1776* (Madison, 1909), 6.

1: "The Hand of Popery in This Hellish Conspiracy": The Legacy of Anti-Catholicism in Colonial New York

1. Petition of sundry free born subjects of Spain, New York Council Papers, New York State Archives, Albany, microfilm roll #19, 58, 24. Governor Hunter to the Board of Trade, March 14, 1713, *N.Y. Col. Docs.*, 5: 357. *Catholics in Colonial Law*, ed. Francis Curran (Chicago, 1953), 90. quoted in William Harper Bennett, *Catholic Footsteps in old*

*New York: A Chronicle of Catholicity in the City of New York from 1524 to 1808* (New York, 1909; reprint, 1973), 249.

2. Thomas J. Davis, *A Rumor of Revolt: The "Great Negro Plot" in Colonial New York* (New York, 1985), 2, 22–34. William Smith, Jr., *The History of the Province of New York*, 2 vols., ed. Michael Kammen (Cambridge, Massachusetts, 1972) 2: 53. N.Y. Col. Docs., 6: 188. Thomas J. Davis, ed., *Rumor of Revolt*, Daniel Horsmanden, *The New York Conspiracy* (1741; repr. Boston, 1971), x, 211–12. Lieutenant Governor Clarke to the Board of Trade, April 22, and to the Duke of Newcastle, June 20th, 1741, N.Y. Col. Docs., 6: 186, 196.

3. Daniel Horsmanden, *The Trial of John Ury* (1741; repr. Philadelphia, 1899), 10. Lieutenant Governor Clarke to the Board of Trade, August 24, 1741, N.Y. Col. Docs., 6: 7, 9. Horsmanden, *The New York Conspiracy*, 383, 410, 415–16.

4. Lieutenant Governor Clarke to the Board of Trade, June 20, 1741, N.Y. Col. Docs., 6: 198. Warrant to Commit John Ury, New York Council Papers, New York State Archives, Albany, microfilm roll number 74: 80. "Dr. John Gilmary Shea on the Trial of John Ury," appended to Horsmanden, *The Trial of John Ury*, 54, 216, 230. Extract from the Journal of John Ury, New York Council Papers, 74: 135a.

5. Horsmanden, *The New York Conspiracy*, 342, 343. Ury claimed that "I protest that the witnesses are perjured, I never knew the perjured witnesses but at my tryall." Extract from the Journal of John Ury, New York Council Papers, 74: 135a.

6. Lieutenant Governor Clarke to the Board of Trade, August 24, 1741, N.Y. Col. Docs. 6: 198, 201. These Hughsons were eventually banished from the province. See Horsmanden, *The New York Conspiracy*, appendix, "A List of White Persons Taken into Custody on the Account of the Conspiracy, in 1741." Horsmanden, *The New York Conspiracy*, 378.

7. Paul Gilje, *The Road to Mobocracy: Popular Disorder in New York City, 1763–1834* (Chapel Hill, 1987), 25–30. I. N. Phelps Stokes, *Iconography of Manhattan Island*, 6 vols. (New York, 1915–28), 6: 554. *New-York Gazette*, November 7, 10, 1748.

8. Quoted in John Tracy Ellis, *Catholics in Colonial America* (Baltimore, 1965), 369. Thomas Jones, *History of New York during the Revolutionary War* 2 vols. (c. 1785; repr. New York, 1879), 1: 2.

9. Richard Pointer, *Protestant Pluralism and the New York Experience* (Bloomington, 1988), 59–60. quoted in Bennett, *Catholic Footsteps in Old New York*, 329. Proclamation for Apprehending French Subjects, October 1, 1755, New York Council Papers, 83: 126. Governor Charles Hardy to the Board of Trade, September 5, 1756, N.Y. Col. Docs., 7: 125. Sister Mary Augustina Ray, *American Opinion of Roman Catholicism in the Eighteenth Century* (New York, 1936), 235.

10. Linda Colley, *Britons: Forging the Nation, 1707–1837* (New Haven, 1992), 326. Dunn was a "romish priest" according to Rev. John Ogilvie, an Anglican chaplain to the king's army. "The Diary of the Rev. John Ogilvie," September 23, 1756, in *The Bulletin of the Fort Ticonderoga Museum,* 5 (February 1961): 375. *New York Gazette and Weekly Mercury,* December 12, 1774. *New-York Gazette,* January 2, 1758. In 1746, during King George's War, Patrick Brooten, Thomas Flanagan, and Law Rice, three Irish (and likely Catholic) soldiers fled their posts at Fort George in New York City. *The New-York Gazette; or Weekly Post-Boy,* December 8, 1746. Sir William Johnson to the Board of Trade, May 28th, 1756, *N.Y. Col. Docs.,* 7: 87–88.

11. *New York Mercury,* July 25, 1763. Jon Butler, *Awash in a Sea of Faith: Christianizing the American People* (Cambridge, Mass., 1990), 177. Morgan Dix, *A History of the Parish of Trinity Church in the City of New York, Part I* (New York, 1898), 304.

12. Joyce Goodfriend, "Upon a bunch of straw: The Irish in Colonial New York," in *The New York Irish,* ed. Ronald Bayor and Timothy Meagher (Baltimore, 1996), 37. Charles Z. Lincoln, *The Constitutional History of New York,* 5 vols. (Rochester, 1906; repr. Buffalo, 1994), 1: 542. Pointer, *Protestant Pluralism,* 4–8. *New York Gazette and Weekly Mercury,* February 28, 1774. Bennett, *Catholic Footsteps in Old New York,* 249. St. Peter's Church Records, Box 1, Register, 1768–75, 2, New York State Library, Albany. John Jenkins, baptized in St. Peter's on June 6, 1756, "John Jenkins File," Colonial Albany Social History Project, New York State Museum, Albany. Thomas Barry "entered as a new Communicant," September 6, 1772, St. Peter's Church Records, Box 1, Register 1768–75, 2. *Philadelphia Sunday Dispatch* (1883), quoted in *American Catholic Historical Researches,* 1 (October 1906): 334. Most Rev. Michael Augustine, "The Catholic Cemeteries of New York," *Records and Studies,* 1 (1900): 370.

13. Stokes, *Iconography of Manhattan Island,* 1: 330–31, 5: 1189. John Gilmary Shea, *Life and Times of the Most Reverend John Carroll* (New York, 1888), 72. Pointer, *Protestant Pluralism,* 4–7. John Carroll, "Response to Smyth," in *The Papers of John Carroll* (hereafter *Carroll Papers*), ed. Thomas Hanley (Notre Dame, 1976), 3 vols., 1: 345. Rev. Michael Augustine Corrigan, "Register of the Clergy Laboring in the Archdiocese of New York from Early Missionary Times to 1885," *Records and Studies,* 1 (1900): 192–93. Rev. Robert Molyneux, "A Funeral Sermon on the Death of the Rev. Ferdinand Farmer" (Philadelphia 1786), Georgetown University Special Collections, Maryland Province Archives, Society of Jesus, Box 25, Folder 5.

2: "The Encouragement Popery Had Met With": Catholics and Religious Liberty in Revolutionary New York

1. Thomas Jones, *History of New York during the Revolutionary War,* 2 vols. (c. 1785; repr. New York, 1879), 1: 6.

2. Bernard Bailyn, *The Ideological Origins of the American Revolution* (Cambridge, Mass., 1967), 98, n. 3. Peter Shaw referred to the November 5 festivities as "New England's Pope Day," which obscures its practice in New York. See his *American Patriots and the Rituals of Revolution* (Cambridge, Mass., 1981), 15–18. "Journals of Captain John Montresor," *Collections of the New-York Historical Society, 1881*, 338.

3. Patricia Bonomi, *A Factious People: Politics and Society in Colonial New York* (New York, 1971), 248, 249. *The New York Gazette; or Weekly Post-Boy*, November 28, 1768, January 9 and May 1, 1769. Burrows and Wallace, *Gotham* (New York, 1999), 214.

4. *The New York Gazette; or Weekly Post-Boy*, March 20, 1769, November 28, 1768, June 13, 1768.

5. *Historical Researches*, 6 (October 1889): 164; "Extract of a letter to a Gentlemen in London," New York, June 1774, in *American Archives*, ed. Peter Force, 4th and 5th ser. (Washington, D.C. 1837–53),1: 300. "No Placemen, etc" by Phileleutheros, March 13, 1775, Broadside Collection, New York Historical Society.

6. "An Act for Making More Effectual Provision for the Government of the Province of Quebec in North America," in Charles Metzger, *The Quebec Act: A Primary Cause of the American Revolution* (New York, 1936), 211. Robert Middlekauff, *The Glorious Cause: The American Revolution: 1763–1789* (New York, 1982), 231. Alan Heimert, *Religion and the American Mind: From the Great Awakening to the Revolution* (Cambridge, Mass., 1966), 387.

7. Anthony Cogliano, *No King, No Popery: Anti-Catholicism in Revolutionary New England* (London, 1995), 42, 46–52. Charles Metzger, S.J., *Catholics and the American Revolution* (Chicago, 1962), 33. Metzger, *The Quebec Act*, 48, 141, 143. "TO THE KING'S MOST EXCELLENT MAJESTY" and "The humble Petition of the General Assembly of the Colony of New York," in Thomas Jones, *History of New York during the Revolutionary War*, 2 vols.(1783; repr., 1879), 1: 535, 531.

8. Alexander Hamilton, *A Full Vindication of Measures of Congress From Calumnies of their Enemies, 1774*, in *Historical Researches*, 6 (April 1889): 160. "The Humble Address of the General Committee of Association for the City and County of New-York," in *American Archives*, ed. Force, 4th ser., 2: 533–34.

9. Cogliano, *No King, No Popery*, 49, see 41–59 for New Englanders' rejection of George III. *Massachusetts Spy*, March 17, 1775. Jones, *History of New York*, 1: 43.

10. Thomas Paine, *Common Sense* (1776; repr., Garden City, 1960), 22, 29, 32.

11. Rev. Edward Kelley, "The Reverend John McKenna, Loyalist Chaplain," *Report of the Canadian Historical Association*, 1933: 34. James Thomas Flexner, *Lord of the Mohawks: A Biography of Sir William*

*Johnson* (Boston, 1959), 9. Rev. Richard Mosley to Rev. Dr. Richard Hind, July 25, 1774, in *The Papers of William Johnson*, ed. Alexander Flick (Albany, 1933), 8: 1195.

12. Philip Ranlet, *The New York Loyalists* (Knoxville, 1986), 121. Sydney to Lt. Gov., June 24, 1785. "Memorial of Roderick MacDonnell." *Historical Researches*, 2 (October 1906): 327. Sir William Johnson himself died in 1774, and his sons Guy and John adhered to their father's politics. Kelly, "The Reverend John McKenna, Loyalist Chaplain," 35–36. *Catholics and the American Revolution*, 3 vols., ed. Martin I. J. Griffin (Ridley Park, Penn., 1907), , 2: 138–39. Peter Guilday, "Father John McKenna a Loyalist Priest," *New Catholic World* (April 1931): 24. See Martin J. Becker, *A History of Catholic Life in the Diocese of Albany, 1609–1864* (New York, 1975), 21.

13. Cogliano, *No King, No Popery*, 67. John Carroll to Eleanor Carroll, May 1, 1776, in *Carroll Papers*, 1: 47. Gayle K. Brown, "The Impact of the Colonial Anti-Catholic Tradition on the Canadian Campaign, 1775–1776," *The Journal of Church and State*, 35 (Summer 1993): 573.

14. Burrows and Wallace, *Gotham*, 222. *Journal of the Provincial Convention*, March 20, 1777.

15. John W. Pratt, *Religion, Politics and Diversity: The Church–State Theme in New York History* (Ithaca, 1967) 85. William Jay, *The Life of John Jay* (New York, 1833), 3–4.

16. Pratt, *Religion, Politics and Diversity*, 93, 96. Charles Z. Lincoln, *The Constitutional History of New York* (1906; repr., Buffalo, 1994), 171. *Journal of the Provincial Convention*, 846, 853.

17. Metzger, *Catholics and the American Revolution*, 278, 244–49. *Journals of Captain John Montresor, Collections of the New York Historical Society* (1881), 489. Joseph Kirlin, *Catholicity in Philadelphia* (Philadelphia, 1909), 104. Stokes, *Iconography of Manhattan Island*, 6 vols., 5: 1070.

18. Charles P. Hanson, *Necessary Virtue: The Pragmatic Origins of Religious Liberty in New England* (Charlottesville, 1998), 119–53.; *Minutes of the Commissioners for Detecting and Defeating Conspiracies in the State of New York, Albany County Sessions, 1778–1781*, ed. Victor Hugo Paltsits (Albany, 1909–10). For the Commission, see Edward Countryman, *A People in Revolution: The American Revolution and Political Society in New York* (Baltimore, 1981), 118, 121–22.

19. *New York Gazette and Weekly Mercury*, August 2, 1779. Burrows and Wallace, *Gotham*, 235, 248–49.

20. *New York Gazette and Weekly Mercury*, August 2, 1779. Alfred F. Young, *Democratic Republicans of New York: The Origins, 1763–1797* (Chapel Hill, 1967), 16. For Anglican Loyalists in New York, see Ranlet, *The New York Loyalists*, 141–44. Bonomi, *A Factious People; Rivington's Royal Gazette*, October 7, 1778.

21. *The Other Side of the Question; or a Defence of the Liberties of North America,* by a citizen, *Historical Researches,* 6 (October 1889): 162. *Rivington's Royal Gazette,* June 20, 1778, February 17, 1779, March 1, 1780, October 14, 1778. "A Loyalist Journal," *The New York Genealogical and Biographical Record,* 105 (October 1974): 201.

22. *Records of the American Catholic Historical Society,* 45 (March 1934): 53. "Letters of Papinian," in *Historical Researches,* 5 (January 1888): 59. The account further noted that "members of Congress followed the righteous example of their proselyted President," *Rivington's Royal Gazette,* May 20, 1780, December 5, 1781.

23. *Rivington's Royal Gazette,* March 1, 1780.

24. One of Arnold's most recent biographers makes no mention of any religious motives for his treason. See James Kirby Martin, *Benedict Arnold: Revolutionary Hero* (New York, 1997). Cogliano, *No King, No Popery,* 83. *Rivington's Royal Gazette,* October 25, 1780.

25. John D. Crimmins, *Irish-American Historical Miscellany* (New York, 1905), 113–20. Michael J. O'Brien, *A Hidden Phase of American History: Ireland's Part in America's Struggle for Liberty* (New York, 1921): 393–526, *New York in the Revolution,* ed. Berthold Fernow (Albany, 1926; repr., Cottonport, N.Y., 1972), 1: 166–67, 173, 106. *Laws of the State of New York,* I: 62.

26. *New York Gazette and Weekly Mercury,* December 30, 1776, February 16, 1778, February 7, 1780. Stokes, *Iconography of Manhattan Island,* 5: 1098. *Rivington's Royal Gazette,* September 30, 1780, March 31, 1779, October 1, 1783. "Prisoners of the Provost Marshal, 1783," *New York Genealogical and Biographical Record,* 104 (January 1973): 5. William A. Polf, *Garrison Town: The British Occupation of New York City, 1776–1783* (Albany, 1976), 38. Records of the Society the Friendly Sons of St. Patrick, American Irish Historical Society, New York City, Box 11, Folder 16.

27. John G. Shea, *Life and Times of the Most Rev. John Carroll* (New York, 1888), 72. Arthur J. Weiss, S.J., "Jesuit Mission Years in New York State, 1654 to 1879," *Woodstock Letters,* 75 (1946): 21.

3: "No Foreign Ecclesiastical Authority": Catholics and Republican Citizenship

1. The list of petitioners and the body of the petition itself have not survived. However, it was assumed by the turn of the century by Catholic historians, and reasonably so, that the petition related to the "illiberality of the New York Constitution limiting the rights of Catholics." *Historical Researches* 19 (April 1902): 67. John Carroll to Leonardo Antonelli, March 1, 1785, *Carroll Papers,* 1: 179.

2. Rev. Charles Whelan to Propaganda Fide, January 28, 1785, *Records of the American Catholic Historical Society* (hereafter *RACHS*), 37 (Sep-

tember 1926): 245–46. "An Early Page in the Catholic History of New York," *The Catholic Historical Review* 1, (April 1915): 69. John Gilmary Shea, *The Catholic Churches of New York City* (New York, 1878), 587. Patrick Carey, *People, Priests, and Prelates: Ecclesiastical Democracy and the Tensions of Trusteeism* (Notre Dame, 1987), 8.

3. Rev. Charles Whelan to Propaganda Fide, January 28, 1785, *RACHS*, 246. New York Catholics to Hector St. John de Crevecoeur, February 3, 1785, quoted in Leo Ryan, *Old St. Peter's: The Mother Church of Catholic New York (1785–1935)* (New York, 1935), 42. Carey, *People, Priests, and Prelates*, 9. "Humble Petition of the Roman Catholic Inhabitants of the Said City," presented by St. John, Consul De France to Common Council of the City of New York, March 4, 1785, in Ryan, *Old St. Peter's*, 43. *Minutes of the Common Council* (New York City) 1: 137. Julia Post Mitchell, *St. Jean De Crevecoeur* (New York, 1916), 147.

4. Carey, *People, Priests, and Prelates*, 9. *Laws of the State of New York* (Albany, 1886), 1: 614; The literature on trusteeism is extensive; for the traditional view of Catholic historians that it was an American corruption of Catholicism, see G. C. Treacy, "The Evils of Trusteeism," *Historical Records and Studies*, 8 (1915), and John G. Shea, *The History of the Catholic Church in the United States*, 4 vols. (New York, 1886–92). For a more contemporary and impartial treatment, see Carey, *People, Priests, and Prelates*. Quoted in Rev. Michael Augustine Corrigan, D.D., "Register of the Clergy Laboring in the City of New York," *Records and Studies*, 1 (1900): 197. "Letter of humble dedication sent by the administrator in the name of the Roman Catholics of New York City to Señor Don Diego de Gardoqui, Minister of His Majesty," *Catholic Historical Review*, 1 (April 1915): 71.

5. "Letter of humble dedication sent by the administrator in the name of the Roman Catholics of New York City to Señor Don Diego de Gardoqui, Minister of His Majesty," *Catholic Historical Review*, I (April 1915): 71.

6. *New York Independent Journal or General Advertiser*, November 5, 1785. Shea, *The Catholic Churches of New York City*, 589; Rev. Charles Whelan to Propaganda Fide, January 28, 1785. Thomas F. Meehan, "Some Pioneer Catholic Laymen in New York—Dominick Lynch and Cornelius Heeney," *Records and Studies*, 4 (October 1906): 286. John May, April 22, 1788, quoted in Meehan, "Some Pioneer Catholic Laymen," 287. *New York Independent Journal or General Advertiser*, May 26, 1786.

7. July 14, 1783, August 5, 1784, March 3, 1784, Letter Book of Dominick Lynch, New York Historical Society. Edward Countryman, *A People in Revolution: The American Revolution and Political Society in New York, 1760–1790* (Baltimore, 1981), 221–51; Alexander Hamilton, Do-

minick Lynch, et al. to Patrick Murdoch, September 7, 1790, *Papers of Alexander Hamilton*, ed. Harold C. Syrett (New York, 1961–87), 7: 25, 3: 609. I have borrowed the term "popular Whigs" to describe the predecessors to New York's Anti-Federalists from Alfred F. Young in *The Democratic Republicans of New York* (Chapel Hill, 1967).

8. Reverend Charles Whelan to Propaganda Fide, January 28, 1785. *New York Independent Journal or General Advertiser*, November 4, 1786. Anne Hartfield, "Profile of a Pluralistic Parish: Saint Peter's Roman Catholic Church," *Journal of American Ethnic History* 12 (Spring 1993): 35–37.

9. Rev. Charles Whelan to Propaganda Fide, January 28, 1785. Hartfield, "Profile of a Pluralistic Parish," 35. John Carroll to Dominick Lynch and Thomas Stoughton, January 24, 1786, and to Charles Plowden, December 15, 1785, *Carroll Papers*, 1: 205, 196–97. "Register of the Clergy," *Records and Studies*, 1: 199–200.

10. Ferdinand Farmer to John Carroll, August 11, 1785, *Historical Researches*, 5 (January 1888): 31.

11. John Carroll to Charles Plowden, December 15, 1785, *Carroll Papers*, 1: 196–97. Ferdinand Farmer to John Carroll, August 11, 1785, *Historical Researches*, 5 (January 1888): 31. John Carroll to Dominick Lynch and Thomas Stoughton, January 24, 1786, *Carroll Papers*, 1: 203, 204.

12. John Carroll to Dominick Lynch and Thomas Stoughton, January 24, 1786, *Carroll Papers*, 1: 204, 205. Carey, *People, Priests and Prelates*, 12, 13.

13. Carroll later referred to an "untoward event which has prevented me from receiving in time the invitation with which I was honored by the Congregation," November 14, 1786, in *Catholic Historical Review*, 1 (April 1915): 77. It is possible that Carroll's remarks were read for him at the opening of St. Peter's; John Carroll, "On the dedication of St. Peter's Church," American Catholic Sermon Collection, Maryland Province Archives, S.J., Special Collections, Georgetown University, Box 5, Folder 17. "Another Letter sent by the Minister to Floridablanca, November 7, 1786, describing the ceremony which took place on St. Charles Day," *Catholic Historical Review*, 1 (April 1915): 74–75. New York City Directory for 1786, New York Historical Society. *New York Packet*, November 7, 1786.

14. Patrick Carey, *People, Priests and Prelates*, 15; John Carroll to William O'Brien, December 8, 1787, *Carroll Papers*, 1: 271.

15. John Carroll to Charles Plowden, March 1, 1788, and to William O'Brien, December 8, 1787, *Carroll Papers*, 11: 272, 271. William H. Bennett, *Catholic Footsteps in Old New York* (New York, 1909; repr., 1973), 383. Carey, *People, Priests, and Prelates*, 15, 16. January 4, 1790 Meeting of Board of Trustees of St. Peter's, quoted in Ryan, *Old St. Peter's*, 55.

16. April 13, 1789, Records of St. Peter's Church, New York Genealogical
    and Biographical Society. *Laws of the State of New York*, 1: 614. *New
    York Packet*, July 10, 1786. Bennett, *Catholic Footsteps in Old New
    York*, 396–97. Rev. James H. McGean, "The Earliest Baptismal Register
    of St. Peter's Church, New York City, I," *Records and Studies*, 1 (1900):
    99, 102; 2: 391.
17. The terms "agrarians," "Clintonians" (Governor George Clinton was
    considered their leader), and "Anti-Federalists" are used interchange-
    ably to identify the same party in New York during the 1780s. Saul
    Cornell, "Aristocracy Assailed: The Ideology of Backcountry Anti-Fed-
    eralism," *Journal of American History*, 76., 4 (March 1990): 1171.
    Countryman, *A People in Revolution*, 224–25.
18. Countryman, *A People in Revolution*, 224–25.
19. New York Constitution of 1777, in *Sources and Documents of United
    States Constitutions*, ed. William F. Swindler (Dobbs Ferry, 1973–88),
    7: 174. *New York Daily Advertiser*, January 26, 1787, February 1, 1787.
20. *New York Daily Advertiser*, February 1, 1787.
21. Alexander Hamilton, January 29, 1787, *Papers of Alexander Hamilton*,
    4: 30. Alexander Hamilton, January 24, 1787, in *Alexander Hamilton
    and the Founding of the Nation*, ed. Richard B. Morris (New York,
    1957), 472–73. *Daily Advertiser*, January 26, 1787.
22. January 29, 1787, *Papers of Alexander Hamilton*, 4: 30. Stanley Elkins
    and Eric McKitrick, *The Founding Fathers: Young Men of the Revolu-
    tion* (Washington, D.C., 1962), 24–25. Jack N. Rakove, *James Madison
    and the Creation of the American Republic* (Glenview, Illinois, 1990),
    24–26.
23. *Laws of the State of New York*, 2: 45. *Journal of the Senate* (New York),
    January 1788, 8, 10.
24. John W. Pratt, *Religion, Politics and Diversity: The Church-State
    Theme in New York History* (Ithaca, 1967), 107. Cecelia M. Kenyon,
    "Men of Little Faith: Anti-Federalists on the Nature of Representative
    Government," *William and Mary Quarterly*, 12 (January 1955): 39, 17.
25. Robert A. Gross, "White Hats and Hemlocks: Daniel Shays and the
    Legacy of the Revolution," in *The Transforming Hand of Revolution*,
    ed. Ronald Hoffman and Peter J. Albert (Charlottesville, 1995), 336–39.
26. "Publius," *Federalist No. 19* (Hamilton and Madison), in *The Federal-
    ist*, ed. Edward Mead Earle (New York, 1937), 118–19. Alfred F. Young,
    *The Democratic Republicans of New York* (Chapel Hill, 1967), 86.
27. *Poughkeepsie Country Journal and Poughkeepsie Advertiser*, April 8,
    1788, quoted in Staughton Lynd, *Anti-Federalism in Dutchess County,
    New York* (Chicago, 1962), 15. Robert Yates to George Mason, June 21,
    1788, quoted in Young, *Democratic Republicans of New York*, 94.
28. *The Documentary History of the Ratification of the Constitution* (here-
    after *DHRC*), ed. John P. Kaminski and Gaspare J. Saladino (Madison,

1984), 3: 367. Antoine de la Forest to Comte de Montmorin, New York, September 28, 1787, *DHRC*, 3: 259. John Carroll as "Pacificus," in the *Gazette of the United States*, June 10, 1789, *John Carroll Papers*, 1: 366.

29. John Carroll to Andrew Nugent, July 18, 1786, *Carroll Papers*, 1: 215.
30. Robin Brooks, "Alexander Hamilton, Melancton Smith and the Ratification of the Constitution in New York," *William and Mary Quarterly*, 24 (July 1967): 347. *The Debates in the Several State Conventions on the Adoption of the Federal Constitution*, ed. Jonathan Elliott (Philadelphia, 1881), 2: 250, 251.
31. Stephen A. Marini, "Religion, Politics, and Ratification," in *Religion in a Revolutionary Age*, ed. Ronald Hoffman and Peter J. Albert (Charlottesville, 1994), 184–217.
32. Linda K. Kerber, *Federalists in Dissent: Imagery and Ideology in Jeffersonian America* (Ithaca, 1970), 175–77.

4: "Federalists and Tories Carrying Everything with a High Hand":
Catholics and the Politics of the 1790s

1. Martha Lamb, Mrs. Burton Harrison, *History of the City of New York*, 2 vols. (New York, 1877; repr., 1896), 2: 338. I.N. Phelps Stokes, *Iconography of Manhattan Island*, 5: 1239. Rev. James H. McGean, "The Earliest Baptismal Register of St. Peter's Church, New York City, I," *Records and Studies*, 1 (1900): 102.
2. John Carroll, Charles Carroll of Carrollton, Daniel Carroll, Thomas Fitzsimons, and Dominick Lynch to George Washington, undated, late 1789, in *Documents of American Catholic History*, ed. John Tracy Ellis (Milwaukee, 1956), 175. Georgia abolished its Protestants only clause in 1789. Edwin S. Gaustad, *Neither King nor Prelate: Religion and the New Nation: 1776–1826* (Grand Rapids, Michigan, 1993), 161–74. Francis Newton Thorpe, *The Federal and State Constitutions, Colonial Charters, and Other Organic Laws* (1909; repr., Buffalo, 1993), 5: 2793.
3. George Washington to American Catholics, March 12, 1790, in *Documents of American Catholic History*, 176. John Carroll as "Pacificus," in the *Gazette of the United States*, June 10, 1789, in *Carroll Papers*, 1: 368.
4. "Address to the Sons of Liberty, March 9, 1789," "Preface to the Tammany Constitution, November 10, 1817," Edwin P. Kilroe Collection, Box 25. "Minutes of Tammany Hall, December 27th, 1792," Box 23, Butler Library, Columbia University. Stokes, *Iconography of Manhattan Island*, 5: 1217. John Pintard to Jeremy Belknap, October 11, 1790, quoted in Young, *Democratic Republicans of New York*, 202. Edwin P. Kilroe, *Saint Tammany and the Origin of the Society of Tammany* (New York, 1913), 143, 149.
5. "Preface to the Tammany Constitution." New York City Directory for 1796, New York Historical Society. Patrick Carey is the latest to claim

Mooney was a Catholic. See Carey, *People, Priests and Prelates,* 9. *New York Evening Post,* January 2, 1802. O'Brien, *In Old New York,* 69. *Heads of Families* (Washington, 1908), 118, 125, 128.

6. *Journal and Patriotic Register,* July 2, 1794, July 5, 1796. Gayle K. P. Brown, "A Controversy Not Merely Religious: The Anti-Catholic Tradition in Colonial New England" (Ph.D. diss., University of Iowa, 1990), 30–35. Sean Wilentz, *Chants Democratic: New York City and the Rise of the American Working Class, 1788–1850* (New York, 1984), 77–78. Len Travers, *Celebrating the Fourth: Independence Day and the Rites of Nationalism in the Early Republic* (Amherst, Mass. 1997), 43. Kilroe, *Saint Tammany,* 214–24. The Tammanyites also visited churches on the anniversary of their society in 1794; they went to hear a sermon by one of their members at the New Dutch Church; *Journal and Patriotic Register,* May 10, 1794. In 1800, the Mechanics' Society celebrated the Fourth of July in St. Paul's Episcopal Church, which had been founded during the colonial era. *Annals of the General Society of Mechanics and Tradesmen of the City of New York, From 1785–1880,* ed. Thomas Earle and Charles T. Congdon (New York, 1882), 36. A reading of the Declaration of Independence was held at Trinity Church on July 4, 1798. *Journal and Patriotic Register,* July 7, 1798.

7. *New York Weekly Museum,* December 29, 1792. John Carroll to Stephen Zacharie, December 2, 1791, John Carroll to Charles Plowden, September 27, 1790, *Carroll Papers,* 1: 546, 466. James M. Banner, "France and the Origins of American Political Culture," *Virginia Quarterly Review,* 64 (1988): 651–670. Simon P. Newman, *Parades and Politics of the Street: Festive Culture in the Early Republic* (Philadelphia, 1997), 120–151. William Doyle, *The Oxford History of the French Revolution* (Oxford, 1989), 259–61.

8. Jay Dolan, *The American Catholic Experience* (New York, 1985), 117. "Oration on the Death of General George Washington," February 22, 1800, *Records and Studies,* 2 (October 1900): 200, 196.

9. Gary Nash, "The American Clergy and the French Revolution," *William and Mary Quarterly,* 22, 3 (July 1965): 408, 411. [Noah Webster], *The Revolution in France considered in Respect to Its Progress and Effects* (New York, 1794), 20, 29.

10. *New York Journal and Patriotic Register,* February 1, 1794. Ruth Block, *Visionary Republic: Millenial Themes in American Thought: 1765–1800* (Cambridge, Massachusetts, 1985), 173, 172. New York Baptist Association to Philadelphia Baptist Association, May 23, 1794, quoted in Richard Pointer, *Protestant Pluralism and the New York Experience* (Bloomington, 1988), 131. Matthew Adgate, *A Northern Light, or New Index to the Bible* (Troy, New York, 1800), 80.

11. Bloch, *Visionary Republic,* 173. CIRCULAR, DEMOCRATIC SOCIETY OF NEW YORK to the Democratic Society of Philadelphia, in *The*

*Democratic-Republican Societies, 1790–1800: A Documentary Source-book,* ed. Philip S. Foner (Westport, 1976), 187, 22, 23. John McKnight, *God, the Author of Promotion* (New York, 1794).

12. Kerby Miller, *Emigrants and Exiles: Ireland and the Irish Exodus to North America* (New York, 1985), 187, 188, 171, 173. "Meeting of the Commissioners of the Almshouse and Bridewell in the City of New York," February 1, 1796, New York City Municipal Archives, Common Council Papers, Box 14, folder marked "February, 1796." "Memorial of 121 Catholics of New York sent to Bishop Carroll by the Trustees in 1796," *Historical Researches,* 8: 133–34.

13. Dr. Richard Bayley, *An Account of the Epidemic Fever* (New York, 1796), 91. Matthew Davis, *A Brief Account of the Epidemical Fevers* (New York, 1796), 7. Extract from a Letter of Father O'Brien, in Bayley, *An Account of the Epidemic Fever,* 89–91. "Meeting of the Commissioners of the Almshouse and Bridewell in the City of New York," February 1, 1796.

14. Elkins and McKitrick, *The Age of Federalism,* 415, 416. Grant Thorburn, *Forty Years Residence in America* (Boston, 1834), 38, 40. Alfred Young, "The Mechanics and the Jeffersonians: New York, 1789–1801," *Labor History,* 5 (Fall 1964): 259. The Whiteboys were secret, agrarian, Irish societies comprised of Catholics from the lower ranks of the country's economic order that emerged in the late eighteenth century. They attempted, often violently, to impose popular justice on Protestant land-Board and merchants whom they found particularly oppressive. See Miller, *Emigrants and Exiles,* 61–67.

15. Young, *The Democratic Republicans of New York,* 476–80; 477. *American Citizen,* September 1, 1801. Wilentz, *Chants Democratic,* 76–77. *Journal and Patriotic Register,* December 30, 1795. Anne Hartfield, "Profile of a Pluralistic Parish: Saint Peter's Roman Catholic Church, New York City, 1785–1815," *Journal of American Ethnic History,* 12 (Spring 1993): 47.

16. New-York Hibernian Volunteers Minute Book, January 12, 1796, February 6, 1796, New York Historical Society. Newman, *Parades and the Politics of the Streets,* 161.

17. Records of the Society of Friendly Sons of St. Patrick's, American Irish Historical Society, Boxes 11 and 12. Eugene P. Link, *Democratic-Republican Societies, 1790–1800* (Morningside Heights, N.Y., 1942), 184. New-York Hibernian Volunteers Minutes Book. Elkins and McKitrick, *The Age of Federalism,* 484–85. Thomas Gaston, Supplement to the New York Hibernian Volunteers Minute Book, New York Historical Society.

18. John Jay to Timothy Pickering, May 13, 1798. Henry P. Johnston, *The Correspondence and Public Papers of John Jay* (New York, 1890; repr., 1970), 4: 241. Quoted in Elkins and McKitrick, *The Age of Federalism,*

694, also see 591. *Journal and Patriotic Register*, July 11, 1798. Kieran McShane, "A Study of Two New York Irish-American Newspapers in the Early Nineteenth Century," *New York Irish History*, 8, 1993–94: 15–18.

19. Martha J. F. Murray, "Memoir of Stephen Louis Le Couteulx De Caumont," *Publications of the Buffalo Historical Society*, 9 (1906): 440, photograph following 442. *The Papers of Alexander Hamilton*, 27 vols., Harold C. Syrett (New York, 1961–87), 3: 227. William E. Rowley, "The Irish Aristocracy of Albany, 1798–1878," *New York History* (July 1971): 279. Thomas Barry to John Carroll, July 28, 1807, *American Catholic Historical Researches*, 18 (January 1901): 12–13. Thomas Barry to Bishop John Carroll, November 29, 1802, *American Catholic Researches*, 18 (January 1901): 9. Minute Book of St. Mary's, Albany, N.Y., Board of Trustees, 1812–15.

20. *Albany Gazette*, September 8, 1796, in Joel Munsell, *Annals of Albany*, 10 vols. (Albany, 1850–69), 3: 135.

21. Rowley, "The Irish Aristocracy of Albany, 1798–1878," 279–82. At least seven of the first nine trustees of St. Mary's lived in the city of Albany. See Sally Light, *Canals and Crossroads: A Sesquicentennial History of the Albany Diocese* (Albany, 1997), 36, 37. The two other men were of French background. Rev. John J. Dillon, *The Historic Story of St. Mary's* (New York, 1933), 93. Five of the eight trustees elected in 1813 were from Albany. St. Mary's Trustee Minutes, Albany, New York.

22. Ira Rosenwaike, *Population History of New York City* (Syracuse, 1972), 27. One early Catholic historian placed the figure at 14,000 in 1807, out of a total population of approximately 70,000. See William H. Bennett, *Catholic Footsteps in Old New York* (1909; repr., New York, 1973), 458. Elkins and McKitrick, *The Age of Federalism*, 732.

23. Elkins and McKitrick, *The Age of Federalism*, 692, 733. James Rogers Sharp, *American Politics in the Early Republic: The New Nation in Crisis* (New Haven, 1993), 233. Craig Hanyan, *De Witt Clinton: Years of Molding, 1769–1807* (New York, 1988), 164–65. *American Citizen*, April 29, April 26, 1800.

24. *Commercial Advertiser*, April 30, 1800. *Daily Advertiser*, April 28, 1800.

25. "Oration on the Death of General George Washington," *Records and Studies*, 2 (October 1900): 197, 199, 200.

26. Records of St. Peter's Church, New York Genealogical and Biographical Society. Thomas F. Meehan, "Some Pioneer Catholic Laymen in New York—Dominick Lynch and Cornelius Heeney," *Historical Records and Studies*, 4 (October 1906): 292, 296.

27. Paul Gilje, *The Road to Mobocracy: Popular Disorder in New York City, 1763–1834* (Chapel Hill, 1987), 129. Burrows and Wallace, *Gotham*,

401. *Daily Advertiser*, April 28, 1800. Jeffrey L. Pasley, *"The Tyranny of Printers": Newspaper Politics in the Early American Republic* (Charlottesville, 2001), 231–32.

28. Marshall Smelser, "The Jacobin Phrenzy: Federalism and the Menace of Liberty, Equality, and Fraternity," *Review of Politics*, 13, (1951), 481–82. Elkins and McKitrick, *The Age of Federalism*, 692. Sharp, *American Politics in the Early Republic*, 233–34. Philip Livingston to Jacob Read, February 23, 1801, reprinted in *Columbia University Quarterly*, 23 (June, 1931): 200. Alfred F. Young, "The Mechanics and the Jeffersonians: New York, 1789–1801," 5, 3 (Fall 1964): 264. *Historical Researches*, 7 (1890): 62. Hartfield, "Profile of a Pluralistic Parish," 39–41.

29. Peter J. Galie, *Ordered Liberty: A Constitutional History of New York* (New York, 1996), 67, 69, n. 13. John Webb Pratt, *Religion, Politics and Diversity* (Ithaca, N.Y., 1967), 123. *Journal of the Assembly of the State of New York*, 24th Session, March 30, 1801. *Laws of New York* (Albany, 1887), April 2, 1801.

30. Newman, *Parades and Politics of the Street*, 3.

5: "In All Countries Such Distinctions Are Odious: In None More So Than This": Political Equality in the Early Republic

1. Michael Durey, *Transatlantic Radicals and the Early American Republic* (Lawrence, 1997), 113–14, 195–96. *Temple of Reason*, November 8, December 6, 1800, January 3, 1801. Matthew, 16:18–19.

2. Alfred F. Young, "The Mechanics and the Jeffersonians, 1789–1801," *Labor History*, 5 (Fall 1964): 249. Jerome Mushkat, *Tammany: The Evolution of a Political Machine, 1789–1865* (Syracuse, 1971), 28.

3. John D. Crimmins, *St. Patrick's Day: Its Celebration in New York and other American Places, 1737–1845* (New York, 1902), 103. Evan Cornog, *The Birth of Empire: DeWitt Clinton and American Experience, 1769–1828* (New York, 1998), 45. Rev. William O'Brien to Bishop John Carroll, November 16, 1801, in Ryan, *Old St. Peter's*, 77.

4. John Wood, *A Full Exposition on the Clintonian Faction and the Society of the Columbian Illuminati* (Newark, New Jersey, 1802), 45. Durey, *Transatlantic Radicals*, 197, 9, 195. J. C. D. Clark, *English Society, 1688–1832* (Cambridge, 1985), 277–78. William P. Van Ness, *An Examination of the Charges Exhibited against Aaron Burr* (New York, 1803), 38.

5. Wood, *A Full Exposition on the Clintonian Faction*, 43, 41.

6. Wood, *A Full Exposition on the Clintonian Faction*, 20–21, 13–14. *Dictionary of American Biography*, ed. Dumas Malone (New York, 1934), 6: 153–54. Durey, *Transatlantic Radicals*, 93, 96, 99, 125–26. Constitution of the Hibernian Provident Society of New York, in John D. Crim-

mins, *St. Patrick's Day: Its Celebration in New York and Other American Places* (New York, 1902), 145.

7. Crimmins, *St. Patrick's Day*, 146. *American Citizen*, March 22, 1803. Simon P. Newman, *Parades and the Politics of the Street* (Philadelphia, 1997), 29–30. Waldstreicher, *In the Midst of Perpetual Fetes*, 26, 130.

8. *Minutes of the Common Council of the City of New York* (New York, 1917), March 7, 1803, 3: 228. *Morning Chronicle*, March 16, 1803. William Palmer, "Gender, Violence and Rebellion in Tudor and Early Stuart Ireland," *Sixteenth Century Journal*, 23 (Winter 1992): 708–10.

9. Edmund P. Willis, "Social Origins of New York City's Political Leadership from the Revolution to 1815," (Ph.D. diss., University of California at Berkeley, 1967), 192. *Minutes of the Common Council*, 3: 157. *New York City's Longworth's Directory, 1806,* New York Historical Society. *Annals of the General Society*, 23. *Morning Chronicle*, March 21, 1803. John Carroll to James Barry, August 25, 1803, *Carroll Papers* 2: 422, 425. "Earliest Baptismal Register of St. Peter's," *Records and Studies*, 2 (1900): 391. Hartfield, "Profile of a Pluralistic Parish" *Journal of American Ethnic History*, 12 (Spring 1993): 47.

10. Sidney I. Pomerantz, *New York: An American City, 1783–1803* (New York, 1938) 65, 66. "A Citizen," in *The New York Gazette and Federal Advertiser*, January 3, 1803, from *New-York Historical Society Collections* (1885), 306.

11. *N-YHS Collections* (1885), 311–17. Burrows and Wallace, *Gotham*, 330–31. *New-York Evening Post*, April 28, 1802.

12. Records of St. Peter's Church, New York Genealogical and Biographical Society. *American Citizen*, April 20th, 1805. John Carroll to James Barry, July 21, 1806, 2:52; John Carroll to Elizabeth Ann Seton, December 2, 1807, 3: 32, *John Carroll Papers*.

13. Pomerantz, *New York: An American City*, 385. One early Catholic historian placed the figure at 14,000 in 1807, out of a total population of approximately 70,000. See William H. Bennett, *Catholic Footsteps in Old New York* (New York, 1909; repr., 1973), 458. Craig Hanyan, *De Witt Clinton: Years of Molding, 1769–1807* (New York, 1988), 362.

14. William H. Bennett, "Francis Cooper: New York's First Catholic Legislator, *Historical Records and Studies*, 12, (June 1918): 29–30. Wilentz, *Chants Democratic*, 71. Howard Rock, *Artisans of the New Republic: The Tradesmen of New York City in the Age of Jefferson* (New York, 1979), 103. A list of nearly 500 members of the Mechanics' Society in 1798 contained the names of only a dozen Catholics, at the most. Congdon and Earle, *Annals of the General Society*, 236–40, 401, 39, 40, 46.

15. Father Michael Hurley to Bishop John Carroll, January 6, 1806, *Records of the American Catholic Historical Society*, 20 (September 1909): 279.

16. John W. Pratt, *Religion, Politics and Diversity: The Church-State Theme in New York History* (Ithaca, New York, 1967), 124. The list of

those who signed the petition was destroyed in a fire in 1911 at the New York State Library in Albany. For the use of petitions by women in the early republic, see Linda K. Kerber, *Women of the Republic* (New York, 1980), 85–87.

17. Father Michael Hurley to Bishop John Carroll, January 6, 1806.
18. "Petition of the Catholics of New York in 1806 against a Religious Test for Office," *Historical Researches*, 11 (October 1894): 183, 182.
19. Ibid., 182–83.
20. Ibid., 183.
21. Ibid. Eamon Duffy, *Saints and Sinners: A History of the Popes* (New Haven, 1997), 203–13.
22. Pratt, *Religion, Politics and Diversity*, 124–25. *American Citizen*, February 4, 1806.
23. Joanne B. Freeman, *Affairs of Honor: National Republics in the New Republic* (New Haven, 2001), 185. *American Citizen*, February 10, 1806. William W. Van Ness is not to be confused with William P. Van Ness, a close associate of Aaron Burr, who acted as Burr's second at the duel with Hamilton. Trustees of St. Peter's to Bishop Carroll, February 13, 1806, *Historical Researches*, 11 (October 1894): 184. Fr. Hurley to Fr. John Carroll, 1806, *RACHS*, 20: 275–76. Dixon Ryan Fox, *The Decline of Aristocracy in the Politics of New York, 1801–1840* (1919; repr, 1965), 44.
24. David Hackett Fischer, *The Revolution of American Conservatism: The Federalist Party in the Era of Jeffersonian Democracy* (New York, 1965), xviii, xix, 318, 319.
25. Annabelle M. Melville, *Elizabeth Bayley Seton, 1774–1821* (New York, 1961), 104.
26. *American Citizen*, February 12, 10, 1806.
27. *Morning Chronicle*, February 8, 1806. *American Citizen*, February 10, 1806.
28. Neither Michael Durey in *Transatlantic Radicals and the Early American Republic* nor Richard Twomey in *Jacobins and Jeffersonians: Anglo-Americans in the United States 1790–1820* mention exiled British radicals in connection with American Catholics. Lance Banning, *The Jeffersonian Persuasion: The Evolution of a Party Ideology* (Ithaca, N.Y., 1978), 227, 265–66. In 1800, the state provided monies to the Episcopalian, Presbyterian, United German, Scotch Presbyterian, Methodist, and African schools. Common Council Papers, New York City Municipal Archives, file named "Churches and Schools." Moses Younglove, a Republican assemblyman from Columbia County, reported the petition favorably out of his committee. March 24, 1802, *Journal of the Assembly of the State of New York, 25th session*, 233–34. Hurley to Carroll, 1806, *RACHS*, 20, 276. February 24, March 7, 1806, *Journal of the*

*Assembly of the State of New York, 1806, 29th Session.* March 21, 1806, *Laws of the State of New York,* chapter 63.

29. Hurley to Carroll, 1806, *RACHS,* 20, 276.

6: "A Middle Party?": Catholics and Republican Nationalism

1. *New York Evening Post,* December 26, 1806. *American Register, 1807,* in *Historical Researches,* 16 (January 1899): 149. *People's Friend,* November 20, 1806. Melville, *Elizabeth Bayley Seton,*104; Gilje, *The Road to Mobocracy,* 130.

2. Richard Stott, ed., William Otter, *History of My Own Times* (1834; repr., Ithaca, 1995), 43. *Morning Chronicle,* December 27, 1806. New York County District Attorney Indictment Papers, January 7, 1807, New York City Municipal Archives, New York City. Gilje, *Road to Mobocracy,* 131–32.

3. *Morning Chronicle,* December 29, 27, 1806. Quoted in Melville, *Elizabeth Bayley Seton,* 104. Robert Troup to Rufus King, January 7, 1807, *The Life and Correspondence of Rufus King* (New York, 1971), 5: 4.

4. *New-York Evening Post,* December 26, 1806.

5. Harvey Strum, "Federalist Hibernophobes in New York, 1807," *Eire-Ireland,* 16 (1981): 7–13. Robert Kelley, *The Cultural Pattern in American Politics: The First Century,* (New York, 1979), 173.

6. *Morning Chronicle,* April 29, May 6, 1806, April 28, April 10, 1807.

7. *New-York Evening Post,* April 4, April 27, 1807.

8. *People's Friend,* April 9, 20, 21, 1807.

9. Ibid., April 6, 21, 1807.

10. Ibid., April 21, 1807;

11. Strum, "Federalist Hibernophobes," 13. *People's Friend,* April 28, 1807. *New-York Evening Post,* May 1, 1807.

12. Elizabeth Seton to Antonio Filicchi, April 6, 1805, Archives of the Sisters of Charity of St. Vincent De Paul, Mount Saint Vincent on the Hudson, New York. Quoted in William H. Bennett, *Catholic Footsteps in Old New York* (1909;, repr., 1973), 445.

13. *American Citizen,* April 25, 1807.

14. Ibid.

15. Ibid., April 25, 30, 1807.

16. Ibid., April 30, 1807.

17. *New-York Evening Post,* April 25, 1807. *People's Friend,* April 15, 1807. William Sampson to Grace Clarke Sampson, April 18, 1807, William Sampson Papers, Library of Congress.

18. *Morning Chronicle,* April 9, 10, 1807. *New-York Evening Post,* April 4, 1807.

19. Thomas Addis Emmet to Rufus King, April 1807, *Life and Correspondence of Rufus King,* 5: 15–23. *American Citizen,* April 9, 4, 1807. King maintained that he was wary of encouraging the emigration of men to

the United States whom he believed were allied with revolutionary France at a time when the U.S. seemed to be moving toward war with France. Rufus King, unpublished address, *Life and Correspondence of Rufus King*, 5: 27.

20. *New-York Evening Post*, April 20, 17, 10, 6, 1807.
21. Ibid., April 27, 1807. *Morning Chronicle*, April 30, 1807.
22. Rev. Michael Augustine Corrigan, "Register of the Clergy Laboring in the Archdiocese of New York from Early Missionary Times to 1885," *Records and Studies*, 1 (1900): 207–8. The other new dioceses were Philadelphia, Boston, and Bardstown, Kentucky.
23. Sermon of Fr. Anthony Kohlmann, January 2, 1809, December 4, 1808, Archives of the Archdiocese of Boston. *New-York Evening Post*, May 1, 1807. Strum, "Federalist Hibernophobes," 12.
24. *New-York Evening Post*, May 22, 1807. Harvey Strum, "Property Qualifications and Voting Behavior in New York, 1807–1816," *Journal of the Early Republic*, 1 (Winter 1981): 361. *People's Friend*, May 2, 1807. *American Citizen*, May 2, 1807. Waldstreicher, *In the Midst of Perpetual Fetes*, 332.
25. *American Citizen*, May 4, 1807. *People's Friend*, May 4, 1807.
26. *New-York Evening Post*, May 4, April 29, 1808. Strum, "Federalist Hibernophobes," 12.
27. *American Citizen*, September 21, 19, 1808.
28. Ibid., September 13, 21, 1808, July 19 and 20, 1809. Durey, *Transatlantic Radicals*, 272. Rock, *Artisans of the New Republic*, 124. Jerome Mushkat, *Tammany: The Evolution of a Political Machine* (Syracuse, New York, 1971), 1, 34.
29. *American Citizen*, September 19, 21, 1808. *Longworth's New-York Register for 1800*, 308.
30. *Public Advertiser*, April 26, 1809.
31. *American Citizen*, April 15, April 24, 1809.
32. Ibid., April 20, 1809.
33. In the sixth ward alone, the margin for the Republicans dropped from 350 to 65. *American Citizen*, May 1, 1809. *Public Advertiser*, April 29, May 2, 1809.
34. Durey, *Transatlantic Radicals*, 272. *American Citizen*, April 16, 26, 23, 1810. To make sure that none of his readers missed the point, Cheetham added that Hopper meant that Swanton "is not a Roman Catholic." *American Citizen*, April 25, 1810.
35. *American Citizen*, April 23, 1810. *Columbian*, April 21, 1810.
36. *American Citizen*, April 21, 23, 1810. *Public Advertiser*, April 25, 1810.
37. *Public Advertiser*, April 25, 18, 1810. *Columbian*, April 18, 1810.
38. *Public Advertiser*, April 20, 1810. *Columbian*, April 26, 1810. *American Citizen*, April 26, 1810.

39. Burrows and Wallace, *Gotham*, 415. *Longworth's New York Directory*, 1810, 316. Records of St. Peter's Church, New York Genealogical and Biographical Society, Reel 1, trustee election results, 1789–1810.

40. *Public Advertiser*, April 24, 1810. *Columbian*, April 21, 1810.

41. Strum, "Federalist Hibernophobes," 12–13. *Public Advertiser*, April 19, 1810. *American Citizen*, April 24, 26, 1810.

42. *New-York Evening Post*, April 27, and 28, 1810. *American Citizen*, May 1, 1810. *Public Advertiser*, May 7, 1810.

7: "The Great Chain of National Union": Catholics and the Republican Triumph

1. *The Trial of John Ury* (1810), *American Catholic Historical Researches*, 16 (January 1899): 3.

2. *The Trial of John Ury*, 4.

3. Ibid.; Joseph Coppinger, "The Catholic Religion Vindicated" (New York, 1813), 16, 20.

4. *Columbian*, April 12, 1812. *Public Advertiser*, April 25, 28, 1812.

5. Kieran McShane, "A Study of Two New York Irish-American Newspapers in the Early Nineteenth Century," *New York Irish History*, 8 (1993–94): 14. *Shamrock*, January 18, 1812, December 14, 1811.

6. *Shamrock*, July 11, September 5, 1812.

7. *Shamrock*, December 15, 1810, January 21, 1815. William Gribbin, *The Churches Militant: The War of 1812 and American Religion* (New Haven and London, 1973), 108. Donald Hickey, *The War of 1812: A Forgotten Conflict* (Urbana, Illinois, 1989), 101.

8. *Shamrock*, March 13, 1813, September 26, 1812, June 18, 1814.

9. John Lambert, *Travels through Canada and the United States of North America in the Years 1806, 1807, 1808*, 2 vols. (London, 1814), 2: 53. William E. Rowley, "The Irish Aristocracy of Albany, 1798–1878," *New York History*, (July 1971): 281. *Shamrock*, December 19, 1812, August 20, 1814. David A. Wilson, *United Irishmen, United States: Immigrant Radicals in the Early Republic* (Ithaca, 1998), 84–85.

10. *Western Star and Harp of Erin*, July 18, 1812. *Shamrock*, July 11, 1812, February 17, 1816, March 20, 1813, September 17, December 3, 1814. John Rodman, "An Oration Delivered Before the Tammany Society and Hibernian Provident Societies, July 5, 1813," Edwin Kilroe Collection, Butler Library, Columbia University Archives. McKeon was buried in the cemetery at St. Patrick's Church in New York City. See John Shea, *The Catholic Churches of New York City* (New York, 1878), 101.

11. *Laws of the State of New York* (Albany, 1813), 2: 253.

12. Walter J. Walsh, "Religion, Ethnicity, and History," in *The New York Irish*, ed. Ronald H. Bayor and Timothy J. Meagher (Baltimore, 1996), 53–54. William Sampson, *The Catholic Question in America* (1813; repr., New York, 1974), 25. Fr. Anthony Kohlmann to Fr. Anthony

Grassi, April 1, 1813, Georgetown University Archives, Society of Jesus, Maryland Province Archives, Box 58, Folder 25. Board of Trustees of St. Peter's Church, April 19, 1812, in Sampson, *The Catholic Question in America*, 53–54.

13. Sampson, *The Catholic Question in America*, 35.

14. Ibid., 83, 85.

15. Wilson, *United Irishmen, United States*, 167–68, 8, 10, 95. Sampson gathered all the documents relevant to the case and published them as *The Catholic Question in America* (1813). Sampson, *The Catholic Question in America*, 80, 81. Walsh, "Religion, History and Ethnicity," 58, 59. Quoted in Wilson, *United Irishmen, United States*, 168.

16. Sampson, *The Catholic Question in America*, 26.

17. Ibid., 44.

18. Ibid., 97, 110, 111, 112, 114. *New York Times*, A19, February 16, 2002.

19. Shea, *Catholic Churches of New York City*, 86; Ryan, *Old St. Peter's*, 118. *New York Gazette*, May 5, 1815, quoted in Ryan, *Old St. Peter's*, 118.

20. *Columbian*, July 17, 1812. Emily Clark, " 'By All the Conduct of Their Lives': A Laywomen's Confraternity in New Orleans, 1730–1744," *William and Mary Quarterly*, 3rd Ser., 54, 4, (October 1997): 774–75. John Pintard to Eliza Noel Pintard Davidson, April 20, 1821, in *Letters from John Pintard to His Daughter*, 4 vols. (New York, 1940), 2: 32. "Sisters of Charity Missioned to New York 1817–1846," Archives of the Daughters of Charity, Albany, New York, Record Group 11–2, Box M-1, Folder 1. Melville, *Elizabeth Bayley Seton*, 255–56.

21. *Shamrock*, June 5, 1813.

22. *New-York Evening Post*, April 25, 1815. *Columbian*, April 25, 26, 1815.

23. *Columbian*, April 26, 1815.

24. Gustavus Myers, *The History of Tammany Hall* (New York, 1901), 50. *Shamrock*, May 4, April 27, April 6, 1816.

25. Thomas F. Meehan, "Some Pioneer Catholic Laymen in New York—Dominick Lynch and Cornelius Heeney," *Records and Studies*, 4: (October 1906): 296, 297. C. M. Burke, *Biographical Sketch of Cornelius Heeney* (New York, 1875), 22–23. *Shamrock*, June 1, March 2, May 4, 1816. William MacNeven to DeWitt Clinton, February 27, 1816, *De-Witt Clinton Papers*, Reel 2, Columbia University.

26. John Pintard to Eliza Noel Pintard Davidson, May 1, 1817, *Letters from John Pintard to His Daughter*, 4 vols. (New York, 1940), 1: 63. *Columbian*, April 26, 1817. Mushkat, *Tammany*, 5. Minutes of the Tammany Society, May 8, 1817, Edwin P. Kilroe Papers, Box 23, Butler Library, Columbia University.

27. *Shamrock*, May 3, 1817. John Pintard to Eliza Noel Pintard Davidson, May 1, 1817, *Letters from John Pintard to His Daughter*, 1: 63.

28. *Columbian*, May 5, April 22, 1817.

29. *Shamrock*, April 5, 1817. *A Plain and Rational Account of the Catholic Faith* (Albany, 1814), Special Collections, Georgetown University Archives, 1817. Clintonian election broadside (misidentified as 1812), reprinted in *New-York Historical Society Quarterly* 61, 2, (April 1972): 127. Carol Sheriff, *The Artificial River: The Erie Canal and the Paradox of Progress, 1817–1862* (New York, 1996), 36–40. *Columbian*, April 22, 30, 1817.

30. Mushkat, *Tammany*, 59. *Columbian*, May 6, 8, 1817.

31. Robert V. Remini, *Martin Van Buren and the Making of the Democratic Party* (New York, 1959), 5. Mushkat, *Tammany*, 59–66.

32. Peter J. Galie, *Ordered Liberty: A Constitutional History of New York* (New York, 1996), 71. *Columbian*, April 28, May 5, 1820.

33. Fox, *The Decline of Aristocracy*, 233. in New York City's sixth ward the vote for a convention was 694 to 141. In Albany's second ward, the vote was 336 to 87. *Reports of the Proceedings and Debates of the New York Constitutional Convention, 1821* (1821; repr., 1970), 679–80. Lincoln, *The Constitutional History of New York*, 212.

34. Galie, *Ordered Liberty*, 77. William E. Rowley, "The Irish Aristocracy of Albany, 1798–1878," *New York History*, 52 (July 1971): 281–82.

35. Galie, *Ordered Liberty*, 76–77.; Evan Cornog, *The Birth of Empire: DeWitt Clinton and the American Experience, 1769–1828* (New York, 1998), 143.

36. Petition of the Catholics of New York City to Pius VII, 1821, Archives of the Propaganda Fide, Special Collections, Catholic University of America.

37. Petition of the Roman Catholics of the City of New York to the Holy Father, 1821, Archives of the Propaganda Fide, Special Collections, Catholic University of America.; Report of Bishop Plessis, September 6, 1820, quoted in Peter Guilday, "Trusteeism," *Historical Records and Studies*, 18 (1917): 59–60. Carey, *People, Priests, and Prelates*, 113–14. Ryan, *Old St. Peter's*, 145–46. New York City Catholics to Propaganda Fide, May 21, 1819, quoted in Carey, *People, Priests, and Prelates*, 86.

38. Catholics of New York to Pius VII, 1821. M. Sorbieu to Pierre Toussaint, June 1, 1820, in Ryan, *Old St. Peter's*, 143–44. Kerby A. Miller, *Emigrants and Exiles: Ireland and the Irish Exodus to North America* (New York, 1985), 193–94. Extract from the notebook of Bishop John Connolly, February 25, 1818, in Rev. J. R. Bayley, *A Brief Sketch of the Early History of the Catholic Church on the Island of New York* (1870; repr., 1973), 92. Bishop Plessis of Quebec on a visit to New York City in 1815 estimated the Catholic population to be about 15,000. See Peter Guilday, "Trusteeism," *Historical Records and Studies*, 18 (1917): 48, 50, n. 79. According to the 1820 U.S. census, the population of New York City was 123,706. See Ira Rosenwaike, *Population History of New York City* (Syracuse, 1972), 36. Ryan, *Old St. Peter's*, 152.

39. Carey, *People, Priests, and Prelates:* 113–14. *Columbian,* July 30, 1819.
40. *Columbian,* July 30, 1819.
41. Ryan, *Old St. Peter's,* 150, 144. *An Address of the Roman Catholics of New-York: To the Right Rev. Doctor John Connolly* (New York, 1821), 6.

Conclusion: "A Most Democratic and Republican Class"

1. Cynthia J. Hinckley, "Tocqueville on Religion and Modernity: Making Catholicism Safe for Liberal Democracy," in *Tocqueville's Political Science: Classic Essays,* ed. Peter A. Lawler (New York, 1992), 197–98.
2. Alexis de Tocqueville, *Democracy in America* (New York, 1966), 1: 300.
3. Tocqueville, *Democracy in America,* 301.
4. *Reports of the Proceedings and Debates of the Convention of 1821, Assembled for the Purpose of Amending the Constitution of the State of New York* (Albany, 1821), 375.

# Bibliography

Primary Sources

Albany County Hall of Records
    Election Records
    Common Council Papers
    Naturalizations/Declarations of Intent
    Oaths
American Irish Historical Society
Archives of the Archdiocese of Boston
    Sermons of Rev. Anthony Kohlmann, S.J.
Archives of the Archdiocese of New York
    Correspondence of Archbishop Hughes
    Correspondence of Bishop DuBois
Archives of the Congregation de Propaganda Fide
    Robert Walsh Papers
Archives of the Maryland Province of the Society of Jesus
    Diary of Fr. Thomas C. Levins
    Woodstock Letters
Archives of the Sisters of Charity of St. Vincent De Paul of New York
    Elizabeth Seton Papers
Archives of the Society of the Friendly Sons of St. Patrick
Archives of the University of Notre Dame
Catholic University of America Archives
    Papers of John Hughes
    Propaganda Fide Files
Columbia University, Butler Library
    DeWitt Clinton Papers
Edwin Kilroe Collection—Tammany Hall

Henry Browne Collection
Georgetown University Archives
Library of Congress
    William Sampson Papers
Mount St. Vincent College, Bronx, New York
New York City Municipal Archives and Record Center
    Common Council Papers (clerk's filed papers) 1784–97
        Court of General Sessions Records
        District Attorney Indictment Papers
        Register of Deaths
New York Genealogical and Biographical Society
New York Historical Society
    Broadside Collection
    Dominick Lynch Letter Book
    New York City Directories
    New York City Lists, 1816 and 1819 (microfilm)
    New-York Hibernian Volunteers Minute Book
New York State Archives
    New York Council Papers
New York State Library
    Canvass of Votes, 1820
    Church Patents, 1784–1842
    Election Result Books, 1787–1815
    Records of St. Peter's Church, Albany
New York University
    Jacob Leisler Papers
St. Mary's Church, Albany, New York
    Board of Trustees Minute Book
St. Peter's Church—Marriage, Baptism, and Trustee Records

Published Sources

Adams, Abigail, and John Adams. *Familiar Letters of John Adams His Wife Abigail Adams during the Revolution, With a Memoir of Mrs. Adams.* Edited by Charles Francis Adams. Boston: Houghton Mifflin, 1875.

*An Act to Incorporate the Members of the Religious Society of Roman Catholics Belonging to the Congregation of St. Patrick's Cathedral in the City of New York.* New York: George Forman, 1817.

*An Address of the Roman Catholics of New-York: To the Right Rev. Doctor John Connolly.* New York, 1821.

Adgate, Matthew. *A Northern Light, or New Index to the Bible.* Troy, New York, 1800.

Andrews, Charles, ed. *Narratives of the Insurrection, 1675–1690.* Edited by Charles Andrews. New York: C. Scribner's Sons, 1915.

Assembly of the State of New York. *Journals.*

Bayley, Dr. Richard. *An Account of the Epidemic Fever.* New York, 1796.

"Catholicism in the Revolution," *Historical* Researches 23 (1906): 1–40.

*Civil List and Constitutional History of the Colony and State of New York.* Albany, 1879.

Colden, Cadwallader. *The History of the Five Indian Nations Depending on the Province of New-York in America.* New York, 1727. Collections of the New York Historical Society.

*Colonial Laws of New York,* Albany, N.Y., 1896.

Coppinger, Joseph. *The Catholic Religion Vindicated.* New York, 1813.

Corrigan, Rev. Michael Augustine. "Register of the Clergy Laboring in the Archdiocese of New York from the Early Missionary Times to 1885." *Records and Studies* 1 (1900): 191–217; (October 1900): 36–81.

Crevecoeur, J. Hector St. John de. *Letters from an American Farmer.* London, 1782. Reprint, New York, 1904.

Curran, Francis, ed. *Catholics in Colonial Law.* Chicago: Loyola University Press, 1963.

Davis, Matthew. *A Brief Account of the Epidemical Fever.* New York, 1796.

De Tocqueville, Alexis. *Democracy in America.* New York: Knopf, 1966.

"Documents relating to the Founding of St. Peter's from the Shea Collection at Georgetown." *Catholic Historical Review* 1 (1915): 69–77.

Dwight, Timothy. *Travels in New England and New York.* 1808. Reprint, Cambridge, Mass.: Harvard University Press, 1969.

Earle, Thomas, and Charles T. Congdon, eds. *Annals of the General Society of Mechanics and Tradesmen of the City of New York from 1785 to 1880.* New York, 1882.

Elliott, Jonathan, ed. *The Debates in the Several State Conventions on the Adoption of the Federal Constitution.* Philadelphia: J. B. Lippincott & Co., 1881.

Ellis, John Tracy, ed. *Documents of American Catholic History.* Milwaukee: The Bruce Publishing Company, 1956.

"Extracts from Early Records of St. Peter's Church, New York City," *Records and Studies* 3 (1901): 143–48.

"Extracts from Journal of Bishop Plessis." Translated by Abbe Lionel Lindsay. *Records of the American Catholic Historical Society,* 15 (December 1904): 377–402.

Foner, Philip, ed. *The Democratic Republican Societies, 1970–1800.* Westport, Conn.: 1976.

Force, Peter, ed. *American Archives.* 4th and 5th ser. Washington, D.C., 1837–53.

Gleason, Philip, ed. *Documentary Reports on Early American Catholicism.* New York: Arno Press, 1978.

Griffin, Martin I. J. *Catholics and the American Revolution.* 3 vols. Ridley Park, Pa., 1907.

Guilday, Peter, ed. *The National Pastorals of the American Hierarchy (1792)*. Washington, D.C.: National Catholic Welfare Council, 1923.

Hall, Michael, ed. *The Glorious Revolution in America: Documents on the Colonial Crisis of 1689*. Chapel Hill: University of North Carolina Press, 1969.

Hamilton, Alexander. *The Papers of Alexander Hamilton*. Edited by Harold C. Syrett, et. al. 27 vols. New York: Columbia University Press, 1961–87.

Hanley, Thomas, ed. *The Papers of John Carroll*. 3 vols. South Bend, Ind.: University of Notre Dame Press, 1976.

Harcourt, Felice, ed. and trans. *Memoirs of Madame de la Tour du Pin*. New York, 1971.

Hastings, Hugh, and E. T. Corwin, eds. *Ecclesiastical Records of the State of New York*. 7 vols. Albany, N.Y.: J. E. Lyon Co., 1901–6.

Herbermann, Charles. "An Interesting Relic," *Records and Studies* 4 (October 1906): 319–26.

Horsmanden, Daniel. *The New York Conspiracy*. Edited by Thomas J. Davis. Boston: Beacon Press, 1971.

———. *The Trial of John Ury*. Philadelphia: Martin I. J. Griffin, 1899.

Hughes, John. *The Catholic Chapter in the History of the United States. Address Delivered in New York City, March 8, 1852*.

———. *A Lecture on the Importance of a Christian Basis for the Science of Political Economy and Its Application to the Affairs of Life*. New York, 1844.

Hughes, Thomas, ed. *The History of the Society of Jesus in North America: Documents*. London and New York, 1908.

Jay, William. *The Life of John Jay*, New York, 1833.

Johnston, Henry P., ed. *The Correspondence and Public Papers of John Jay, 1763–1826*. New York: De Capo Press, 1971.

Jones, Thomas. *History of New York during the Revolutionary War*. 2 vols. New York: New York Historical Society, 1879.

*Journal of the Provincial Congress, Provincial Convention, Committee of Safety of the State of New York 1775–1777*. 2 vols. Albany, N.Y.: Thurlow Weed, 1842.

Kaminski, John P., and Gaspare J. Saladino. *The Documentary History of the Ratification of the Constitution*. Madison: State Historical Society of Wisconsin, 1984.

Kehoe, Lawrence, ed. *Complete Works of the Most Rev. John Hughes, D.D.* New York: The Catholic Publications House, 1866.

King, Rufus. *Life and Correspondence of Rufus King*. New York: De Capo Press, 1971.

Kline, Mary-Jo, ed. *Political Correspondence and Public Papers of Aaron Burr*. 2 vols. Princeton, New Jersey: Princeton University Press, 1983.

Lambert, John. *Travels through Canada and the United States of North America in the Years 1806, 1807, 1808.* 2 vols. London, 1814.

"Letter-Book of Captain McDonald of the Royal Highland Emigrants, 1775–1779." *Collection of the New York Historical Society for the Year 1882.* New York, 1882.

"Letters from the Archiepiscopal Archives at Baltimore, 1790–1814." *Records of the American Catholic Historical Society* 20 (1909): 275–76.

Lincoln, Charles Z. *The Constitutional History of New York.* Rochester, New York. 1906. Reprint, Buffalo: William S. Hein, 1994.

"A Loyalist Journal." *New York Genealogical and Biographical Record* 105 (October 1974): 193–202.

Marryat, Frederick. *A Diary in America, With Remarks on Its Institutions.* Edited by Sydney Jackman. New York: Alfred A. Knopf, 1962.

Merrill, Michael, and Sean Wilentz, eds. *The Key of Liberty: The Life and Democratic Writings of William Manning, "A Laborer," 1747–1814.* Cambridge, Mass.: Harvard University Press, 1993.

McGean, Rev. James. "The Earliest Baptismal Register of St. Peter's Church, New York City." *Records and Studies* 1 (1899): 97–107, 387–99; 2 (1900): 148–62, 454–63; 3 (1901): 143–48, 217–25, 506–15.

McGee, Thomas Darcy. *A History of the Irish Settlers in North America.* 1851.

McKnight, John. *God, the Author of Promotion.* New York, 1794.

Miller, John. *New York Considered and Improved, 1695.*

*Minutes of the Common Council of the City of New York, 1675–1776.* New York: Dodd, Mead and Company, 1905.

*Minutes of the Common Council of the City of New York, 1784–1831.* New York: Published by the City, 1917.

Morris, Richard B., ed. *Alexander Hamilton and the Founding of the Nation.* New York: The Dial Press, 1957.

Munsell, Joel. *The Annals of Albany.* 10 vols. Albany, N.Y., 1850–59.

———. *Collections on the History of Albany.* 4 vols. Albany, N.Y., 1871.

Murray, Martha. *Memoir of Stephen Louis LeCouteulx De Caumont.* Publications of the Buffalo Historical Society 9 (1906): 432–83.

Nolan, Hugh J. *Pastoral Letters of the United States Catholic Bishops. Volume I: 1792–1940.* Washington, D.C.: National Conference of Catholic Bishops, 1984.

O'Brien, Thomas Hanley, ed. *The John Carroll Papers.* 3 Vols. South Bend, Ind.: Notre Dame University Press, 1976.

O'Callaghan, Edmund B., ed. *The Colonial Laws of New York from the Year 1664 to the Revolution.* 5 vols. Albany, N.Y.: Weed, Parsons, and Company, 1868.

———. *The Documentary History of the State of New York.* 4 vols. Albany, 1849–51.

————. *Documents Relative to the Colonial History of the State of New York*. 15 vol.s. Albany, N.Y.: Weed and Parsons, 1853–87.

Ogilvie, John. "The Diary of the Rev. John Ogilvie." *The Bulletin of the Fort Ticonderoga Museum* 5 (February 1961): 331–81.

Otter, William Sr. *History of My Own Times*, Emmitsburg, Maryland, 1834. Reprint, Ithaca, N.Y., 1995.

Paine, Tom. *Common Sense*. 1776. Reprint, Garden City, New York: Doubleday, 1960.

Palsits, Victor H., ed. *Minutes of the Commission for Detecting and Defeating Conspiracies in the State of New York: Albany County Sessions 1778–1781*. 3 vols. Albany, N.Y.: J. B. Lyon, 1909–10.

"Petition of the Catholics of New York in 1806 against a Religious Test for Office." *American Catholic Historical Researches* 11 (January 1894): 182–84.

"Petition of the Catholics of New York to the Continental Congress, December 1783." *Historical Researches* 19 (April 1902): 67.

"Petition of the German Roman Catholics of the City of New York to Bishop Carroll of Baltimore for a German Pastor, March 2 1808." *Records and Studies* 2 (1900): 194–95.

Pintard, John. *Letters from John Pintard to His Daughter*. 4 vols. New York Historical Society, 1940.

*Plain and Rational Account of the Catholic Faith*. Albany, New York, 1814.

Power, John P., ed. *The Laity's Directory to the Church Service*. New York: Creagh, 1822.

*Reports of the Proceedings and Debates of the Convention of 1821, Assembled for the Purpose of Amending the Constitution of the State of New York*. Albany, New York: E. and E. Hosford, 1821.

Rodman, John. "An Oration Delivered before the Tammany Society and Hibernian Provident Societies July 5, 1813."

"St. Peter's Church, New York City; Its Corporations and Its Property. The Old Trustee System. *Records and Studie*, 1 (1899): 356–65.

Sampson, William. *The Catholic Question in America*. 1813. Reprint, New York: De Capo Press, 1974.

Senate of the State of New York. *Journals*.

Smith, William Jr. *The History of the Province of New York*. Edited by Michael Kammen. Cambridge, Mass.: Harvard University Press, 1972.

Smyth, Rev. Patrick. *The Present State of the Catholic Missions Conducted by the Ex-Jesuits in North America*, Dublin, 1788.

Society of the Friendly Sons of St. Patrick. *Charter, Constitution . . . Officers, . . . Roll of Members*. New York: W. P. Mitchell and Sons, 1909.

Stokes, I. N. Phelps. *Iconography of Manhattan Island*. 6 vols. New York, 1915–28.

Storing, Herbert J., ed. *The Complete Anti-Federalist*. Chicago: University of Chicago Press, 1981.

Sullivan, James., ed. *The Minutes of the Albany Committee of Correspondence, 1775–1778*. 2 vols. Albany, N.Y.: University of the State of New York, 1923.

Swindler, William F., ed. *Sources and Documents of United States Constitutions*. Dobbs Ferry, New York: Oceana Publications, 1973–88.

Taylor, William. *An Address to the Roman Catholic Congregation of New York*. New York: Charles A. Baldwin, 1821.

Thorburn, Grant. *Forty Years Residence in America*. Boston, 1834.

Thorpe, Francis Newton. *The Federal and State Constitutions, Colonial Charters, and Other Organic Laws*. Chicago: Callaghan & Company, 1901.

United States Department of Commerce. Bureau of Census. *Heads of Families of the First Census of the United States Taken in 1790: New York*. Washington, D.C.: U.S. Government Printing Office, 1908.

———. *Heads of Families of the Second Census of the United States Taken in 1800: New York*. Washington, D.C.: U.S. Government Printing Office, 1908.

———. *U.S. Census, Third, 1810: New York*. Washington, D.C.: U.S. Government Printing Office, 1811.

———. *U.S. Census, Fourth, 1820: New York*. Washington, D.C.: U.S. Government Printing Office, n.d.

Van Ness, William P. *An Examination of the Charges Exhibited against Aaron Burr*. New York, 1803.

Webster, Noah. *The Revolution in France Considered in Respect to Its Progress and Effects*. New York, 1794.

Wood, John. *A Full Exposition on the Clintonian Faction and the Society of the Columbian Illuminati*. Newark, New Jersey, 1802.

Zanca, Kenneth J., ed. *American Catholics and Slavery, 1789–1866*. Lanham, Md.: University Press of America, 1994.

Secondary Sources

*Books*

Adams, W. F. *Ireland and Irish Emigration to the New World from 1815 to the Famine*. New Haven: Yale University Press, 1932.

Agnito, Joseph. *The Building of the Catholic Church: The Episcopacy of John Carroll*. New York: Garland Publishing Inc. 1968.

Albert, Peter, and Ronald Hoffman, eds. *Religion in a Revolutionary Age*. Charlottesville, Va: University of Virginia Press, 1994.

Alexander, DeAlva. *A Political History of the State of New York*. New York: Henry Holt and Company, 1906.

Archdeacon, Thomas F. *New York City, 1664–1710: Conquest and Change*. Ithaca, New York: Cornell University Press, 1976.

Bailyn, Bernard. *The Ideological Origins of the American Revolution.* Cambridge, Mass.: Harvard University Press, 1967.

Banning, Lance. *The Jeffersonian Persuasion: Evolution of a Party Ideology.* Ithaca, New York: Cornell University Press, 1978.

Bayley, Joseph. *The Catholic Church on the Island of New York.* 1870. Reprint, New York: U.S. Catholic Historical Society, 1973.

Bayor, Ronald H., and Timothy Meagher,eds. *The New York Irish.* Baltimore: Johns Hopkins University Press, 1996.

Becker, Carl L. *The History of Political Parties in the Province of New York, 1760–1776.* Madison: University of Wisconsin Press, 1909.

Becker, Martin J. *A History of Catholic Life in the Diocese of Albany, 1609–1864.* New York: United States Catholic Historical Society, 1975.

Bennett, William H. *Catholic Footsteps in Old New York.* New York: Schwartz, Kirwin and Fauss, 1909.

Benson, Lee. *The Concept of Jacksonian Democracy: New York as a Test Case.* Princeton: Princeton University Press, 1961.

Billington, Ray Allen. *The Protestant Crusade, 1800–1860: A Study of the Origins of American Nativism.* New York: The Macmillan Company, 1938.

Bloch, Ruth. *Visionary Republic: Millennial Themes in American Thought: 1756–1800.* Cambridge: Cambridge University Press, 1985.

Bonomi, Patricia. *A Factious People: Politics and Society in Colonial New York.* New York: Columbia University Press, 1971.

———. *Under the Cope of Heaven: Religion, Society and Politics in Colonial America.* New York: Oxford University Press, 1986.

———. *The Lord Cornbury Scandal: The Politics of Reputation in British America.* Chapel Hill: University of North Carolina Press, 1998.

Bridenbaugh, Carl. *Mitre and Sceptre: Transatlantic Faiths, Ideas, Personalities and Politics, 1689–1775.* New York: Oxford University Press, 1962.

Bridges, Amy. *A City in the Republic: Antebellum New York and the Origins of Machine Politics.* New York: Cambridge University Press, 1984.

Burke, C. M. *Biographical Sketch of Cornelius Heeney, Founder of the Brooklyn Benevolent Society.* New York, 1875.

Butler, Jon. *The Huguenots in America: A Refugee People in New World Society.* Cambridge, Mass.: Harvard University Press, 1983.

———. *Awash in a Sea of Faith: Christianizing the American People.* Cambridge, Mass.: Harvard University Press, 1990.

Carey, Patrick. *People, Priests, and Prelates: Ecclesiastical Democracy and the Tensions of Trusteeism.* South Bend, Ind.: University of Notre Dame Press, 1987.

Chambers, William N. *Political Parties in a New Nation.* New York: Oxford University Press, 1963.

Charles, Joseph. *The Origins of the American Party System.* New York: Harper & Brothers, 1956.

Childs, Frances S. *French Refugee Life in the United States, 1790–1800: An American Chapter of the French Revolution.* Baltimore: The Johns Hopkins Press, 1940.

Clark, J. C. D. *The Language of Liberty, 1660–1832: Political Discourse and Social Dynamics in the Anglo-American World.* Cambridge: Cambridge University Press, 1994.

Cogliano, Francis D. *No King, No Popery: Anti-Catholicism in Revolutionary New England.* London: Greenwood Press, 1995.

Connolly, S. J. *Priests and People in Pre-Famine Ireland, 1780–1845.* New York: St. Martin's Press, 1982.

Countryman, Edward. *A People in Revolution: The American Revolution and Political Society in New York.* Baltimore: Johns Hopkins University Press, 1981.

Cornog, Evan. *The Birth of Empire: DeWitt Clinton and the American Experience, 1769–1828.* New York: Oxford University Press, 1998.

Crimmins, John D. *St. Patrick's Day: Its Celebration in New York and Other American Places, 1737–1845.* New York, 1902.

Cunningham, Noble. *The Jeffersonian Republicans: The Formation of Party Organization, 1789–1801.* Chapel Hill: University of North Carolina Press, 1957.

Curry, Thomas J. *The First Freedoms: Church and State in America to the Passage of the First Amendment.* New York: Oxford University Press, 1986.

Davis, Thomas, J. *A Rumor of Revolt: The "Great Negro Plot" in Colonial New York.* New York: The Free Press, 1985.

Dillon, Rev. John J. *The Historic Story of St. Mary's, Albany, N.Y.* New York: P. J. Kenedy & Sons, 1933.

Diner, Hasia. *Erin's Daughters in America: Irish Immigrant Women in the Nineteenth Century.* Baltimore: Johns Hopkins University Press, 1983.

Dirvin, Joseph I. *Mrs. Seton: Foundress of the American Sisters of Charity.* New York: Farrar, Straus and Cudahy, 1962.

Dix, Morgan. *A History of the Parish of Trinity Church in the City of New York.* New York: Knickerbocker Press, 1898.

Dolan, Jay P. *The Immigrant Church: New York's Irish and German Catholics, 1815–1865.* Baltimore: Johns Hopkins University Press, 1975.

———. *The American Catholic Experience: A History from Colonial Times to the Present.* New York: Doubleday, 1985.

Doyle, William. *The Oxford History of the French Revolution.* Oxford: Oxford University Press, 1989.

Duffy, Eamon. *Saints and Sinners: A History of the Popes.* New Haven: Yale University Press, 1997.

Durey, Michael. *Transatlantic Radicals and the Early American Republic.* Lawrence,: University of Kansas Press, 1997.

Elkins, Stanley, and Eric McKitrick. *The Founding Fathers: Young Men of the Revolution.* Washington, D.C.: Washington Service Center for Teachers of History, 1962.

———. *The Age of Federalism: The Early American Republic 1788–1800.* New York: Oxford University Press, 1993.

Ellis, John Tracy. *Catholics in Colonial America.* Baltimore: Helicon Press for the American Benedictine Academy, 1965.

Fischer, David Hackett. *The Revolution of American Conservatism: The Federalist Party in the Era of Jeffersonian Democracy.* New York: Harper and Row, 1965.

———. *Paul Revere's Ride.* New York: Oxford University Press, 1994.

Flexner, James Thomas. *Lord of the Mohawks: A Biography of Sir William Johnson.* Boston: Little & Brown, 1959.

Foner, Eric. *Tom Paine and Revolutionary America.* New York: Oxford University Press, 1976.

Formisano, Ronald. *The Transformation of Political Culture: Massachusetts Parties, 1790s–1840s.* New York: Oxford University Press, 1983.

Fox, Dixon Ryan. *The Decline of Aristocracy in the Politics of New York, 1801–1840.* New York: Harper Torchbooks, 1965.

Franchot, Jenny. *Roads to Rome: The Antebellum Protestant Encounter with Catholicism.* Berkeley: University of California Press, 1994.

Freeman, Joanne B. *Affairs of Honor: National Politics in the New Republic.* New Haven: Yale University Press, 2001.

Galie, Peter J. *Ordered Liberty: A Constitutional History of New York.* New York: Fordham University Press, 1996.

Gaustad, Edwin S. *Neither King nor Prelate: Religion and the New Nation: 1776–1826.* Grand Rapids, Michigan, 1993. W. B. Eerdmans Pub. Co.

Gilje, Paul. *The Road to Mobocracy: Popular Disorder in New York City, 1763–1834.* Chapel Hill: University of North Carolina Press, 1987.

Goodman, Paul. *The Democratic-Republicans of Massachusetts: Politics in a Young Republic.* Cambridge, Mass.: Harvard University Press, 1964.

Gorman, Father Robert. *Catholic Apologetical Literature in the United States 1784–1858.* Washington: Catholic University of America Press, 1939.

Gribbin, William. *The Churches Militant: The War of 1812 and American Religion.* New Haven: Yale University Press, 1973.

Hackett, David G. *The Rude Hand of Innovation: Religion and the Social Order in Albany, New York, 1652–1836.* New York: Oxford University Press, 1991.

Handlin, Oscar. *Boston's Immigrants.* Cambridge, Mass.: Harvard University Press, 1959.

Hanson, Charles P. *Necessary Virtue: The Pragmatic Origins of Religious Liberty in New England.* Charlottesville: University of Virginia Press, 1998.

Hanyan, Craig. *DeWitt Clinton: Years of Molding, 1769–1807.* New York: Garland Publishing, Inc. 1988.

Hatch, Nathan. *The Democratization of American Christianity.* New Haven: Yale University Press, 1989.

Heimert, Alan. *Religion and the American Mind From the Great Awakening to the Revolution.* Cambridge, Mass.: Harvard University Press, 1966.

Hennessey, James. *American Catholics: A History of the Roman Catholic Community in the United States.* New York, Oxford University Press, 1981.

Hickey, Donald R. *The War of 1812: A Forgotten Conflict.* Urbana: University of Illinois Press, 1989.

Hodges, Graham R. *New York City Cartmen, 1667–1850.* New York: New York University Press, 1986.

Hoffman Richard, and Peter J.Albert, eds. *The Transforming Hand of Revolution: Reconsidering the American Revolution as a Social Movement.* Charlottesville: University of Virginia Press, 1995.

Hofstadter, Richard. *The Idea of a Party System: The Rise of Legitimate Opposition in the United States, 1780–1840.* Berkeley: University of California Press, 1969.

———. *America at 1750: A Social Portrait.* New York: Knopf, 1971.

Howe, Daniel Walker. *The Political Culture of the American Whigs.* Oxford: Oxford University Press, 1979.

Ignatiev, Noel. *How the Irish Became White.* New York: Routledge, 1995.

Ireland, Owen. *Religion, Ethnicity and Politics: Ratifying the Constitution in Pennsylvania.* University Park: Penn State University Press, 1995.

Johnson, Paul. *A Shopkeeper's Millennium: Society and Revivals in Rochester, New York, 1815–1837.* New York: Hill and Wang, 1978.

Kass, Alvin. *Politics in New York State, 1800–1830.* Syracuse: Syracuse University Press, 1965.

Keane, John. *Tom Paine: A Political Life.* Boston: Little & Brown, 1995.

Kelley, Robert. *The Cultural Pattern in American Politics: The First Century.* New York: Knopf, 1979.

Kenneally, James J. *The History of American Catholic Women.* New York: Crossroad, 1990.

Kerber, Linda K. *Federalists in Dissent: Imagery and Ideology in Jeffersonian America.* Ithaca: Cornell University Press, 1970.

———. *Women of the Republic: Intellect and Ideology in Revolutionary America.* New York: W. W. Norton & Company, 1980.

Kilroe, Edwin P. *Saint Tammany and the Origin of the Society of Tammany or Columbian Order in the City of New York.* New York, 1913.

Knobel, Dale. *Paddy and the Republic: Ethnicity and Nationality in Antebellum America.* Middletown, Conn.: Wesleyan University Press, 1986.

Light, Dale B. *Rome and the New Republic: Conflict and Community in Philadelphia Catholicism between the Revolution and the Civil War.* South Bend, Ind.: Notre Dame University Press, 1996.

Light, Sally. *Canals and Crossroads: An Illustrated History of the Albany, New York Roman Catholic Diocese.* Albany, New York: Albany Catholic Press Association, 1997.

Link, Eugene Perry. *Democratic-Republican Societies, 1790–1800.* New York: Columbia University Press, 1965.

Livermore, Shaw Jr. *The Twilight of Federalism: The Disintegration of the Federalist Party, 1815–1830.* New York: Gordian Press, 1972.

Lovejoy, David. *The Glorious Revolution in America.* New York: Harper & Row, Publishers, 1972.

Lustig, Mary Lou. *Privilege and Prerogative: New York's Provincial Elite.* Madison: Fairleigh Dickinson University Press, 1995.

Lynd, Staughton. *Anti-Federalism in Dutchess County, New York.* Chicago: Loyola University Press, 1962.

Maier, Pauline. *The Old Revolutionaries: Political Lives in the Age of Samuel Adams.* New York: Vintage Books, 1980.

Maynard, Theodore. *The Story of American Catholicism.* New York: The Macmillan Company, 1941.

Melville, Annabelle. *Elizabeth Bayley Seton, 1774–1821.* New York: Charles Scribner's Sons, 1951.

Metzger, Charles. *The Quebec Act: A Primary Cause of the American Revolution.* New York: United States Catholic Historical Society, 1935.

———. *Catholics and the American Revolution.* Chicago: Loyola University Press, 1962.

Middlekauf, Robert. *The Glorious Cause: The American Revolution 1763–1789.* New York: Oxford University Press, 1982.

Miller, John C. *Crisis in Freedom: The Alien and Sedition Acts.* Boston: Little, Brown and Company, 1951.

Miller, Kerby A. *Emigrants and Exiles: The Irish Exodus to North America.* New York: Oxford University Press, 1985.

Mohl, Raymond A. *Poverty in New York, 1783–1825.* New York: Oxford University Press, 1971.

Morris, Charles R. *American Catholic: The Saints and Sinners Who Built America's Most Powerful Church.* New York: Times Books, 1997.

Murphy, Richard, and Laurence T. Mannion. *The History of the Friendly Sons of Saint Patrick in the City of New York, 1784–1955.* New York, 1962. J. C. Dillon Co. Inc.

Mushkat, Jerome. *Tammany: The Evolution of a Political Machine 1789–1865.* Syracuse: Syracuse University Press, 1971.

Myers, Gustavus. *The History of Tammany Hall.* New York, 1901.

Newman, Simon. *Parades and Politics of the Street: Festive Culture in the Early Republic.* Philadelphia: University of Pennsylvania Press, 1997.

O'Brien, Michael J. *A Hidden Phase of American History: Ireland's Part in America's Struggle for Liberty.* New York, 1921.

Pasley, Jeffrey L. *"The Tyranny of Printers": Newspaper Politics in the Early American Republic.* Charlottesville: University of Virginia Press, 2001.

Pointer, Richard W. *Protestant Pluralism and the New York Experience.* Bloomington: Indiana University Press, 1988.

Pomerantz, Sidney. *New York: An American City, 1783–1802.* New York: Columbia University Press, 1938.

Pratt, John Webb. *Religion, Politics, Diversity: The Church–State Theme in New York History.* Ithaca: Cornell University Press, 1967.

Ranlet, Philip. *The New York Loyalists.* Knoxville: The University of Tennessee Press, 1986.

Ray, Sister Mary Augustina. *American Opinion of Roman Catholicism in the Eighteenth Century.* New York: Columbia University Press, 1936.

Reich, Jerome R. *Leisler's Rebellion: A Study of Democracy in New York, 1664–1720.* Chicago: University of Chicago Press, 1953.

Remini, Robert V. *Martin Van Buren and the Making of the Democratic Party.* New York: Columbia University Press, 1959.

Ritchie, Robert C. *The Duke's Province: A Study of New York Politics and Society, 1664–1691.* Chapel Hill, University of North Carolina Press, 1977.

Rock, Howard. *Artisans of the Republic: The Tradesman of New York City in the Age of Jefferson.* New York: New York University Press, 1979.

Roediger, David R. *The Wages of Whiteness: Race and the Making of the American Working Class.* London: Verso: 1991.

Rosenwaike, Ira. *Population History of New York City.* Syracuse: Syracuse University Press, 1972.

Ryan, Leo R. *Old St. Peter's: The Mother Church of [the] Catholic Church [of New York] (1785–1935).* New York: The United States Catholic Historical Society, 1935.

Sellers, Charles. *The Market Revolution: Jacksonian America, 1815–1846.* New York: Oxford University Press, 1991.

Shannon, William V. *The American Irish.* London: The Macmillan Company, 1963.

Sharp, James Roger. *The New Nation on Trial: Opposition Politics in the United States, 1789–1801.* New Haven: Yale University Press, 1993.

Shaughnessy, Gerald. *Has the Immigrant Kept the Faith? A Study of Immigration and Catholic Church Growth in the U.S., 1790–1920.* New York: Macmillan Company, 1925.

Shaw, Peter. *American Patriots and the Rituals of Revolution.* Cambridge, Mass.: Harvard University Press, 1981.

Shea, John Gilmary. *The Catholic Churches of New York City.* New York: Lawrence G. Goulding & Co., 1878.

Sheriff, Carol. *The Artificial River: The Erie Canal and the Paradox of Progress, 1817–1862.* New York: Hill and Wang, 1996.

Smith, James M. *Freedom's Fetters: The Alien and Sedition Laws and American Civil Liberties.* Ithaca: Cornell University Press, 1956.

Spaulding, E. Wilder. *New York in the Critical Period, 1783–1789.* New York: Columbia University Press, 1932.

Stansell, Christine. *City of Women: Sex and Class in New York, 1789–1860.* Urbana: University of Illinois Press, 1987.

Taylor, Alan. *William Cooper's Town: Power and Persuasion on the Frontier of the Early American Republic.* New York: Knopf, 1995.

Tiedemann, Joseph S. *Reluctant Revolutionaries: New York City and the Road to Independence.* Ithaca: Cornell University Press, 1998.

Travers, Len. *Celebrating the Fourth: Independence Day and the Rites of Nationalism in the Early Republic.* Amherst, Mass.: University of Massachusetts Press, 1997.

Twomey, Richard J. *Jacobins and Jeffersonians: Anglo-American Radicalism in the United States, 1790–1820.* New York: Garland, 1989.

Vidal, Gore. *Burr: A Novel.* Toronto: Bantam Books, 1973.

Waldstreicher, David. *In the Midst of Perpetual Fetes: The Making of American Nationalism, 1776–1820.* Chapel Hill, University of North Carolina Press, 1997.

Walsh, Sister Marie De Lourdes. *The Sisters of Charity of New York, 1809–1959.* Vol. 1. New York: Fordham University Press, 1960.

Warner, William H. *At Peace with All Their Neighbors: Catholics and Catholicism in the National Capital, 1787–1860.* Washington, D.C.: Georgetown University Press, 1994.

Watson, Harry. *Liberty and Power: The Politics of Jacksonian America.* New York: The Noonday Press, 1990.

White, Shane. *Somewhat More Independent: The End of Slavery in New York City.* Athens: University of Georgia Press, 1991.

Wilentz, Sean. *Chants Democratic: New York City and the Rise of the American Working Class, 1788–1850.* New York: Oxford University Press, 1984.

Wilson, David A. *United Irishmen, United States: Immigrant Radicals in the Early Republic.* Ithaca: Cornell University Press, 1998.

Young, Alfred F. *The Democratic Republicans of New York: The Origins, 1763–1797.* Chapel Hill: University of North Carolina Press, 1967.

————, ed. *Beyond the American Revolution: Explorations in the History of American Radicalism.* De Kalb: Northern Illinois University Press, 1993.

*Articles and Essays*

Agnito, Joseph. "Ecumenical Stirrings: Catholic–Protestant Relations During the Episcopacy of John Carroll." *Church History* 45 (September 1976): 358–73.

Augustine, Rev. Michael. "The Catholic Cemeteries of New York," *Records and Studies* 1 (1900): 369–78.

Balmer, Randall. "Traitors and Papists: The Religious Dimensions of Leisler's Rebellion." *New York History* 70 (October 1989): 341–72.

Banner, James M. "France and the Origins of American Political Culture." *Virginia Quarterly Review* 64 (1988): 651–70.

Bennett, W. H. "Francis Cooper: New York's First Catholic Legislator." *Records and Studies* 2 (June 1918): 29–38.

Bosworth, Timothy W. "Anti-Catholicism as a Political Tool in Mid-Eighteenth Century Maryland." *Catholic Historical Review* 61 (October 1975): 539–63.

Brown, Gayle K. "The Impact of the Colonial Anti-Catholic Tradition on the Canadian Campaign, 1775–1776." *The Journal of Church and State* 35 (Summer 1993): 559–75.

Brown, Thomas More. "The Image of the Beast: Anti-Papal Rhetoric in Colonial America." In *Conspiracy: The Fear of Subversion in American History*, edited by Richard Curry and Thomas Brown, 1–20. New York: Holt, Rinehart and Winston, Inc., 1972.

Carey, Patrick. "Republicanism within American Catholicism, 1785–1860." *Journal of the Early Republic, 1785–1860* (Winter 1983): 413–37.

Carter, Edward C. II, "A 'Wild Irishman' under Every Federalist's Bed: Naturalization in Philadelphia, 1789–1806." *The Pennsylvania Magazine of History and Biography* 94 (1970): 332–46.

Casino, Joseph J. "Anti-Popery in Colonial Pennsylvania." *Pennsylvania Magazine of History and Biography* 105 (July 1981): 279–309.

Christoph, Peter R. "The Time and Place of Jan Van Loon: A Roman Catholic in Colonial Albany, Part II." *De Halve Maen* 60 (December 1987): 8–11.

Clark, Emily. "'By All the Conduct of Their Lives: A Laywomen's Confraternity in New Orleans, 1730–1744." *William and Mary Quarterly* 54 (October 1997): 769–94.

Cornell, Saul. "Aristocracy Assailed: the Ideology of Backcountry Anti-Federalism," *Journal of American History* 76 (March 1990): 1148–72.

Corrigan, Most Rev. Michael Augustine. "Register of the Clergy Laboring in the Archdiocese of New York from the Early Missionary Times to 1885." *Records and Historical Studies* (1899): 191–217; 2 (1900): 227–67.

Davis, David Brion. "Some Themes of Counter-Subversion: An Analysis of Anti-Masonic, Anti-Catholic and Anti-Mormon Literature." *The Mississippi Valley Historical Review* 47 (1960): 205–24.

Devitt, Rev. E. I. "The Planting of the Faith in America." *Records of the American Catholic Historical Society* 6 (1894): 137–79.

D'Innocenzo, Michael. "The Popularization of Politics in Irving's New York." In Andrew B. Myers, *The Knickerbocker Tradition: Washington Irving's New York*, 12–35. Tarrytown, New York: Sleepy Hollow Restorations, 1974.

Dolan, Jay P. "A Critical Period in American Catholicism." *Reviews of Politics* 35 (1973): 523–36.

Doyle, David N. "The Irish in North America, 1776–1845." In *A New History of Ireland*, edited by W. E. Vaughan, 682–725. Oxford: Clarendon Press, 1989.

Durey, Michael. "Thomas Paine's Apostles: Radical Emigres and the Triumph of Jeffersonian Republicanism." *William and Mary Quarterly* 44 (October 1987): 661–88.

Foil, Paul J., C.S.C. "Pioneer Efforts in Catholic Journalism in the United States (1809–1840)." *Catholic Historical Review* 1 (October 1915): 258–270.

Formisano, Ronald. "Deferential-Participant Politics: The Early Republic's Political Culture, 1789–1840." *American Political Science Review* 68 (1974): 473–87.

Gienapp, William. "Nativism and the Creation of a Republican Majority in the North before the Civil War." *Journal of American History* 72 (December 1985): 529–59.

Guilday, Peter. "Father John McKenna: A Loyalist Priest." *New Catholic World.* April 1931.

———. "The Restoration of the Society of Jesus in the United States (1806–1815)." *Records of the American Catholic Historical Society* 32: 171–232.

Hardy, Beatriz Betancourt. "A Papist in a Protestant Age: The Case of Richard Bennett, 1667–1749." *The Journal of Southern History* 60 (May 1994): 203–28.

Hartfield, Anne. "Profile of a Pluralistic Parish: Saint Peter's Roman Catholic Church, New York City, 1785–1815." *Journal of American Ethnic History* 12 (Spring 1993): 30–59.

Hinckley, Cynthia J. "Tocqueville on Religion and Modernity: Making Catholicism Safe for Liberal Democracy." In *Tocqueville's Political Science: Classic Essays*, edited by Peter A. Lawler, 197–213. New York: Garland Publishing, Inc. 1992.

Hoffman, Ronald. "Marylando-Hibernus; Charles Carroll the Settler, 1660–1720." *William and Mary Quarterly*, 45 (April 1988): 207–36.

Kelley, Rev. Edward. "The Reverend John McKenna, Loyalist Chaplain." *Report of the Canadian Historical Association*. 1933.

Kenny, Kevin."Religion and Immigration: The Irish Community in N.Y.C., 1815 to 1840." *The Recorder* 3 (Winter 1989): 4–49.

Kenyon, Cecelia M. "Men of Little Faith: The Anti-Federalists on The Nature of Representative Government." *William and Mary Quarterly* 12 (January 1955): 3–43.

Kerber, Linda K. "Abolitionists and Amalgamators: The New York City Race Riots of 1834." *New York History* 48 (January 1967): 28–39.

King, Ethel. "The New York Negro Plot of 1741." *Records and Studies* 20 (1931): 173–180.

Klein, Milton M. "Origins of the Bill of Rights in Colonial New York." *New York History* 72 (October 1991): 389–405.

Le Beau, Bryan F. "Saving the West from the Pope: Anti-Catholic Propaganda and the Settlement of the Mississippi River Valley." *American Studies* 32 (Spring 1991): 101–14.

Lenhart, Rev. John M, "Contributions to the Life of Rev. Charles Whelan, O.M.Cap. (D. 1806), First Resident Pastor of New York City." *Records of the American Catholic Historical Society*, 37: 242–48.

Maier, Pauline. "The Pope at Harvard: The Dudleian Lectures, Anti-Catholicism, and the Politics of Protestantism." *Proceedings of the Massachusetts Historical Society* 97 (1985): 16–41.

McAvoy, Thomas T. "The Catholic Minority in the United States, 1789–1821," *Records and Studies* 39/40 (1952): 33–50.

McShane, Joseph M., S.J. "John Carroll and the Appeal to Evidence: A Pragmatic Defense of Principle," *Church History* (June 1988): 298–309.

McShane, Kieran. "A Study of Two New York Irish-American Newspapers in the Early Nineteenth Century." *New York Irish History* 8 (1993–94): 13–21.

Meehan, Thomas F. "Some Pioneer Catholic Laymen in New York—Dominick Lynch and Cornelius Heeney," *Records and Studies* 4 (October 1906): 285–301.

———. "New York's First Catholic Newspaper." *Records and Studies* 3 (January 1903): 115–30.

———. "Tales of Old New York." *Records and Studies* 18 (March 1928): 121–69.

Miller, Rev. Norbert, "Pioneer Capuchin Missionaries in the United States (1784–1816)." *Records and Studies* 21 (1932): 170–234.

Nash, Gary. "The American Clergy and the French Revolution." *William and Mary Quarterly*, 22 (July 1965): 392–412.

O'Hanley Thomas. "Archbishop Carroll and the French Revolution." *Records of the American Catholic Historical Society of Philadelphia* 71 (September–December 1960): 67–73.

O'Toole, James M. "From Advent to Easter: Catholic Preaching in New York City, 1808–1809." *Church History* 63 (September 1994): 365–77.

Otterness, Philip. "The New York Naval Stores Project and the Transformation of the Poor Palatines, 1710–1712." *New York History* 75 (April 1994): 133–56.

Paulson, Peter. "The Tammany Society and the Jeffersonian Movement in New York City, 1795–1800." *New York History* 34 (January 1953): 72–84.

Quirk, Rev. John. "Father Ferdinand Farmer, S.J." *Records and Studies* 6 (December 1912): 238–48.

Rowley, William E. "The Irish Aristocracy of Albany, 1798–1878." *New York History* 52 (July 1971): 275–304.

Ryan, Leo R. "Pierre Toussaint, God's Image Carved in Ebony." *Records and Studies* 25 (1935): 39–58.

Shelley, Thomas J. "Black and Catholic in Nineteenth Century New York City: The Case of Pierre Toussaint." *Records of the American Catholic Historical Society of Philadelphia* 102 (1991): 1–17.

Smelser, Marshall. "The Jacobin Phrenzy: Federalism and the Menace of Liberty, Equality, and Fraternity." *Review of Politics* 13 (1951): 457–82.

———. "The Jacobin Phrenzy: The Menace of Monarchy, Plutocracy, and Anglophilia, 1789–1798." *Review of Politics* 21 (1959): 239–58.

Strum, Harvey. "Federalist Hibernophobes in New York, 1807." *Eire-Ireland* 16 (1981): 7–13.

Tentler, Leslie W. "On the Margins: The State of American Catholic History." *American Quarterly* 45 (March 1993): 104–27.

Voorhees, David William. "The 'Fervent Zeale' of Jacob Leisler." *William and Mary Quarterly* 51 (July 1994): 447–72.

Weiss, Arthur J., S.J. "Jesuit Mission Years in New York State, 1654–1879." *Woodstock Letters* 75 (1946): 124–39.

Young, Alfred F. "The Mechanics and the Jeffersonians: New York, 1789–1801. *Labor History* 5 (1964): 247–76.

*Unpublished Works*

Baumann, Roland M. "The Democratic Republicans of Philadelphia: The Origins, 1776–1797." Ph.D. diss., Pennsylvania State University, 1970.

Blau, Alan Lee. "New York City and the French Revolution, 1789–1797: A Study of French Revolutionary Influence." Ph.D. diss., City University of New York, 1973.

Bric, Maurice. "Ireland, Irishmen, and the Broadening of the late 18th Century Philadelphia Polity." Ph.D. diss., Johns Hopkins University, 1991.

Brown, Gayle Kathleen Pluta. "A Controversy Not Merely Religious: The Anti-Catholic Tradition in Colonial New England." Ph.D diss., University of Iowa, 1990.

Carter II, Edward C. "The Political Activities of Matthew Carey, Nationalist, 1760–1814." Ph.D. diss., Bryn Mawr College, 1962.

Clute, Florence E. "Discrimination against Catholics, Quakers and Jews in New Netherlands and Colonial New York." Master's thesis, St. Louis University, 1940.

Doyle, Richard. "The Irish in Pre-Revolutionary New York, 1664–1775." Ph.D. diss., St. Louis University, 1932.

Hardy, Beatriz. "Papists in a Colonial Age: The Catholic Gentry and Community in Colonial Maryland, 1689–1776." Ph.D. diss., University of Maryland, 1993.

Manfra, Jo Ann. "The Catholic Episcopacy in America, 1789–1852." Ph.D. diss., University of Iowa, 1975.

Otterness, Philip L. "The Unattained Canaan: The 1709 Palatine Migration and the Formation of German Society in Colonial America." Ph.D. diss., University of Iowa, 1996.

Pine, Tricia. "Maryland Catholic Community, 1690–1775." Ph.D. diss., Catholic University of America, 1996.

Redempta, Mary. "Catholics in the Revolutionary War." Master's thesis, St. John's University, 1927.

Voorhees, David W. "In Behalf of the True Protestants['] Religion: The Glorious Revolution in New York." Ph.D. diss., New York University, 1988.

Wheeler, William Bruce. "Urban Politics in Nature's Republic: The Development of Political Parties in the Seaport Cities in the Federalist Era." Ph.D. diss., University of Virginia, 1967.

Willis, Edmund. "The Social Origins of New York City's Political Leadership from the Revolution to 1815." Ph.D. diss., University of California at Berkeley, 1967.

Winking, Lawrence H. "The Catholic Church in Congressional Debate, 1789–1837." Master's thesis, Catholic University, 1930.

# Index